G000060190

TOTUS TUUS

STUDIES AND TEXTS—NO. I

ARTHUR BURTON CALKINS

TOTUS TUUS

John Paul II's Program of Marian Consecration and Entrustment

ACADEMY OF THE IMMACULATE
LIBERTYVILLE, ILLINOIS

Nihil Obstat: Rev. Terry J. Tekippe
Censor

Imprimatur: ✠ Most Rev. Francis B. Schulte
Archbishop of New Orleans
September 15, 1992

The *Nihil Obstat* and *Imprimatur* are the Church's declarations that a work is free from error in matters of faith and morals, but in no way do they imply that the Church endorses the contents of the work.

Cover art by Jean Mirailhet
Courtesy of Musée d'Art et d'Histoire, Palais Massèna

ISBN 0–9635345–0–5
Library of Congress catalogue number 92–74257
Printed in the United States of America

ACADEMY OF THE IMMACULATE STUDIES AND TEXTS

Among the many projects Saint Maximilian M. Kolbe planned for his Niepokalanów to promote a greater knowledge and love of the Immaculate and thereby the final triumph of the Kingdom of the Heart of Jesus was an Academy of the Immaculate.[1] It was to foster study of the mystery of the Immaculate and of her vocation to be maternal Mediatress in the economy of salvation and study of the Militia of the Immaculate—which he once defined as a global vision of Catholic life under a new form, that of our link with the Immaculate, our Mediatress with Jesus.[2] Among its various activities would be the formation of theologians at the doctoral level with a specialization in Mariology; the cultivation of research into the mystery of Mary and of her intervention in the affairs of mankind; the establishment of a library of the Immaculate; and the publication of studies resulting from diligent and persevering research, extending our knowledge and understanding of the Queen of heaven and earth.

World War II and the saint's death in the Auschwitz concentration camp prevented his realization of that Academy. And in the half-century since his martyrdom nothing more has been done to implement those projects. To honor Saint Maximilian on the 75th anniversary of the founding of the M.I., and to foster some part of the saint's vast plans for

[1] St. Maximilian Kolbe, O.F.M. Conv., *Gli Scritti di Massimiliano Kolbe: eroe di Oświęcim e Beato della Chiesa*, 3 vols., trans. Cristoforo Zambelli (Florence: Città di Vita, 1975–1978), 508, 647.

[2] Ibid., 1220.

enhancing the influence of Our Lady in the intellectual and theological world, the National Center of the Militia of the Immaculate in the United States, under the direction of Fr. James McCurry, O.F.M. Conv., is inaugurating a new series of studies and texts.

The series will admit of considerable variety in the volumes included within it: practical as well as speculative, manuals as well as original research, popular as well as erudite. All, however, will be marked by fidelity to Catholic tradition and the magisterium and by solid scholarship; all will deal in some way or another with the mystery of the Immaculate, Mediatress of all graces, and of that total consecration which is the heart of our link with her as our Mother and Mediatress. Fittingly, the first number of the series is a learned—and in many ways exhaustive—dissertation on that consecration in the teaching and pastoral program of the present Holy Father, Pope John Paul II.

May the Immaculate Virgin be pleased with these efforts to promote her cause. May she deign to use them as instruments for the salvation of souls, for the ever greater incorporation of the mystery of her Immaculate Conception into the fabric of human life: in every person, in every community, for the greater glory of her Son and Savior and the triumph of His Kingdom.

CONTENTS

PART ONE: MARIAN CONSECRATION IN THE SPIRITUAL JOURNEY OF THE CHURCH

PART III: ASSESSMENT

ABBREVIATIONS

AA	*Apostolicam Actuositatem* (Vatican II Decree on Apostolate of Lay People)
AAS	*Acta Apostolicae Sedis* (1909–)
Africa Ap	*Africa: Apostolic Pilgrimage* (Boston: St. Paul Editions, 1980)
AG	*Ad Gentes* (Vatican II Decree on Church's Missionary Activity)
Argentina	*Pope John Paul II in Argentina* (Boston: St. Paul Editions, 1983)
ASC	*Alma Socia Christi: Acta Congressus Mariologici-Mariani Romae Anno Sancto MCML Celebrati* (Rome: Pontificia Academia Mariana Internationalis, 1953)
ASS	*Acta Sanctae Sedis* (1865–1908)
Brazil	*Brazil: Journey in the Light of the Eucharist* (Boston: St. Paul Editions, 1980)
BSFEM	*Études Mariales: Bulletin de la Société française d'Études Mariales*
Carlen 2	Claudia Carlen, I.H.M., *The Papal Encyclicals 1878–1903* (Raleigh, N.C.: McGrath Publishing Co., "Consortium Book", 1981)

Carlen 3 — *The Papal Encyclicals 1903–1939* (Raleigh, N.C.: McGrath Publishing Co., "Consortium Book", 1981)

CD — *Christus Dominus* (Vatican II Decree on the Pastoral Office of Bishops in the Church)

"Cons." — Stefano De Fiores, "Consacrazione", in *Nuovo Dizionario di Mariologia*, ed. Stefano De Fiores, S.M.M., and Salvatore Meo, O.S.M. (Milan: Edizioni Paoline, 1985), 394–417

Denz-Schon. — Henricus Denzinger and Adolfus Schonmetzer, S.J., eds., *Enchiridion Symbolorum Definitionum et Declarationum de Rebus Fidei et Morum*, 32nd ed. (Freiburg-im-Breisgau: Herder, 1963)

DSp — Marcel Viller, S.J., et al., *Dictionnaire de Spiritualité Ascétique et Mystique* (Paris: Beauchesne et Ses Fils, 1937–)

DV — *Dei Verbum* (Vatican II Dogmatic Constitution on Divine Revelation)

Far East — *The Far East: Journey of Peace and Brotherhood* (Boston: St. Paul Editions, 1981)

Flan. — Austin Flannery, O.P., ed., *Vatican Council II: The Conciliar and Post Conciliar Documents* (Collegeville, Minn.: Liturgical Press, 1975)

France — *France: Message of Peace, Trust, Love and Faith* (Boston: St. Paul Editions, 1980)

Inseg — *Insegnamenti di Giovanni Paolo II* (1978–), (Vatican City: Libreria Editrice Vaticana, 1979–)

Ireland — *Ireland "In the Footsteps of St. Patrick"* (Boston: St. Paul Editions, 1979)

LG — *Lumen Gentium* (Vatican II Dogmatic Constitution on the Church)

Maria — Hubert du Manoir, S.J., ed., *Maria: Études sur la Sainte Vierge*, 8 vols. (Paris: Beauchesne et Ses Fils, 1949–1971)

Mariology — Juniper B. Carol, O.F.M., ed., *Mariology*, 3 vols. (Milwaukee: Bruce Publishing Co., 1955–1961)

Messages — *Messages of John Paul II: Servant of Truth* (Boston: St. Paul Editions, 1979)

MSS — *Maria in Sacra Scriptura: Acta Congressus Mariologici-Mariani, in Republica Dominicana Anno 1965 Celebrati* (Rome: Pontificia Academia Mariana Internationalis, 1967)

NCE — *New Catholic Encyclopedia*, 15 vols. (New York: McGraw-Hill Book Co., 1967)

NDM — Stefano De Fiores, S.M.M., and Salvatore Meo, O.S.M., eds., *Nuovo Dizionario di Mariologia* (Milan: Edizioni Paoline, 1985)

OL — *Our Lady: Papal Teachings*, trans. Daughters of St. Paul (Boston: St. Paul Editions, 1961)

Omelie — Karol Wojtyła, *Maria: Omelie*, trans. Janina Korzeniewska (Vatican City: Libreria Editrice Vaticana, 1982)

OR — *L'Osservatore Romano*, daily Italian edition

ORE	*L'Osservatore Romano*, weekly edition in English. First number = cumulative edition number; second number = page
PC	*Perfectae Caritatis* (Vatican II Decree on the Up-to-Date Renewal of Religious Life)
PG	J. P. Migne, *Patrologia Graeca*
PL	J. P. Migne, *Patrologia Latina*
PO	*Presbyterorum Ordinis* (Vatican II Decree on the Ministry and Life of Priests)
Poland	*Pilgrim to Poland* (Boston: St. Paul Editions, 1979)
Portugal	*Portugal: Message of Fatima* (Boston: St. Paul Editions, 1983)
RSV	Revised Standard Version of the Holy Bible
SC	*Sources Chrétiennes* (Lyons)
ST	*Summa Theologiae*
Talks	*Talks of John Paul II* (Boston: St. Paul Editions, 1979)
Theotokos	Michael O'Carroll, C.S.Sp., *Theotokos: A Theological Encyclopedia of the Blessed Virgin Mary* (Wilmington: Michael Glazier, Inc.; Dublin: Dominican Publications, 1982)
TPS	*The Pope Speaks* (1954–)

Unger	Dominic Unger, O.F.M. Cap., ed. and trans., *Mary, Christ and the Church* (Bay Shore, N.Y.: Montfort Publications, 1979)
U.S.A.	*U.S.A.—The Message of Justice, Peace and Love* (Boston: St. Paul Editions, 1979)
VI	*Virgo Immaculata: Acta Congressus Mariologici-Mariani Romae Anno MCMLIV Celebrati* (Rome: Pontificia Academia Mariana Internationalis, 1956)

FOREWORD

It gives me great joy to write a few words of introduction to this book in which Father Arthur B. Calkins examines John Paul II's program of Marian consecration and entrustment, highlighting particularly the fact that this program takes its origin from the will of Christ and is ultimately directed to Him. Having worked closely with Father Calkins for almost three years, I have had ample opportunity to appreciate his overall theological preparation, his particular familiarity with Mariology, his careful judgment, and his facility in expressing complex matters with clarity.

Father Calkins has chosen a most important topic, one which helps us to appreciate more profoundly this characteristic note of the spirituality which is lived by so many and which has become a special hallmark of the pontificate of Pope John Paul II. One must also recognize that this spirituality of consecration or entrustment to the Mother of God is a "sign of contradiction" (cf. Lk 2:34) for not so few among our separated brothers and even those within the Church. My hope is that those who have difficulties with this practice might consider attentively its scriptural bases as they are indicated by the Holy Father and faithfully presented by Father Calkins. But for those, as well, who are already disposed in one way or another to the prospect of giving themselves entirely into the hands of Our Lady in order to belong more completely to her Divine Son, I believe that this work may prove to be of great value.

Without being exhaustive, I find Father Calkins' treatment of Marian consecration in the spiritual journey of the

Church very interesting and informative. I would single out for particular attention his handling of two important developments in the modern period. He has indicated the significant role of the Marian Congregations promoted since the sixteenth century by the Society of Jesus and the importance of their formula of consecration to Our Lady (even if one might regret the recent modification of their title), and he has established the fact very clearly that by the formula "Marian consecration" Saint Louis-Marie Grignion de Montfort always understood the consecration of oneself to Christ through the hands of Mary.[1]

What Father Calkins corroborates in de Montfort and, indeed, in all the other major proponents of entrustment to Mary is the right understanding of "through Mary". For instance, when de Montfort speaks of Mary's mediation or of our going to Christ through her, he is not setting up Our Lady as a barrier which must be overcome before reaching Our Lord, nor as a hurdle which must be surmounted before arriving at our goal, nor of any chronological process. Rather, according to de Montfort, with Mary we reach Jesus more quickly, love Him more tenderly, and serve Him more faithfully. The "through Mary" brings about a more intensely immediate union with the Eternal and Incarnate Wisdom. Mary does not stand in the way. Far from it, she is the "mysterious milieu", the atmosphere in which our union with God is readily facilitated.

I would also like to highlight the importance of Father Calkins' book precisely in this postconciliar period in which we live. Indeed, the Council had rightly insisted on seeing and understanding Mary in terms of her role in the mystery of Christ (something which the Church has consistently striven to do in every era), but what happened instead in not so few places was the virtual elimination of Marian devotions including the centuries-old practice of Marian con-

[1] Cf. *Redemptoris Mater*, no. 48.

secration. This negative, even if perhaps well-intentioned, program was carried out in the name of Christocentrism, conciliar renewal, and a "return to the basics". Happily, I believe that at the moment we are beginning to witness a "Marian revival", and I believe that this owes no little to the efforts of our present Holy Father.

In point of fact, the Council Fathers had specifically stated that the practice and exercises of devotion toward Our Lady "recommended by the teaching authority of the Church in the course of centuries be highly esteemed".[2] In order to emphasize this and that the Council had not "downgraded" the position of Our Lady in any way, Pope Paul VI wrote his apostolic exhortation *Marialis Cultus* in 1974 and publicly renewed the entrustment of the Church to Our Lady the following year. By carefully tracing the major outlines of the history of Marian consecration in the life of the Church and showing their remarkable convergence in what Father Calkins refers to as Pope John Paul II's "program of entrustment", he has, I believe, performed a very valuable service.

On the level of both academic theology and pastoral practice, the author has done well to elucidate what he considers the two fundamental principles which allow one to speak of and practice consecration and entrustment to Mary: the principle of analogy and that of mediation. Even more, I believe he has convincingly shown how these principles underlie the whole tradition of "giving oneself into the hands of Mary" as it has come down to us in the Church and as it is tirelessly preached and carried out by Pope John Paul II.

Likewise Father Calkins has not hesitated to grapple with the issue of "entrustment versus consecration". While he readily acknowledges that our Holy Father has a certain preference for the word "entrust" and appropriately notes the specific shadings of the Polish equivalent *zawierzać*, he

[2] *Lumen Gentium*, no. 67.

wisely draws our attention to the fact that Pope John Paul II uses these terms synonymously and concludes that they both express the spiritual reality of "belonging to Mary", though with somewhat different nuances which are not contradictory but complementary. Hence, after centuries of being "consecrated by use", the expression "consecration to Mary" is still legitimate today.

I believe that future scholars will be indebted to this work for the major lines which it traces, for the solidity of its argumentation, for the affinity of the author with the theme of his study, and, not least, for the impressive bibliography which Father Calkins has consulted and which can obviously serve also as a useful quarry for future studies. For this reason it seems to me that this book is an excellent choice with which to launch the new series, Academy of the Immaculate: Studies and Texts. But even more, I hope that it will help many—priests, religious, and above all the interested members of the faithful—to understand the ineffable gift of His Mother given by the dying Lord to His beloved disciple (Jn 19:25–27).

Finally, as this study presents and synthesizes so strikingly one of the very important ways in which our Holy Father "strengthens his brethren" (Lk 22:32), I fondly hope that it will also elicit for him who truly bears the burden of all the churches (2 Cor 11:28) a great outpouring of appreciation, support, and filial love.

— ✠ Paul Augustine Cardinal Mayer, O.S.B.

PREFACE

The theme of consecration to Mary came to the fore in my life virtually simultaneously with the beginning of the pontificate of Pope John Paul II. The day I made my personal consecration to the Mother of God, the Feast of the Immaculate Conception, 1978, was the day that the Pope launched what I refer to as his "program of Marian consecration and entrustment" from the Patriarchal Basilica of Saint Mary Major. On that day he said:

> The Pope, at the beginning of his episcopal service in St. Peter's Chair in Rome, wishes to entrust the Church particularly to her in whom there was accomplished the stupendous and complete victory of good over evil, of love over hatred, of grace over sin; to her of whom Paul VI said that she is "the beginning of the better world;" to the Blessed Virgin. He entrusts to her himself, as the servant of servants, and all those whom he serves, all those who serve with him. He entrusts to her the Roman Church, as token and principle of all the churches in the world, in their universal unity. He entrusts it to her and offers it to her as her property.[1]

Curiously, I was not aware when I made that act of consecration to Mary in Warwick Neck, Rhode Island, that a major feature of the papal service of John Paul II was being established, propelling the whole Church in the same direction that I, too, had by God's grace deliberately taken that day. In a relatively short period of time I became conscious of a new dimension in my life, a new confidence in God's

[1] *Insegnamenti Giovanni Paolo II* (1978), (Vatican City: Libreria Editrice Vaticana, 1979–), 313 (hereafter cited as *Inseg*); *Talks of John Paul II* (Boston: St. Paul Editions, 1979), 424 (hereafter cited as *Talks*).

providence, a new freedom; I sensed the gentle, maternal, yet powerful presence of Mary.

Perhaps not so strangely, because of my initiation into the formal discipline of theology in those stormy years immediately after the Council, even though I felt drawn to put my life entirely in Mary's hands, I was also hesitant. Would such an act not stand in the way of my relationship with Jesus? Father George Kosicki, C.S.B., then coordinator of Bethany House of Intercession for Priests, made two comments to me which I have never forgotten. The first was an accommodation of the text of Matthew 1:20: "Do not fear to take Mary to yourself because that which is conceived in her is of the Holy Spirit." [2] The second was in the nature of a personal testimony made by Cardinal Leo Josef Suenens to this effect: "If God has entrusted a special role to His Mother in our salvation, who are we to tell Him that He can't?" [3] Both of these reflections helped me over my theological hurdles and providentially smoothed the way for me to make the total gift of myself to Mary in order to belong ever more completely to Jesus.

When the time was made available for me to do further graduate work in theology with a specialization in Mariology, I was already deeply convinced of the value of Marian consecration for leading the Christian life and wanted to illustrate why this is necessarily so. Through much reading and discussions with Father Théodore Koehler, S.M., then Director of the International Marian Research Institute at the University of Dayton and Curator of the university's Marian Library, I came to the subject of the program of the Marian consecration and entrustment of the Pope. Could one discover a theological rationale in the homilies, addresses, and writings of John Paul II? I wanted to find out.

[2] Cf. George W. Kosicki, C.S.B., *Born of Mary: Testimonies, Tensions, Teachings* (Stockbridge, Mass.: Marian Press, 1985), xiii, 6–7.

[3] Cf. ibid., 6.

Besides recognizing my debt of gratitude to Fathers George Kosicki and Théodore Koehler for guiding me along a rich and fruitful path, I would also like to acknowledge the never-failing encouragement I received from Father Peter Damian Fehlner, O.F.M. Conv., who arranged for the publication of the licentiate thesis which I had written under Father Koehler's direction in *Miles Immaculatae*[4] and subsequently became the moderator of this doctoral study. His help has been unstinting, positive, and generous in every phase of this work—even beyond the defense. Would that every doctoral student could have such a director! I am also grateful to Father Giovanni Iammarrone, O.F.M. Conv., president of the Seraphicum, for his welcoming me into the academic community of the Pontifical Faculty of Saint Bonaventure and the interest he showed in my work, and Father Maurizio Wszołek, O.F.M. Conv., for his helpful comments regarding methodology and the organization of this work.

While I cannot name all those to whom I am indebted for their support in the course of these past six years, I cannot neglect to mention their Excellencies, the Most Reverend Philip M. Hannan, Archbishop Emeritus of New Orleans, and his successor, the Most Reverend Francis B. Schulte, who allowed me to undertake and continue this study. I am also pleased to acknowledge my debt of gratitude to the Most Reverend Constantino Luna, O.F.M., Bishop Emeritus of Zacapa, Guatemala, and international president of the World Apostolate of Fatima, whose encouragement and fatherly kindness have been a constant source of support to me since I first met him in 1984. It is also my happy task to acknowledge with deep appreciation the kindness and generosity of Father Herman J. Schnurr, a faithful priest for over half a century and a fervent lover of the Mother of

[4] "John Paul II's Consecration to the Immaculate Heart of Mary: Christological Foundation", *Miles Immaculatae* 23 (1987): 88–116, 364–417.

God, whose generous benefactions made it possible for me to spend 1989 as a year of research and writing in Rome along with the inestimable benefit of my library and computer.

It was also a great privilege for me to benefit from the priestly example and paternal concern of Paul Augustine Cardinal Mayer, first president of the Pontifical Commission "Ecclesia Dei", during the time of the writing of this thesis, and I am especially grateful to His Eminence for gracing its defense with his presence.

Finally I must thank those "behind the scenes": my mother, Mrs. Shirley Kopf; Miss Deborah Ann DeDuck; Father James McCurry, O.F.M. Conv.; the Carmelites of Erie, Flemington, and Regina Carmeli in Rome; the Colettine Poor Clares of Newport News; and the many friends in North America and in Rome whose names remain "in pectore".

INTRODUCTION

The theological problem

The placing of oneself in the hands of Mary, the gift of oneself to her, is, as we shall see, an ancient tradition in the Church, attested to in every era of her life. Yet at the same time this custom raises a "theological problem": How can one give, entrust, or consecrate oneself to a human person when only God is the ultimate goal of our lives? Has the "tradition" of the Church in this regard actually been a "corruption" which needs to be purged of impure elements that divert our full attention from Christ who is the only "way" to the Father (cf. Jn 14:6)? As a young theology student in the years immediately following the Second Vatican Council I was inclined to think so.

It seemed obvious that the goal of the Council was to bring us back to our roots, to sweep away unnecessary accretions, to reset our goals. From this perspective, consecration to Mary seemed to be missing the mark. Why consecrate oneself to Mary? Why not simply go straight to Jesus? Why multiply expendable "go-betweens"? The question continues to be asked today.

Happily, the history of Catholic theology provides answers to these questions as we shall see in our survey of Marian consecration in the spiritual journey of the Church. Two great protagonists and theorists of this practice come readily to mind, although they are far from being the only ones: Saints Louis-Marie Grignion de Montfort and Maximilian-Maria Kolbe. Although their veneration for Mary was very great and they called themselves respectively her "slave" and her "possession and property", they cannot in justice be accused of "mariolatry" because in their vision Jesus was never eclipsed by His Mother.

Nonetheless, from a "negative" perspective, it is still useful in every era to ask the crucial questions again because they are perennial and we gain in understanding as we work our way through them. Not only that, but there are many Catholics today who fear that the gift of oneself to Mary is at best an indirect way to Jesus or at worst an obstruction. Further, there are many of our separated Christian brothers and sisters for whom the very idea of consecrating or entrusting oneself to Mary appears as a disturbing deviation from Gospel Christianity. Indeed, is there a Christological foundation for such a practice?

From the "positive" perspective as well, there is value in raising the question anew. What is the hidden spiritual dynamism which explains the phenomenal growth of movements like the Legion of Mary and Maximilian Kolbe's Niepokalanów, which can topple oppressive regimes in places as disparate as Poland and the Philippines? Why is the Pope so doggedly persistent in entrusting every local church, country, and the universal Church to the Mother of God? Is there a Christological perspective which justifies such deportment?

The purpose of this study

Hence the explicit purpose of this study is to analyze the act of consecration or entrustment to Mary in order to discover its basis in the mystery of Christ the Incarnate Word and in the eternal plan of God—and to do so explicitly in terms of the teaching and practice of the Church's supreme pastor, Pope John Paul II.

Since his election to the papacy on October 16, 1978, he has not hesitated to bring the role of Mary to the forefront of Catholic life and thought. The newly elected Pope John Paul II, speaking spontaneously from the central loggia of Saint Peter's Basilica on the occasion of his first public appearance as Pope, said:

> I was afraid to accept this nomination, but *I did it in the spirit of obedience to our Lord Jesus Christ and of total confidence in His Mother, the most holy Madonna.* . . . I present myself to you all to confess our common faith, our hope, *our confidence in the Mother of Christ and of the Church*, and also to start anew on this road of history and of the Church, with the help of God and with the help of men.[1]

Not only did the newly elected Supreme Pontiff break with precedent in addressing himself to the estimated throng of 200,000 who had gathered in Saint Peter's Square that evening to discover the identity of the 263rd successor of Peter and to receive his first blessing, but he also sounded one of the most persistent notes of his pontificate: *total confidence in Mary*.

This had already been signaled twenty years before with his episcopal coat of arms whose primary feature is a cross "which does not correspond to the customary heraldic model",[2] but which is "enough off center to make room for the initial of Mary, symbolically standing at the foot of the Cross of her Son",[3] thus underscoring her unique role in the Redemption. In iconographic language the statement cannot be missed—even if it may be a source of chagrin to experts in ecclesiastical heraldry. But if the symbolism were not enough, the motto would clearly bring the matter home; its simple words "Totus tuus" are transposed and excerpted from a Latin prayer composed by Saint Louis-Marie Grignion de Montfort: *tuus totus ego sum, et omnia mea tua sunt, O Virgo super omnia benedicta*,[4] and rendered into English: "I belong to you entirely, and all that I possess is yours, Virgin blessed above all."[5]

[1] *Inseg* I (1978), 3; *Talks*, 48–49; my emphasis.

[2] Cf. *Talks*, 47.

[3] George Huntston Williams, *The Mind of John Paul II: Origins of His Thought and Action* (New York: Seabury Press, 1981), 279.

[4] *Oeuvres complètes de saint Louis-Marie Grignion de Montfort* (Paris: Éditions du Seuil, 1982), 839.

[5] *God Alone: The Collected Writings of St. Louis Mary de Montfort* (Bay Shore, N.Y.: Montfort Publications, 1987), 515.

Indeed it cannot be doubted that Pope John Paul II has brought the figure of Mary and her maternal relationship with the followers of her Son to the fore in the course of his pontificate in ways that surpass those of all his predecessors. And chief among the ways in which he has accomplished this have been the unprecedented and constantly multiplying acts of consecration or entrustment to Mary which he has made and commented upon. Pope John Paul's declaration of the second Marian Year in the history of the Church on January 1, 1987,[6] and the subsequent celebration of that special time of grace[7] for the Church from Pentecost of 1987 to the Feast of the Assumption in 1988 with the issuance of the encyclical letter *Redemptoris Mater*[8] has further created the context in which to study his understanding of the relationship which the Lord Jesus willed between His Mother and His followers.

The unprecedented and constantly multiplying acts of consecration or entrustment to Mary which I alluded to above constitute what I will refer to throughout this study as the Holy Father's "program of entrustment". "If the last popes have spoken in positive terms of Marian consecration," says Stefano De Fiores, "John Paul II has made of it one of the characteristic programmatic points of his pontificate",[9] "a programmatic point of spiritual life and pastoral practice".[10]

[6] *Inseg* X:1 (1987), 6–7; *L'Osservatore Romano*, English ed., 969:5 (hereafter cited as *ORE*).

[7] René Laurentin in the title of his book on the topic describes the Marian Year as *A Year of Grace with Mary*. The English edition, translated by Msgr. Michael J. Wrenn, was published by Veritas, Dublin, in 1987.

[8] *Inseg* X:1 (1987), 678–744; *Mother of the Redeemer: On the Blessed Virgin Mary in the Life of the Pilgrim Church* (Boston: St. Paul Editions, 1987).

[9] Stefano De Fiores, "Consacrazione", in *Nuovo Dizionario di Mariologia*, ed. Stefano De Fiores, S.M.M., and Salvatore Meo, O.S.M. (Milan: Edizioni Paoline, 1985), 406 (my trans.), (hereafter cited as "Cons." and *NDM* respectively).

[10] Stefano De Fiores, S.M.M., "Questi tuoi figli o Madre", *L'Osservatore Romano* 121, no. 285:2 (my trans.), (hereafter cited as *OR*).

The present state of research

While this "program of entrustment" has been duly noted by any number of commentators and scholars such as Father De Fiores, no one has undertaken a systematic study of it. Thus far the most detailed inquiry would seem to be that of Padre Angel Luis, C.SS.R., "La consagración a María en la vida y doctrina de Juan Pablo II", which appeared in *Estudios Marianos* (51:77–112) in 1986, and, while that essay is helpful in signaling some fundamental texts and their magisterial precedents, it rather exposes the topic than treats it thoroughly.

Hence what I wish to present in this study is an in-depth analysis of the papal magisterium of Pope John Paul II with regard to the question of Marian consecration, based on his published statements which occur in homilies, addresses, official documents, and prayers.[11] For the sake of assessing the continuity and consistency of his thought, I have also had recourse to Italian and English translations of his prepapal writings and homilies.[12] Without a doubt there are further riches to be mined in the corpus of his works produced as priest and bishop in Krakow and further studies to be undertaken, but I have limited myself primarily to his papal teaching, which is most important for the life of the universal Church.

The sources

Since his first papal visit to the Patriarchal Basilica of Saint Mary Major on the Feast of the Immaculate Conception in

[11] The principal source for these is *Insegnamenti di Giovanni Paolo II*, published by the Libreria Editrice Vaticana. In the case of English translations I depend almost entirely on the translations provided by the weekly English edition of *L'Osservatore Romano* or convenient collections of those published by the Daughters of St. Paul in the United States (St. Paul Editions).

[12] See the bibliography, where I list prepapal works.

1978, John Paul has hardly passed up an opportunity of placing the Church and her destiny in the hands of Mary.[13] In virtually every country he visits and every region of Italy to which he travels as its Primate, he seeks out a Marian sanctuary in which to renew his entrustment of the Church Universal and the local church there to the Madonna. And his "habitual acts of entrustment" to Our Lady in addresses to the faithful, in Angelus messages, in pontifical documents, and especially in his fraternal discourses to bishops on their "ad limina" visits are simply legion. Documenting these references has, indeed, been a major preoccupation for me since the autumn of 1984. I am indebted to the late Don Domenico Bertetto, S.D.B., for his indefatigable work of chronicling the Pope's Marian teaching for the first six years of the pontificate in his six volumes entitled *Maria nel Magistero di Giovanni Paolo II* (Rome: Libreria Ateneo Salesiano, 1980–1986). While I never had the privilege of meeting Don Bertetto, his work initiated me into the study of the *fontes* and provided helpful orientation.

The method

The method that I utilize in this study is an analysis of the major themes which I have found to be immediately related to the topic of Marian consecration in the thought of the Pope without attempting to superimpose any category on them. I do point out in the historical section how the Pope is at home with the terminology of virtually every major period in the Church's long tradition of Marian consecration, and I attempt as well to signal for special notice springs

[13]The beautiful book, *Affido a Te, O Maria*, ed. Sergio Trasatti and Arturo Mari (Bergamo: Editrice Velar, 1982), just began to chronicle the principal Marian consecrations of the Pope from December 8, 1978, to June 7, 1981. Fr. Bogumil Lewandowski, in his book, *Tutti consacrati alla Madonna* (Rome, 1988), 48–149, provides some of the major national texts up to the entrustment of the United States in Los Angeles on October 16, 1987.

which seem to have contributed particularly to his formation, such as the thought of de Montfort, Kolbe, and Wyszyński, but the major divisions of part two, the heart of this thesis, have emerged from a steady pondering of the texts themselves.

Following the fundamental work of expository analysis, I consider in the third part the teaching of John Paul II on Marian consecration vis-à-vis the contemporary theological context. There I have simply striven to compare the theological synthesis which I have extracted from the corpus of his papal works with representative contemporary theological thought on the subject of Marian consecration. From this comparison I highlight what I consider to be the primary contributions of John Paul II to the theology of Marian consecration. Finally, in the light of the tradition of Marian consecration in the Church, particularly the magisterial tradition, I indicate areas in which the ongoing teaching of John Paul II might continue to develop fruitfully.

Framework of the Pope's program of entrustment

Within the framework of this "program of entrustment", there are certain acts which emerge as particularly solemn and paradigmatic. The first is the text of June 7, 1981. It was made by previous recording for Pentecost Sunday, June 7, 1981,[14] in conjunction with the celebration of the 1600th anniversary of the First Council of Constantinople and the 1550th anniversary of the Council of Ephesus. The event itself had been planned well in advance by the Pope. The double observance had been the object of a pontifical letter, *A Concilio Constantinopolitano I*, addressed to the bishops of the world,[15] in which he spoke of Mary's divine maternity

[14] *Inseg* IV:1 (1981), 1241–47; *ORE* 688:7, 10.

[15] *Inseg* IV:1 (1981), 815–28; *ORE* 678:6–8.

as establishing a "permanent link with the Church" (*perpetuum vinculum maternum cum Ecclesia*).[16] His more active participation in the festivities marking the observance of these two great councils and culminating on Pentecost Sunday, however, was precluded by an assassin's bullet. The circumstances of this act of entrustment to Mary, which addresses her as "entrusted to the Holy Spirit more than any other human being" and "linked in a profound and maternal way to the Church",[17] are particularly poignant, then, and may also be reckoned as the plea of a stricken father on behalf of his family. The very same act was renewed again on the Feast of the Immaculate Conception in 1981 before the icon of the *Salus Populi Romani* in St. Mary Major's.[18]

The above cited act of entrustment became the archetype of two subsequent acts, closely modeled upon it, which gained considerably more public notice. The first of these was made on May 13, 1982, the Feast of Our Lady of Fatima, in that humble village in Portugal where Our Lady

[16] *Inseg* IV:1 (1981), 824; *ORE* 678:7.

[17] *Inseg* IV:1 (1981), 1245; *ORE* 688:10.

[18] *Inseg* IV:1 (1981), 1245–47; *ORE* 688:10. But for one alteration, the text as it appears in *Inseg* IV:2 (1981), 876–79, is identical with the earlier text except that it uses fewer exclamation points and italics (perhaps merely a matter of the typesetter's discretion). A new English translation was also rendered by the staff of the English language edition of *L'Osservatore Romano*; it seems to differ from the earlier one in only minor stylistic variations; cf. *ORE* 714:12.

The one alteration in the text occurs in the seventh paragraph. In the prior version the Pope said: "Embrace with the love of the Mother and Handmaid of the Lord those who most await this embrace, and also those whose act of dedication you too await in a particular way" (*ORE* 688:10). [*Abbracia con l'amore della Madre e della Serva del Signore coloro che questo abbraccio più aspettano, e insieme coloro il cui affidamento Tu pure attendi in modo particolare* {*Inseg* IV:1 (1981), 1246}.] In the version he used on this date he said: "Embrace with the love of the Mother and the Handmaid of the Lord the peoples who await this embrace the most, and likewise the peoples whose consecration you, too, are particularly awaiting" (*ORE* 714:12). [*Abbraccia con l'amore della Madre e della Serva del Signore i popoli che questo abbraccio più aspettano, e insieme i popoli il cui affidamento Tu pure attendi in modo particolare* {*Inseg* IV:2 (1981), 878}.]

had first appeared sixty-five years earlier. It was also the first anniversary of the nearly fatal attempt on his life. These two events have remained closely linked in the mind of the Holy Father as he himself told the people of Portugal:

> I come here today because on this very day last year, in St. Peter's Square in Rome, the attempt on the Pope's life was made, in mysterious coincidence with the anniversary of the first apparition at Fatima, which occurred on May 13, 1917.
>
> I seemed to recognize in the coincidence of the dates a special call to come to this place. And so, today I am here. I have come in order to thank divine Providence in this place which the Mother of God seems to have chosen in a particular way. *Misericordiae Domini, quia non sumus consumpti* ["Through God's mercy we were spared" (Lam 3:22)], I repeat once more with the prophet.[19]

> I had already intended for some time to come to Fatima, as I have already had occasion to say upon my arrival in Lisbon. But after the well-known attempt on my life a year ago in St. Peter's Square, on regaining consciousness, my thoughts turned immediately to this sanctuary to place in the heart of the heavenly Mother my thanks for having saved me from danger. I saw in everything that was happening—I never tire of repeating it—a special motherly protection of our Lady. And in the coincidence—there are no mere coincidences in the plans of divine Providence—I also saw an appeal and, who knows, a reminder of the message which came from here 65 years ago, through three children, children of simple country people, the little shepherds of Fatima, as they became known throughout the world.[20]

The importance of this event had been previously signaled to the bishops of the world by a letter of April 19, 1982,[21] addressed to each of them by Cardinal Agostino Casaroli, secretary of state to His Holiness, informing them that he intended "in spiritual union with all the Bishops of

[19] *Inseg* V:2 (1982), 1569; *Portugal: Message of Fatima* (Boston: St. Paul Editions, 1983), 74 (hereafter cited as *Portugal*).

[20] *Inseg* V:2 (1982), 1537–38; *Portugal*, 49–50.

[21] Secretariat of State, no. 85685.

the world, to renew the two acts whereby Pope Pius XII entrusted the world to the Immaculate Heart of Mary". The Pope also announced his intentions to the faithful in the course of his Regina Caeli message of May 9, 1982.[22] The act itself was preceded by a finely-wrought homily[23] on Mary's role in the Christian life, her spiritual maternity, and the meaning of consecration to her and was renewed again on October 16, 1983, after the Canonization Mass of Saint Leopold Mandić of Castelnovo, in the presence of all the bishops who were attending the Synod on Reconciliation and Penance.[24]

The second of the acts deriving from that of Pentecost Sunday, 1981, was given more advance publication, and correspondingly more emphasis was placed on the collegial nature of the act. It was announced in a pontifical letter to all the bishops of the world, dated from the Vatican on December 8, 1983, but only published on February 17, 1984.[25] It was intended to be one of the crowning acts of the Holy Year of the Redemption which began on March 25, 1983, and concluded on Easter Day, April 22, 1984. John Paul presented the rationale to his brother bishops in this way:

> In the context of the Holy Year of the Redemption, I desire to profess this [infinitely salvific] power [of the Redemption] together with you and with the whole Church. I desire to profess it through the Immaculate Heart of the Mother of God, who in a most particular degree experienced this salvific power. The words of the Act of consecration and entrusting which I enclose, correspond, with a few small changes, to those which I pronounced at Fatima on 13 May 1982. I am profoundly convinced that the repetition of this Act in the course of the Jubilee Year of the Redemption cor-

[22] *Inseg* V:2 (1982), 1460-61; *ORE* 734:2.

[23] *Inseg* V:2 (1982), 1567-77; *Portugal* 72–85.

[24] *Inseg* VI:2 (1983), 793–96; *ORE* 735:5–12. This was done with the omission of paragraphs 2–7 of number 1.

[25] *Inseg* VII:1 (1984), 416–18; *ORE* 823:2.

> responds to the expectations of many human hearts, which wish to renew to the Virgin Mary the testimony of their devotion and to entrust to her their sorrows at the many different ills of the present time, their fears of the menaces that brood over the future, their preoccupations for peace and justice in the individual nations and in the whole world.
>
> The most fitting date for this common witness seems to be the Solemnity of the Annunciation of the Lord during Lent 1984. I would be grateful if on that day (24 March, on which the Marian Solemnity is liturgically anticipated, or on 25 March, the Third Sunday of Lent) you would renew this Act together with me, choosing the way which each of you considers most appropriate.[26]

The act itself was carried out by the Pope on Sunday, March 25, 1984, in Saint Peter's Square before the statue of Our Lady of Fatima, which ordinarily occupies the site of Mary's appearances at the Cova da Iria in Fatima, Portugal, and which was flown to the Vatican especially for this occasion. The act of entrustment[27] was recited by the Pope after the Mass commemorating the Jubilee Day of Families.

Again on May 13, 1991, the tenth anniversary of the attempt on his life, the Pope went to Fatima to thank Our Lady for her powerful intervention in sparing his life and to renew once more the consecration of the world to her. The text of this act of entrustment was quite independent of those of 1982 and 1984 from a literary perspective and considerably briefer. In the course of this prayer of dedication, he spoke personally to the Virgin as "*My Mother* for ever, and especially on 13 May 1981, when I felt your helpful presence at my side", while addressing her also as "Mother

[26] *Inseg* VII:1 (1984), 417–18; *ORE* 823:2.

[27] *Inseg* VII:1 (1984), 774-77; *ORE* 828:9–10. The text is exactly the same as that earlier transmitted to all the bishops of the Church (*Inseg* VII:1 [1984], 418–21; *ORE* 823:2, 12) with this exception: that the Pope inserted between the two sentences of the last paragraph of number 2 these additional words when he recited it in St. Peter's Square: "Enlighten especially the peoples whose consecration and entrustment by us you are awaiting" (*ORE* 828:10); [*Illumina specialmente i popoli di cui tu aspetti la nostra consacrazione e il nostro affidamento* {*Inseg* VII:1 (1984), 776}].

of Christ and of the Church", "Mother of all people", "Mother of the nations", and "Mother of life". Concluding this invocation he declared: "In Collegial union with the pastors, in communion with the entire People of God spread to the four corners of the earth, today I renew the filial entrustment of the human race to you. *With confidence we entrust everyone to you.*" [28]

These great events which stand out in the pontificate of Pope John Paul II must not be seen as isolated acts, but rather as special moments in continuity with his whole "program of entrustment". Here is how he spoke of his "program" without calling it such in his address to the College of Cardinals at the end of 1979, his first full year as Pope:

> All this *per Mariam*. I entrusted the beginning of my Pontificate to her, and I brought to her in the course of the year the expression of my filial piety, which I learned from my parents. Mary was the star of my way, in her most famous or most silent sanctuaries: Mentorella and St. Mary Major, Guadalupe and Jasna Gora, Knock and the national Sanctuary of Mary Immaculate at Washington, Loreto, Pompei, Ephesus. I entrust myself to her. To her I entrust the whole Church, now ending a year and awaiting the dawn of the new one. [29]

Again he spoke thus to the Roman Curia on the Vigil of the Feast of Saints Peter and Paul in 1982:

> This year, in a special way, after the attempt on my life which by coincidence occurred on the anniversary of the apparition of the Virgin at Fatima, my conversation with Mary has been, I should like to say, uninterrupted. I have repeatedly entrusted to her the destiny of all peoples: beginning with the act of consecration of 8 December [1981], Feast of the Immaculate Conception, to the consecration to the Virgin of the countries visited: of Nigeria at

[28] *ORE* 1191:7. The act of entrustment was made in Portuguese. An Italian translation was published in *OR* 122, no. 109 (1982): 1.

[29] *Inseg* II:2 (1979), 1497; *ORE* 615:13.

> Kaduna, of Equatorial Guinea at Bata, of Gabon at Libreville, of Argentina at the Sanctuary of Lujan. I remember the visits to the Italian sanctuaries of Our Lady of Montenero in Livorno, and of Our Lady of St. Luke in Bologna; culminating in the pilgrimage to Fatima in Portugal, "Land of St. Mary," which was a personal act of gratitude to Our Lady, almost the fulfillment of a tacit vow for the protection granted me through the Virgin, and a solemn act of consecration of the whole human race to the Mother of God, in union with the Church through my humble service.[30]

There has been no veering from the path of this "program of entrustment" from the beginning of the pontificate nor any suggestion that he considers it finished. For instance, he solemnly consecrated Poland to its Queen on his first return visit as Pope on June 4, 1979,[31] but he also did so again with less external pomp, but no less explicitly, on June 19, 1983.[32] Again on the Feast of the Assumption in 1991 he led a huge international throng of youth in an act of entrustment to Our Lady at Jasna Góra as a major feature of the Sixth World Youth Day.[33] Likewise he entrusted the United States to Mary on October 7, 1979, in Washington, D.C.,[34] and again in Los Angeles on September 16, 1987.[35] It would be possible to adduce other such instances at great length while what I have referred to as the "habitual" entrustments number in the hundreds every year according to the texts supplied in *L'Osservatore Romano* and in the *Insegnamenti*.

[30] *Inseg* V:2 (1982), 2442-43; *ORE* 744:6.

[31] *Inseg* II:1 (1979), 1416–19; *Pilgrim to Poland* (Boston: St. Paul Editions, 1979), 110–15 (hereafter cited as *Poland*).

[32] *Inseg* VI:1 (1983), 1595–1600; *ORE* 791:9–10.

[33] *ORE* 1204:7.

[34] *Inseg* II:2 (1979), 683–84; *U.S.A.—The Message of Justice, Peace and Love* (Boston: St. Paul Editions, 1979), 250–53 (hereafter cited as *U.S.A.*).

[35] *Inseg* X:3 (1987), 593–95.

PART ONE

MARIAN CONSECRATION IN THE SPIRITUAL JOURNEY OF THE CHURCH

I

HISTORICAL FORMS

While it seems indisputable that John Paul II has given an enormous impetus to the promotion of consecration or entrustment to Mary from the outset of his pontificate, it is equally clear that this practice is very ancient in the Church. Further on in this study we will consider the scriptural bases for this practice so deeply rooted in the Church, but for the moment let us look at some of its principal expressions in the life of the Church.

The patristic period

It does not seem presumptuous to see the first adumbrations of the tradition which would come to be known as Marian consecration in the Church in the most ancient recorded prayer to the Mother of God, the *Sub tuum praesidium.*[1] It is the filial prayer of Christians who know Mary's motherly

[1] Discovered in 1917, a papyrus now kept in the John Rylands Library in Manchester, England, contains the text of this Marian prayer which makes it the oldest invocation of the Mother of God which has been found thus far. Cf. Gerard S. Sloyan, "Marian Prayers", in *Mariology*, ed. Juniper B. Carol, vol. 3 (Milwaukee: Bruce Publishing Co., 1961), 64–68; I. Calabuig Adan, O.S.M., "Liturgia", *NDM,* 778–79; Théodore Koehler, S.M., "Maternité Spirituelle, Maternité Mystique", in *Maria: Études sur la Sainte Vierge*, ed. Hubert du Manoir, S.J., vol. 6 (Paris: Beauchesne et Ses Fils, 1961), 571–74 (latter hereafter cited as *Maria*); Gabriele Giamberardini, O.F.M., *Il culto mariano in Egitto*, vol. 1 of *Secoli I–VI* (Jerusalem: Franciscan Printing Press, 1975), 69–97; Achille M. Triacca, "*Sub tuum praesidium*: nella *lex orandi* un'anticipata presenza della *lex credendi*. La *teotocologia* precede la

mercy (*eusplangchnía* in the Greek text) and therefore do not hesitate to have recourse to her protection (*praesidium* in the Latin text). If it does not speak of belonging to Mary, it is surely not far removed from this concept.

The redoubtable Marian encyclopedist, Father Michael O'Carroll, C.S.Sp., renders this third- or, at the latest, fourth-century prayer according to the reconstruction of Father Gabriele Giamberardini, O.F.M.: "Under your mercy, we take refuge, Mother of God, do not reject our supplications in necessity. But deliver us from danger. [You] alone chaste, alone blessed."[2] This Marian troparion used in almost all the Rites of the Church and cited in the Marian chapter of *Lumen Gentium*[3] is ordinarily rendered into English after the Latin version: "We fly to thy patronage, O holy Mother of God, despise not our petitions in our necessities, but deliver us from all danger, O ever glorious and blessed Virgin."[4]

This ancient Marian invocation is of capital importance from many perspectives. First, it constitutes a remarkable witness to the fact that prayer was already explicitly addressed to Mary as *Theotókos* or "Mother of God" long before the Council of Ephesus vindicated the use of this title in 431. Secondly, it may well reflect a tradition even older than the third century, the era from which many scholars believe the Egyptian papyrus dates, going all the way back to the apostolic period. Thirdly, while this antiphon (called a

---

mariologia?" in *La mariologia nella catechesi dei Padri (età prenicena)*, ed. Sergio Felici (Rome: Libreria Ateneo Salesiano "Biblioteca di Scienza Religiosa", no. 88, 1989), 183–205; R. Iacoangeli, "*Sub tuum praesidium.* La più antica preghiera mariana: filologia e fede", ibid., 207–40.

[2] Michael O'Carroll, C.S.Sp., *Theotokos: A Theological Encyclopedia of the Blessed Virgin Mary* (Wilmington: Michael Glazier; Dublin: Dominican Publications, 1982), 336 (hereafter cited as *Theotokos*).

[3] *Lumen Gentium* (Vatican II Dogmatic Constitution on the Church), no. 66 (hereafter cited as *LG*).

[4] *Theotokos*, 336.

"troparion" according to Byzantine liturgical usage) does not explicitly call Mary "our Mother", it does so in equivalent and very expressive terms.

About this justly famous and most ancient of Marian prayers, Father Quéméneur makes this careful observation:

> Here we do not yet have a consecration properly so called, but we already discern the fundamental elements that characterize Marian consecrations. The *Sub tuum* recognizes the patronage of the Mother of God; it is a spontaneous gesture of recourse to Mary. Originating in Egypt, the *Sub tuum*, with slight variations, will soon be taken up by the other churches; starting with the sixth century, it is inserted into the Byzantine, Ambrosian, and Roman liturgies. We can say that it is the root from which the formulas of other Marian prayers will arise.[5]

It is in the light of the biblical connotation of the Greek root *euspla*——[6] that Father Jean-Marie Salgado, O.M.I., does not hesitate to translate the beginning of the *Sub tuum* as "We take refuge in your merciful heart" or "We have recourse to your merciful heart". It seems highly significant that the living tradition of the Church testified to by her early liturgies in both East and West provides further support for rendering *euspla*[*ngchnian*] as heart.[7] If such a rendition of this prayer can be justified—and I believe that the whole tradition seen in its remarkable continuity may well bear this out—then it would seem that the *Sub tuum* pro-

[5] M. Quéméneur, S.M.M., "Towards a History of Marian Consecration", trans. Br. William Fackovec, S.M., *Marian Library Studies* 122 (March 1966): 4. (This excellent article originally appeared as "La consécration de soi à la Vierge à travers l'histoire", *Cahiers Marials*, no. 14 [1959]: 119–28.)

[6] The remainder of the word is missing on the papyrus.

[7] Cf. H. Koester's article "*splángchnon, splangchnízomai, 'eúsplangchnos*", in *Theological Dictionary of the New Testament*, ed. Gerhard Friedrich (Grand Rapids, Mich.: W. B. Eerdmans, 1971), 548–59; and Jean-Marie Salgado, O.M.I., "Aux Origines de la Découverte des Richesses du Cœur Immaculé de Marie: Du IIIè au XIIè Siècle", *Divinitas* 31 (1987): 229–32.

vides a foundation not only for consecration to Mary, but even more specifically for consecration to her Immaculate Heart.

Significantly, and very conscious that he was standing in the most ancient stream of the Church's tradition, John Paul II framed the first part of his great acts of entrustment in 1982 and 1984 with the words of this antiphon: "We have recourse to your protection, holy Mother of God." [8] Likewise, for the Sixth International World Youth Day celebrated at Częstochowa on the Feast of the Assumption in 1991, he began the act of entrustment to Our Lady with the first Latin words of the *Sub tuum* and recited the entire Latin text in the course of the prayer.[9] Also, on the Feast of the Immaculate Conception in 1991 at the traditional ceremony in the Piazza di Spagna, he invoked Our Lady saying: "Under your protection we take refuge once again, at the end of this year, this century, this millennium." [10]

He has further alluded to or quoted this ancient prayer on numerous other occasions: in a Regina Caeli address in 1982,[11] in his Marian encyclical *Redemptoris Mater*,[12] and in the final paragraph of his encyclical *Sollicitudo Rei Socialis*.[13] He referred to it in his commentary on the doctrine of the *Theotókos* in the course of his Christological catecheses[14] and

[8] *Inseg* V:2 (1982), 1586, 1587; *ORE* 735:5, 12; *Inseg* VII:1 (1984), 774, 775. He also utilized the words "we take refuge under your protection" in the Act of Entrustment of Colombia to Mary on July 3, 1986, *Inseg* IX:2 (1986), 93; *ORE* 948:5.

[9] *ORE* 1204:7.

[10] *OR* 131, no. 284:5; *ORE* 1220:5. On that occasion the Pope prayed: "*Sotto la Tua protezione ci rifugiamo . . .*" which is almost exactly the same as the beginning of the ancient prayer in the standard Italian translation: "*Sotto la tua protezione cerchiamo rifugio . . .*"

[11] *Inseg* VI:1 (1983), 1057; *ORE* 782:2.

[12] *Inseg* X:1 (1987), 717; St. Paul ed., 45.

[13] *Inseg* X:3 (1987), 1611–12; *ORE* 1028:13.

[14] *Inseg* XI:1 (1988), 642; *ORE* 1031:1.

has made it his own prayer for various groups upon whom he has invoked Our Lady's protection.[15]

If the *Sub tuum praesidium* testifies to the Christian's child-like tendency to take refuge under the protection of the *Theotókos*, history will illustrate the truth of this many times over in the course of centuries. The first such recourse of which we are aware involving an entrustment to the Mother of God was made by the Byzantine Emperor Heraclius in 626, according to Saint Germanus of Constantinople. When the city on the Bosphorus was in imminent danger, the Emperor confided it to God and the Virgin Mother and it was spared.[16] This is one of several incidents which would lead to the establishment of the Feast of the Protection of the Holy Mother of God (*Pokrov*) who stretches out her mantle over the peoples,[17] and Father Joseph de Sainte-Marie, O.C.D., did not hesitate to see in this the first known collective Marian consecration in history.[18]

Father O'Carroll informs us that his confrère, Father Henri Barré, C.S.Sp., found evidence for the title *servus Mariae* in African sermons from the fifth and sixth centuries which indicate a personal attitude of belonging to Mary.[19]

[15] To a group of clergy from Novara on March 11, 1988, *ORE* 1032:10; to the youth of Bolivia in Cochabamba on May 11, 1988, *ORE* 1043:13; on the occasion of the *Moleben* in honor of the Mother of God during the celebration of the Millennium of Christianity in the Ukraine on July 9, 1988, *ORE* 1051:4.

[16] Cf. Angelo Cardinal Mai, ed., *Nova Patrum Bibliotheca*, vol. 6 of *Pars Secunda* (Rome: Typis Sacri Consilii Propagando Christiano Nomini, 1853), 423–37 (esp. nos. 1, 5, 6, 7, 9, 12, 16); A. Wenger, A.A., "L'Intercession de Marie en Orient du VIè au Xè siècle", *Bulletin de la Société française d'Études Mariales* (hereafter cited as *BSFEM*) 23 (1966): 58; J. Marangos, S.J., "Le Culte Marial Populaire en Grèce", in *Maria*, 4:810–11; Gabriele Roschini, O.S.M., *Il Culto Mariano*, vol. 4 of *Maria Santissima nella Storia della Salvezza* (Isola del Liri: Tipografia Editrice M. Pisani, 1969), 84–85.

[17] Cf. S. Salaville, A.A., "Marie dans la Liturgie Byzantine ou Gréco-Slave", in *Maria*, 1:280; cf. also Quéméneur, 4, and *Redemptoris Mater*, no. 33.

[18] *Teologia e Spiritualità della Consacrazione a Maria* (Rome: Pontificio Istituto di Spiritualità del Teresianum, lectures, n.d.), 1:13.

[19] *Theotokos*, 107.

Father Stefano De Fiores, S.M.M., also points to the use of this term in Saint Ephrem the Syrian (d. 373) and Pope John VII (d. 707), but indicates that these instances cannot compare to the consistent usage and fervor of Saint Ildephonsus of Toledo (d. 667).[20] Ildephonsus is usually considered the first major representative of the spirituality of "Marian slavery"[21] which eventually develops into what is now known as Marian consecration.[22]

Pope John Paul II himself in his homily in Saragossa on November 6, 1982, immediately prior to the Entrustment of Spain to Our Lady, reviewed what is for us the most relevant information about this Benedictine abbot who became the archbishop of Toledo:

> Saint Ildephonsus of Toledo, the most ancient witness of that form of devotion which we call slavery to Mary, justifies our attitude of being slaves of Mary because of the singular relation she has with respect to Christ. "For this reason I am your slave, because your Son is my Lord. Therefore you are my Lady because you are the slave of my Lord. Therefore, I am the slave of the slave of my Lord, because you have been made the Mother of my Lord. Therefore I have been made a slave because you have been made the Mother of my Maker" [*De virginitate perpetua Sanctae Mariae*, 12: *PL* 96, 108].
>
> As is obvious, because of these real and existing relationships between Christ and Mary, Marian devotion has Christ as its ultimate object. The same Saint Ildephonsus saw it with full clarity: "So in this way one refers to the Lord that which serves his slave. So, what is delivered up to the Mother redounds to the Son; thus passes to the King the honor that is rendered in the service of the Queen" [c. 12: *PL* 96, 108]. Then one understands the double

[20] "Cons.", 400. In the case of Pope John VII one might profitably consult the testimony presented in Roschini, *Maria Santissima,* 4:97–98.

[21] Cf. the excellent article by Théodore Koehler, S.M., "Servitude (saint esclavage)", in Marcel Viller et al., *Dictionnaire de Spiritualité Ascétique et Mystique*, vol. 14 (Paris: Beauchesne et Ses Fils, 1990), 730–45 (latter hereafter cited as *DSp*).

[22] Cf. Patrick J. Gaffney, S.M.M., "The Holy Slavery of Love", in *Mariology*, 3:143-46; Roschini, *Maria Santissima,* 4:85–86.

> employment of the desire expressed in the same blessed formula, speaking with the most Holy Virgin: Grant that I may surrender myself to God and to you, to be the slave of your Son and of you, to serve your Lord and you" [c. 12: *PL* 96, 105].[23]

The next major witness to the development of the tradition is the great Doctor of the Church, Saint John of Damascus (d. c. 750). The last of the great Eastern Fathers of the Church interprets the name of Mary according to Syriac etymology to mean "lady" or "mistress". In his *Exposition of the Orthodox Faith* he says of Mary: "Truly she has become the Lady ruler of every creature since she is the Mother of the Creator." [24] In his first homily on the Dormition of the Mother of God he consequently prays:

> We are present before you, O Lady [*Despoina*], Lady, I say, and again, Lady, binding our souls to our hope in you, and as to a most secure and firm anchor [cf. Heb 6:9], *to you we consecrate* [*anathémenoi*] *our minds, our souls, our bodies* [cf. 1 Th 5:23], *in a word, our very selves,* honoring you with psalms, hymns, and spiritual canticles [cf. Eph 5:19], insofar as we are able—even though it is impossible to do so worthily. If truly, as the sacred Word has taught us, the honor paid to our fellow servants testifies to our good will towards our common Master, how could we neglect honoring you who have brought forth your Master? . . . In this way we can better show our attachment to our Master.
>
> Turn your gaze on us, Noble Lady, Mother of the good Master, rule over and direct at your discretion all that concerns us; restrain the impulses of our shameful passions; guide us to the tranquil harbor of the divine will; make us worthy of future blessedness, of the beatific vision in the presence of the Word of God who was made flesh in you.[25]

[23] *Inseg* V:3 (1982), 1179–80; trans. by Debra Duncan.

[24] Cited in Valentine Albert Mitchell, S.M., *The Mariology of Saint John Damascene* (Kirkwood, Mo.: Maryhurst Normal Press, 1930), 76; cf. also 214.

[25] J. P. Migne, *Patrologia Graeca*, 96, 720C–D, 721A–B (hereafter cited as *PG*); *Sources Chrétiennes*, 80, 118 (hereafter cited as *SC*), (my trans., made with reference to *Theotokos*, 199, and Georges Gharib et al., eds., *Padri e altri autori bizantini*, vol. 2 of *Testi Mariani del Primo Millennio* [Rome: Città Nuova Editrice, 1989], 519–20; my emphasis).

One notes how in language which is redolent with scriptural overtones Saint John makes the total gift of himself and those who are joined with him, of all that they have and are, to Our Lady. He deliberately uses the Greek term *anathémenoi* in order to indicate that "consecration" means "setting aside for sacred use". What is literally signified, according to the use of this word in Leviticus 27:28 and in other places in the Old Testament, is that this "giving of oneself to Mary" is so exclusive, absolute, and permanent that one who would revoke the gift would be "cut off" (i.e., *anathema*) from God and his people. In analyzing this text, Father José María Canal, C.M.F., notes three major points: (1) Damascene's deliberate use of the term "consecration" which pertains to setting aside for sacred use; (2) the comprehensiveness of this act which excludes nothing; and (3) its basis in Mary's unique relationship to her Divine Son by virtue of the divine maternity.[26]

The medieval period

In the feudal setting of the early Middle Ages we find the custom of "patronage" (*patrocinium*) becoming widespread. In order to protect their lives and possessions, freemen would vow themselves to the service of their overlords; in exchange for the assurance of protection and the necessities of life, the client would place himself completely at the disposal of his protector. Here is a description by the well-known liturgical scholar, Josef Jungmann, S.J., of a traditional ceremony by which a vassal would put himself under the patronage and at the service of a suzerain:

[26] P. José María Canal, C.M.F., "La Consagración a la Vírgen y a Su Corazón Inmaculado", in *De Virginis Immaculatae Regalitate Eiusque Corde Materno*, vol. 12 of *Virgo Immaculata: Acta Congressus Mariologici-Mariani Romae Anno MCMLIV Celebrati* (Rome: Pontificia Academia Mariana Internationalis, 1956), 234–35 (latter hereafter cited as *V.I.*). Cf. also Joseph de Sainte Marie, *Teologia*, I:14, I:T–2.

> He put his hands in the enfolding hands of the master, just as is done today by the newly ordained priest when he promises honour and obedience to his bishop at the end of the ordination Mass. The act is also called commendation: *se commendare, se tradere, in manus* or *manibus se commendare (tradere)*, and also *patrocinium se commendare (tradere)*. From the side of the overlord there was the corresponding *suscipere, recipere, manus suscipere* and the like.[27]

Not surprisingly in those ages of faith this relationship of vassalage would provide a way of describing one's relationship to Mary. If Jesus is one's Lord, as we have already seen Saint John of Damascus reason, then it is only logical that Mary becomes one's Lady. Fulbert of Chartres (d. 1028) provides us with a beautiful prayer in which he underscores that his consecration to Christ in baptism also makes of him another "beloved disciple" (cf. Jn 19:26–27) "committed" to Mary:

> Remember, O Lady, that in baptism I was consecrated to the Lord and professed the Christian name with my lips. Unfortunately I have not observed what I have promised. Nevertheless I have been handed over [*traditus*] to you and committed to your care [*commendatus*] by the Lord, the living and true God. Watch over the one who has been handed over to you [*traditum*]; keep safe the one who has been committed to your protection [*commendatum*].[28]

Likewise, a freeman who was in debt or otherwise not prospering in his affairs might present himself to an overlord with "a rope around his neck, a sign that [he] was to become a serf, engaging his person, his family and his goods".[29] This, too, could be transferred into the spiritual realm and appropriated to one's relationship to Our Lady as we see in the case of Saint Odilo, abbot of Cluny (d. 1049), who as a

[27] J. A. Jungmann, S.J., *Pastoral Liturgy* (New York: Herder and Herder, 1962), 298.

[28] Henri Barré, C.S.Sp., *Prières Anciennes de L'Occident à la Mère du Sauveur: Des origènes à saint Anselme* (Paris: Lethielleux, 1963), 159 (my trans.).

[29] Quéméneur, 6.

young man consecrated himself to Our Lady by going to a church dedicated to her and presenting himself at her altar with a rope around his neck and praying:

> O most loving Virgin and Mother of the Savior of all ages, from this day and hereafter take me into your service and in all my affairs be ever at my side as a most merciful advocate. For after God I place nothing in any way before you and I give myself over to you forever as your own slave and bondsman [*tanquam proprium servum, tuo mancipatui trado*].[30]

In a very interesting and original piece of research Father Mark Elvins argues on the basis of a fair amount of converging circumstantial evidence that Richard II solemnly consecrated England to Mary as "her Dowry" on the Saturday after Corpus Christi, 1381. He argues that this is pictorially represented in the famous "Wilton Dyptich" housed in London's National Gallery of Art.[31] If this is so, it would seem to represent the first consecration of a kingdom to Our Lady.

Another beautiful image of the *patrocinium* of the Virgin is that of her "protective mantle" or *Schutzmantel* as it has come to be known in German. We have already seen this in the East in the feast and icon of the *Pokrov*.[32] Here is Jungmann's description of the Marian iconography which would become classical in the medieval West:

> The emblem of Citeaux was the image of the Mother of God with the abbots and abbesses of the order kneeling under her mantle. Caesarius of Heisterbach (d. 1240) also knew this motif as he shows in his description of a Cistercian monk in heaven, looking about in vain for his brothers until Mary opens out her wide mantle and discloses a countless number of brothers and nuns. In the later

[30] Barré, *Prières Anciennes*, 147 (my trans.).

[31] Mark Elvins, "The Origin of the Title 'Dowry of Mary' and the Shrines of Our Lady at Westminster", a paper given to the London branch of the Ecumenical Society of the Blessed Virgin Mary on May 18, 1989.

[32] Cf. above, 45.

> Middle Ages especially, the motif of the protective mantle is widespread, commonly as an expression of protection being sought or hoped for, chiefly in connexion with the image of the Mother of God.[33]

The Pope, also, has used this lovely image of the Virgin's protection on numerous occasions, for instance: in an Angelus address on New Year's Day of 1980,[34] in Brazil the same year,[35] in Belice, Sicily, in 1982,[36] in Vienna in 1983,[37] in Liechtenstein in 1985,[38] and in supplication for the Armenians in 1987.[39] Among yet other instances,[40] he concluded an audience with pilgrims from Derry in Northern Ireland on April 13, 1989, praying: "May our Lady of Knock, Queen of Peace, spread her mantle of peace over the whole land."[41] In a letter directed to Discalced Carmelite Nuns and dated on the Feast of St. Thérèse, 1991, he wrote:

> You [Nuns who follow the Constitutions approved respectively in both 1990 and 1991 as well as Carmelite Fathers and Brothers] all call upon Mary as your common Mother, whom the Order's imagery aptly depicts covering the sons and daughters of Carmel from one side to the other with her mantle.[42]

Arnold Bostius (d. 1499), a Flemish Carmelite, wrote explicitly about Mary's patronage and protection of his order in his major Marian work, *De Patronatu et Patrocinio Beatis-*

[33] Jungmann, 300; cf. also *Theotokos*, 93–94; Georges Gharib, "La Madonna della Misericordia: 'Sotto la tua protezione' ", *Madre di Dio* 59 (May 1991): 13–16.

[34] *Inseg* III:1 (1980), 10; *ORE* 614:4.

[35] *Inseg* III:2 (1980), 104; *Brazil: Journey in the Light of the Eucharist* (Boston: St. Paul Editions, 1980), 83 (hereafter cited as *Brazil*).

[36] *Inseg* V:3 (1982), 1343; *ORE* 761:2.

[37] *Inseg* VI:2 (1983), 527; *ORE* 803:11.

[38] *Inseg* VIII:2 (1985), 639; *ORE* 905:7.

[39] *Inseg* X:3 (1987), 1179; *ORE* 1017:7.

[40] Cf. *Inseg* XI:1 (1988), 757; *ORE* 1035:10; *Inseg* XI:3 (1988), 465; *ORE* 1056:21; *Inseg* XII:1 (1989), 1498; *ORE* 1093:12.

[41] *Inseg* XII:1 (1989), 807; *ORE* 1086:11.

[42] *ORE* 1211:2.

simae Virginis Mariae in Dicatum sibi Carmeli Ordinem. Although he did not use the word "consecration" to describe the Carmelite's relationship to Mary because that meaning had not yet been appropriated to the word, he used all the equivalent Latin expressions such as *dicare, dedicare, devovere, sub qua vivere,* etc.,[43] and he maintained, as Pope Pius XII would in his letter *Neminem Profecto* of February 11, 1950,[44] that the wearing of the Carmelite scapular was an explicit sign of the acceptance of Mary's patronage and protection, of the Carmelite's belonging to her.[45]

An interesting liturgical application of this imagery is found in the medieval ceremonial for the consecration of virgins: after the imposition of the veil, the bishop blessed the newly consecrated and exhorted them to live "without stain beneath the mantle of Holy Mary, Mother of Our Lord Jesus Christ".[46] The language of the *patrocinium* is very well attested to with regard to Mary as even a cursory glance at the index of Father Barré's magisterial anthology of medieval Marian prayers will indicate.[47] It also continues to be used by Pope John Paul II in expressions such as "commit",[48] "commend",[49] "place in the hands of

[43] I. Bengoechea, O.C.D., "Un precursor de la consagración a María en el siglo XV: Arnoldo Bostio (1445–1499)", *Estudios Marianos* 51 (1986): 218; cf. also Redemptus M. Valabek, O. Carm., *Mary, Mother of Carmel: Our Lady and the Saints of Carmel,* vol. 1 (Rome: Institutum Carmelitanum, 1987), 74.

[44] *Acta Apostolicae Sedis* 42 (1950): 390–91 (hereafter cited as *AAS*); *Our Lady: Papal Teachings*, trans. Daughters of St. Paul (Boston: St. Paul Editions, 1961), nos. 452–54 (hereafter cited as *OL*).

[45] Bengoechea, 224–25; Valabek, 76.

[46] R. Metz, "La Consécration des Vierges dans l'église Romaine", in *Études d'histoire de la Liturgie* (P.U.F., 1954), 177, quoted in Quéméneur, 7.

[47] Barré, *Prières Anciennes*, 330–41.

[48] *Committere* continues to be the verb of choice in Latin papal texts which speak of "consecration" to Mary. Cf. *Inseg* II:1 (1979), 364; *Talks,* 165; *Inseg* II:1 (1979), 860–61; *ORE* 577:9; *Inseg* II:1 (1979), 1635; *ORE* 589:2; *Inseg* II:2 (1979), 1093; *ORE* 608:9; *Inseg* IV:2 (1981), 1045; *ORE* 715:18.

[49] Cf. "commend", *Inseg* I (1978), 73; *Talks,* 136; "raccomando", *Inseg* I (1978), 131; *Talks,* 212; "commend", *Inseg* II:1 (1979), 1103; "commendamus", *Inseg* II:1

Mary"[50] or "under the protection of the Holy Mother of God".[51]

The modern period

This heritage of the *patrocinium* of Mary would find expression in the Marian Congregations (sodalities) established by the Belgian Jesuit, Jean Leunis, in 1563 for the students of the Collegio Romano.[52] The admission to the Congregation, which had as its aim the formation of militant Christians after the ideals of Saint Ignatius Loyola and was placed under the patronage of Our Lady, soon became an act of oblation to the Virgin. The text of one of these early admission ceremonies by Father Franz Coster (d. 1619) was published in the *Libellus sodalitatis* in 1586 and is most likely the very formula which he first used to receive students into the Congregation which he had founded at Cologne in 1576. In it the sodalist chooses Mary as "Lady, Patroness and Advocate" and begs her to receive him as her *servum perpetuum*.[53] Father Quéméneur underscores the fact that the Marian Congregations introduce yet another perspective into the question of Marian consecration which is inherited from the late Middle Ages: the corporate dimension.

(1979), 860–61; *ORE* 577:9; "raccomandiamo", *Inseg* II:1 (1979), 1066; *ORE* 581:10; "encomiendo", *Inseg* II:1 (1979), 1315; *ORE* 586:10–11; "recommende", *Inseg* II:2 (1979), 141; "empfehle", *Inseg* II:2 (1979), 184; *ORE* 597:6.

[50] Cf. *Inseg* II:1 (1979), 1391; *Poland*, 72; *Inseg* III:1 (1980), 237–38; *ORE* 619:4; *Inseg* IV:2 (1981), 576, 579; *ORE* 711:10.

[51] Cf. *Inseg* II:1 (1979), 1029; *ORE* 581:6–7; *Inseg* II:2 (1979), 597; *U.S.A.*, 132; *Inseg* II:2 (1979), 1356; *ORE* 614:7–8; *Inseg* II:2 (1979), 1429; *ORE* 616:5; *Inseg* III:1 (1980), 1322; *Africa: Apostolic Pilgrimage* (Boston: St. Paul Editions, 1980), 362 (hereafter cited as *Africa Ap*); *Inseg* III:1 (1980), 1847; *ORE* 640:7.

[52] Cf. E. Villaret, S.J., "Marie et la Compagnie de Jésus", in *Maria*, 2:962–68; "Cons.", 402.

[53] Jungmann, 303.

> Since the Middle Ages there was a tendency for people prompted by sentiments of piety to group together, to form confraternities and various kinds of spiritual associations. There still existed such partly temporal and partly spiritual institutions as trade guilds and professional associations. In these, consecration corresponds to an oath; it is something like the "sacrament" of initiation, the formula for entrance.[54]

In 1622 the Marian Congregation admission formulae of the Italian Jesuit Pietro Antonio Spinelli as well as that of Father Coster were published in the book *Hortulus Marianus* by Father La Croix. The two formulae are described respectively as *modus consecrandi* and *modus vovendi* to the Blessed Virgin. Jungmann comments that this is the first appearance of the word *consecrare* (to consecrate) with the meaning of putting oneself under the *patrocinium* of Mary, and it is taken as being synonymous with the word *devovere* which in classical Latin meant to devote oneself to a deity.[55] In effect, the understanding from the beginning of this usage has been that by the act of consecration to Our Lady, the sodalist places himself at the service of Christ the King through her mediation and under her patronage.[56] The use of the term "consecration" with the meaning of giving oneself completely to Mary in order to belong more perfectly to Christ enters into the common Catholic lexicon from this period and has continued to be used by Pope John Paul II in this sense.[57]

[54] Quéméneur, 8.

[55] Jungmann, 304.

[56] Villaret, 968.

[57] Cf. *Inseg* II:1 (1979), 1036; *ORE* 580:3; *Inseg* II:1 (1979), 1412–19; *Poland*, 103–15; *Inseg* II:1 (1979), 1470–71; *Poland*, 189; *Inseg* II:2 (1979), 177; *ORE* 597:2; *Inseg* II:2 (1979), 290; *ORE* 599:9; *Inseg* II:2 (1979), 468–70; *Ireland "In the Footsteps of St. Patrick"* (Boston: St. Paul Editions, 1979), 88–92 (hereafter cited as *Ireland*); *Inseg* III:1 (1980), 1068–70; *Africa Ap*, 39–42; *Inseg* III:1 (1980), 1253; *Inseg* IV:1 (1981), 128; *Inseg* IV:2 (1981), 458–59; *ORE* 708:5; *Inseg* IV:2 (1981), 1219; *ORE* 718:10 (in this instance the Italian text which the Pope read clearly says "avevo consacrato" whereas the English translation gives "dedicated" instead); *Inseg* IX:2 (1986), 91–94; *ORE* 948:5.

During virtually the same period of time that the Jesuit Marian Congregations were being born, confraternities of the Holy Slavery of Mary were germinating in the soil of Spain. In fact, the earliest of these, founded under the inspiration of Sister Agnes of Saint Paul at the convent of the Franciscan Conceptionists at Alcalá de Henares, dates from August 2, 1595,[58] and thus antedates the foundation of the sodality movement. The first theologian of this "Marian slavery" as it was practiced in Alcalá was the Franciscan Melchor de Cetina "who composed in 1618 what may be called the first 'Handbook of Spirituality' for the members of the confraternity."[59]

As the seventeenth century progressed, the confraternities multiplied and papal approval followed. One of the great promoters and proponents of this spirituality was the Trinitarian, Simón de Rojas (1552–1624),[60] who was canonized by Pope John Paul II on July 3, 1988. Here is how the Holy Father characterized his Marian spirituality in the canonization homily:

> One aspect of our Saint which must be emphasized, is, without a doubt, his most unique and faithful love of Our Lady which he had shown since childhood. This intense Marian experience constantly increased within him. . . . One very typical way he had of living and broadcasting this devotion, was the "servitude" or filial surrender of himself to the Mother of God. . . . In fact, the new Saint is a providential model for us of Marian life, which lies within our reach. He perfectly expressed his will to belong to Mary, in one of

[58] Gaffney, "Holy Slavery", 146; Canal, 250; and especially J. Ordoñez Marquez, "La Cofradía de la Esclavitud en las Concepcionistas de Alcalá", *Estudios Marianos* 51 (1986): 231–48.

[59] Gaffney, "Holy Slavery", 146; Canal, 252–53; Gaspar Calvo Moralejo, O.F.M., "Fray Melchor de Cetina, O.F.M., el primer teólogo de la 'Esclavitud Mariana' (1618)", *Estudios Marianos* 51 (1986): 249–71.

[60] Cf. Juan Pujana, "Simón de Rojas", in *DSp*, 14:877–84; Gaffney, "Holy Slavery", 147; Canal, 253–54.

his favourite exclamations "Our Lady, may I be completely yours, thus I shall have nothing to fear!" [61]

The Augustinian, Bartolomé de los Ríos (1580–1652),[62] extended the work of his friend, de Rojas, into the Low Countries and propagated it by means of his writings which were known and cited by Saint Louis de Montfort.[63] In his *Hierarchia Mariana* he provides this formula of dedication:

> I choose you today, O Holy Virgin, as my Lady, my Queen and my Empress and I recognize in myself what I truly am, your servant and slave, beseeching and begging by the majesty of your most sweet name . . . that you admit me into your family to serve you with the humility of a slave and with the love of a son. . . . Grant, O sovereign Virgin, that this ardent desire to serve you as my Queen and Lady of incomparable greatness until the last breath of my life may never depart from my will.[64]

Perhaps the single most important figure to emerge thus far in our brief consideration of the forms of Marian consecration in the spiritual journey of the Church is Cardinal Pierre de Bérulle (1575–1629), founder of the Oratory of Jesus and promoter of the Teresian reform of Carmel in France. His greatest glory in terms of the history of spirituality is probably one of which he was never conscious, that of being the "founder of the French School" of spirituality. His spiritual paternity would enrich the Church through Saint John Eudes and the Venerable Jean-Jacques Olier, Saints Louis-Marie Grignion de Montfort and Jean-Baptiste de la Salle. His disciples of even the second and third generations would continue to develop his doctrine with their own refinements and emphases. The depth of thought and the

[61] *Inseg* XI:3 (1988), 23; *ORE* 1049:2.

[62] Cf. Quirino Fernandez, "Los Ríos y Alarcón (Bartolomé de)", in *DSp*, 9:1013–18.

[63] Cf. St. Louis-Marie Grignion de Montfort, *True Devotion*, no. 160; Gaffney, "Holy Slavery", 255–59.

[64] Quoted in Canal, 259, trans. by Rodolfo Vargas y Rubio.

ponderousness of his style rendered him somewhat inaccessible so that often his immediate followers such as Olier and Eudes presented the fruits of his contemplation in ways which were much more appealing,[65] but there can be no doubt that he was "le chef d'école".

Of specific interest to us is that while visiting Spain in 1604 Bérulle, who had been a member of the Marian Congregation in his days in the Jesuit College of Clermont, came into contact with the confraternities of the Slaves of the Virgin and in particular with that of Alcalá de Henares where he went to see the General of the Carmelites.[66] This exposure would seem to have had a notable influence on the development of his own spirituality for he would eventually formulate a "vow of servitude" to the Virgin Mary because of his conviction that in the divine design God wished to include in the vocation and predestination of Jesus Christ his divine filiation as well as the divine maternity.[67] Hence Mary, the first to have made the vow of servitude to Jesus, "pure capacity for Jesus filled with Jesus",[68] relates one perfectly to him. Here are Bérulle's words:

> To the perpetual honour of the Mother and the Son, I wish to be in the state and quality of servitude with regard to her who has the state and quality of the Mother of my God. . . . I give myself to her in the quality of a slave in honour of the gift which the eternal Word made of himself to her in the quality of Son.[69]

[65] Raymond Deville, P.S.S., *L'école française de spiritualité*, no. 11 of *Bibliothèque d'Histoire du Christianisme* (Paris: Desclée, 1987), 29.

[66] A. Molien, "Bérulle", *DSp* 1:1547.

[67] *Opuscule de piété*, 93, 1103, quoted in Paul Cochois, *Bérulle et l'École française*, no. 31 of *"Maîtres Spirituels"* (Paris: Éditions du Seuil, 1963), 105. Cf. also William M. Thompson, ed., *Bérulle and the French School: Selected Writings* (New York: Paulist Press, 1989), 14–16, 41–50; Thédore Koehler, S.M., "Servitude", 738–41. This insight of Bérulle is vindicated in *Ineffabilis Deus* (*Pii IX Acta* I:599; *OL*, no. 34); *Munificentissimus Deus* (*AAS* 42 [1950]: 768; *OL*, no. 520); and *LG*, no. 61.

[68] Quoted in Cochois, 105.

[69] M. Rigal, *Les Mystères de Marie*, in *Coll. Les Lettres Chrétiennes* (Paris, 1961), 204, trans. in O'Carroll, *Theotokos*, 80.

He formulated a similar vow to Jesus Christ in honor of the state and "form of a servant"[70] which he took upon himself at the Incarnation,[71] a vow of which Jesus

> himself in his own person is the author and teacher, of which the Holy Virgin is the first and longest professed, and of which the apostles are the first and oldest superiors. . . . It is the vow and solemn profession of Christians at baptism.[72]

The late Father Vincent Vasey, S.M., in his posthumously published paper on the Mariology of Bérulle anticipates the question as to why the vow to Mary should precede the vow to Christ:

> Logically, the vow of servitude to Mary should take place first; the vow to Jesus should come after. In fact, Bérulle introduced the two vows about the same time; the first consecration or vow of service was made to Mary and then a vow of service to Jesus, to respect the due hierarchy in accord with Dionysian categories.
>
> Nothing strange—that Bérulle should consider the Virgin as his intermediary hierarch—for, he considered his own vocation as that of an hierarch with the duty of leading his subjects to a share in Mary's mystical graces and then, through the Virgin, to a participation in the mysteries of Christ, and, finally, through the mysteries of Christ to the life of the Trinity. To summarize his thought: *per Mariam ad Iesum; per Iesu mysteria ad Trinitatem.*[73]

The heritage of Cardinal Pierre de Bérulle would in a certain sense synthesize what had taken place before him and lay a solid foundation for his spiritual children.[74] Surely among them all his most direct heir who has been raised to

[70] Phil 2:7.

[71] Text given in Deville, 43.

[72] *Narré de ce qui s'est passé sur les Élévations à Jésus et à la très sainte Vierge*, 614, quoted in Cochois, 103 (my trans.).

[73] Vincent R. Vasey, S.M., "Mary in the Doctrine of Bérulle on the Mysteries of Christ", *Marian Studies* 36 (1985): 63; cf. Cochois, 107–8.

[74] Cf. M. T. Poupon, O.P., *Le poème de la parfaite consécration à Marie* (Lyon: Librairie de Sacré-Cœur, 1947), 336–74.

the honors of the altar is Saint John Eudes. A member of the Sodality at the Jesuit College in Caen from his youth, formed in the Oratory of Jesus by Bérulle and his immediate successor, Charles de Condren, Eudes was probably the greatest missioner and popularizer of the French School.[75] In his first book, *The Kingdom of Jesus*, a kind of handbook of Bérullian spirituality intended for a wide public, he offers this counsel about how a Christian should relate to Mary:

> You must see and adore her Son in her, and see and adore Him alone. It is thus that she wishes to be honored, because of herself and by herself she is nothing, but her Son Jesus is everything in her, her being, her life, her sanctity, her glory, her power and her greatness. You should thank Our Lord for the glory He has given to Himself through His admirable Mother. You must offer yourself to Him and ask Him to give you to her, causing all your life and all your acts to be consecrated to the honor of her life and her actions. You must pray that He will make you participate in her admirable love for Him and in her other virtues. You must ask Him to employ your life in her honor, or rather to honor Himself in her, in whatever way He pleases.
>
> You must recognize and honor her first as the Mother of God, then as your own Mother and Queen. You must thank her for all the love, glory and perfect service she rendered to Her Son Jesus Christ our Lord. You must refer to her, after God, your being and your life, subjecting yourself entirely to her as her slave, imploring her to direct you in all your affairs and to assume full power over you, as over something belonging entirely to her, and to dispose of you as she pleases, for the greater glory of her Divine Son.[76]

In this carefully measured exhortation the Norman saint highlights the Christocentrism of Bérulle and synthesizes his vows of servitude to Jesus and Mary while retaining his

[75] Cf. Charles Lebrun, C.J.M., *The Spiritual Teaching of St. John Eudes*, trans. Basil Whelan, O.S.B. (London: Sands and Co., 1934), 260.

[76] *Oeuvres Complètes du Vénérable Jean Eudes*, vol. 6 (Vannes: Imprimerie Lafoyle Frères, 1905–1911), 189; St. John Eudes, *The Life and Kingdom of Jesus in Christian Souls*, trans. by a Trappist father (New York: P. J. Kenedy & Sons, 1946), 272.

emphasis on Mary's complete relativity to Christ. Also to be noted is his accent on "Jesus living in Mary", a characteristic of the French School given classic form in the well-known prayer of Jean-Jacques Olier, the founder of the Seminary of Saint-Sulpice.[77] Probably his most mature expression of belonging to Mary is to be found in his "Contract of Holy Matrimony with the Most Blessed Virgin Mary, the Mother of God" which he wrote and signed in his own blood at Caen on April 28, 1668.[78] While the terminology may be initially jarring to modern sensibilities, it should be noted that Bérulle himself proposed to his sons in the Oratory that they should consider their relation to Jesus and Mary as a marriage (alliance).[79] An analysis of the text will indicate the delicacy, Christocentrism, theological precision, and creativity of this document.

Not surprisingly, during this golden era of French spirituality France itself would be consecrated to Mary in 1638 by Louis XIII under the influence of Cardinal Richelieu.[80] Many other nations followed suit as Father Jungmann tells us:

> At the command of King Philip IV of Spain, in 1643 the South American Spanish colonies were dedicated to Mary through a "solemn consecration". In 1664 the same thing was done for Portugal and all her colonies at the instigation of King John IV. . . . Some-

[77] Cf. the analysis of this prayer by Irenée Noye, P.S.S., "O Jesus Living in Mary", trans. Roger M. Charest, S.M.M., *Queen of All Hearts* 32, no. 5 (1982): 9. Pope John Paul II commented briefly, but appreciatively, on this prayer at the close of his annual retreat with the Roman Curia on February 27, 1988, cf. *Inseg* XI:1 (1988), 502; *ORE* 1029:2.

[78] St. John Eudes, *Letters and Shorter Works*, trans. Ruth Hauser (New York: P. J. Kenedy & Sons, 1948), 318–23.

[79] Vasey, 61.

[80] Cf. Maurice Vloberg, "Le Voeu de Louis XIII", *Maria*, 5:519–33; René Laurentin, *Le voeu de Louis XIII: Passé ou avenir de la France 1638–1988* (Paris: O.E.I.L., 1988). In his entrustment of France to Our Lady on August 14, 1983, the Pope made explicit reference to the earlier consecration of France to Mary by Louis XIII, cf. *Inseg* VI:2 (1983), 206; *ORE* 798:4.

> thing similar happened in Austria in the following year at the order of Emperor Ferdinand III. . . . At Mass on Easter day 1674 the missionary to the Indians, Jacques Marquette, S.J., solemnly consecrated the new mission on the Mississippi along with his Indians to the Immaculata.[81]

Into this French ecclesial context, characterized at its highest levels by ardent love for the Mother of God, was born Louis-Marie Grignion (1673–1716) at Montfort-la-Cane. (Wishing to give no impression of self-importance, he would eventually identify himself by the name of the town of his birth and baptism rather than by his family name.) This saint described as "the last of the great Bérullians"[82] and the greatest proponent of Marian consecration produced by the "French School" was first educated at the Jesuit College in Rennes where he was a member of the Marian Congregation[83] and then for eight years under the influence of the Sulpicians founded by Olier.[84] Given this milieu, one finds many strands of his thought which may be traced to the "French School".

If Bérulle had already indicated the link between baptism and his "vow of servitude to Jesus", de Montfort would associate Mary with one's baptismal commitment as well. What he proposes in his classic work *True Devotion to the Blessed Virgin* is a renewal of one's baptismal promises "through the hands of Mary":

> In holy baptism we do not give ourselves to Jesus explicitly through Mary, nor do we give him the value of our good actions.

[81] Jungmann, 305–6.

[82] Deville, 139.

[83] Cf. Stefano De Fiores, S.M.M., *Itinerario spirituale di S. Luigi Maria di Montfort (1673–1716) nel periodo fino al sacerdozio (5 giugno 1700)*, Marian Library Studies, n.s., 6 (Dayton, Oh.: University of Dayton, 1974), 59–81.

[84] Cf. ibid., 142–65, 184–203. Another excellent study which considers the influence of the "French School" on de Montfort is Benedetta Papàsogli, *Montfort: A Prophet for our Times*, trans. Ann Nielsen, D.W. (Rome: Edizioni Monfortane, 1991), esp. 103–13, 379–98.

> After baptism we remain entirely free either to apply that value to anyone we wish or keep it for ourselves. But by this consecration *we give ourselves explicitly to Jesus through Mary's hands* and we include in our consecration the value of all our actions.[85]

If Saint Louis had written a special formula of consecration in conjunction with his treatise, *True Devotion*, it has not thus far come to light. The formula which he has left us in his most theological and central, although far too little known, work, *The Love of Eternal Wisdom*, clearly highlights the fact that Jesus is the goal of the act of consecration which he proposes while Mary is its intermediary:

> Eternal and incarnate Wisdom, most lovable and adorable Jesus, true God and true man, only Son of the eternal Father and of Mary always Virgin, . . . I dare no longer approach the holiness of your majesty on my own. That is why I turn to the intercession and the mercy of your holy Mother, whom you yourself have given me to mediate with you. Through her I hope to obtain from you contrition and pardon for my sins, and that Wisdom whom I desire to dwell in me always. . . .
>
> O admirable Mother, present me to your dear Son as his slave now and for always, so that he who redeemed me through you, will now receive me through you.[86]

While de Montfort readily and very frequently speaks of "consecrating oneself to Mary", this must always be understood as a shorthand form of "consecrating oneself to Jesus through the hands of Mary".[87] It is precisely in these terms that Pope John Paul II presents him as a proponent of authentic Marian spirituality in *Redemptoris Mater*.[88]

[85] *True Devotion*, no. 126; *God Alone*, 329.

[86] *Love of Eternal Wisdom*, nos. 223, 226; *God Alone*, 112–13.

[87] Cf. Reginald Garrigou-Lagrange, O.P., *The Mother of the Saviour and Our Interior Life*, trans. Bernard J. Kelley, C.S.Sp. (St. Louis: B. Herder Book Co., 1957), 256, n. 19.

[88] *Redemptoris Mater*, no. 48.

Perhaps, in the final analysis, the greatest contribution of this Breton saint to the theology of Marian consecration is precisely in his insistence on Mary's mediation as willed by God. This secondary and subordinate, but nonetheless real mediation of Mary described in *Lumen Gentium*, numbers 60 and 62, and presented with such conviction by Saint Louis is well explained by one of his spiritual sons:

> Objection has been raised against this principle of Montfort, primarily because his understanding of "mediatrix," or "through Mary" has been sadly twisted. In the eyes of this missionary, no one is more approachable, more lovable, than the tender Jesus. His chapters on the tenderness, the humanness, the simplicity of Jesus in *The Love of the Eternal Wisdom*, in his *Cantiques* on Jesus—an antiochene element in his Christology—all bear this out. When he speaks of "mediators" or going *through* Mary, he is not setting up Our Lady as a barricade which must be pierced before reaching the Lord; he is not speaking of a hurdle which must be surmounted before arriving at the goal; he is not speaking of any chronological procedure. As he explains it, it is with Mary that we arrive at Jesus more quickly, love Him more tenderly, serve Him more faithfully. In Montfort's eyes, the "through Mary" brings about a more intensely immediate union with the Eternal and Incarnate Wisdom. She does not stand in the way. She is the "mysterious milieu", the atmosphere, as Gerard Manley Hopkins wrote after reading Montfort, which only enhances, intensifies this union. To withdraw from this atmosphere, this milieu which God has given to us, to try to circumvent the quickening catalyst of Mary with which God has so kindly endowed us, is to ignore the role of Mary in salvation history; it is to show disrespect for God. At least implicitly, everyone comes to Jesus through the means He takes to come to us: through Mary. Again, for Montfort, this refers to the ineradicable characteristic of all salvation history: the necessary, representative, salvific, eternal consent of Mary. Far from denying the beauty of Jesus, Mary as Mediator "of intercession" with the "Mediator of redemption" affirms the uniqueness of "the one and only mediator between God and Man, the man Jesus Christ" (1 Tim. 2:5)

while also affirming our own weakness and the will of God in this present order of salvation.[89]

There is a sense in which the life and work of de Montfort may be seen as bringing to its culmination the concept of Marian "servitude" or "slavery" which we have traced from the Spanish confraternities and even earlier. He himself used the term frequently in his writings[90] while maintaining that "we can call ourselves, and become, the loving slaves of our Blessed Lady in order to become more perfect slaves of Jesus."[91] Of course, the term "slavery" or "servitude" grates upon the ears of many in the highly democratized era in which we live. The Pope, a committed disciple of de Montfort's Marian thought, does not hesitate to defend the master's usage in his interview with André Frossard on the subject:

> It is well known that the author of the treatise [on *True Devotion*] defines his devotion as a form of "slavery". The word may upset our contemporaries. Personally I do not see any difficulty in it. I think we are confronted here with the sort of paradox often to be noted in the Gospels, the words "holy slavery" signifying that we could not more fully exploit our freedom, the greatest of God's gifts to us. For freedom is measured by the love of which we are capable.[92]

He spoke similarly on June 4, 1979, while he reviewed the modern history of Poland's consecration to Mary and

[89] J. Patrick Gaffney, S.M.M., "Saint Louis Mary Grignion de Montfort and the Marian Consecration", *Marian Studies* 35 (1984): 142–44.

[90] Cf. *True Devotion*, nos. 55–56, 75–76; *Love of Eternal Wisdom*, nos. 211, 219; *Secret of Mary*, nos. 34, 41, 61.

[91] *True Devotion*, no. 75; *God Alone*, 312–13.

[92] André Frossard, *"Be Not Afraid!": Pope John Paul II Speaks out on His Life, His Beliefs, and His Inspiring Vision for Humanity*, trans. J. R. Foster (New York: St. Martin's Press, 1984), 126. On the Gospel basis of the language of "slavery", cf. Roman Ginn, O.C.S.O., "Slave Talk in St. Paul and St. Louis de Montfort", *Queen of All Hearts* 39 (March–April 1989): 12–13; Donald MacDonald, S.M.M., "From the Slavery of Sin to the Total Consecration to Christ", *Queen of All Hearts* 40 (July–August 1989): 18–19.

supported the use of the term "maternal slavery of love" which was incorporated into the great Act of Consecration made on May 3, 1966, on the occasion of the celebration of the Millennium of Christianity in Poland:

> The act speaks of "servitude." It contains a paradox similar to the words of the Gospel according to which one must lose one's life to find it (cf. Mt. 10:39). For love constitutes the fulfillment of freedom, yet at the same time "belonging," and so not being free is part of its essence. However, this "not being free" in love is not felt as slavery but rather as an affirmation and fulfillment of freedom. The act of consecration in slavery indicates therefore a unique dependence and a limitless trust. In this sense slavery (non-freedom) expresses the fullness of freedom, in the same way as the Gospel speaks of the need to lose one's life in order to find it in its fullness.[93]

In an address of December 17, 1987, to his brother Polish bishops from the metropolitan province of Wrocław on the occasion of their "ad limina" visit, he continued to develop some of the implications of the "maternal slavery of love" which Poland had vowed to Mary, its Queen, on May 3, 1966. Once again, he chose to underscore the paradoxical nature of the language employed:

> Here it is a question not only of verbal paradoxes, but of ontological ones as well. The most profound paradox is perhaps that of life and death, expressed, among other places, in the parable of the seed which must die in order to produce new life. This paradox is definitely confirmed by the paschal mystery.[94]

Further, considering "maternal slavery" as the path of Saints Louis de Montfort and Maximilian Kolbe and the Polish Cardinal Primates Hlond and Wyszyński he said that it

[93] *Inseg* II:1 (1979), 1414; *Poland*, 106; cf. also his further remarks on his taking leave of Jasna Góra on June 6, *Inseg* II:1 (1979), 1470–71; *Poland*, 189.

[94] *Inseg* X:3 (1987), 1436; *ORE* 1022:11.

> must reveal itself as the path towards victory, the price of freedom. For that matter, it is difficult to imagine any being less inclined to "enslave" than a mother, than the Mother of God. And if what we are speaking of is an "enslaving" through love, then from that perspective "slavery" constitutes precisely *the revelation of the fullness of freedom*. In fact, freedom attains its true meaning, that is, its own fullness, through a true good. Love is synonymous with that attainment.[95]

While it may be true to see de Montfort's teaching as the highpoint of the Marian consecration championed by the "French School", it would be unfair to consider the subsequent history of this phenomenon in the life of the Church simply in terms of denouement. The unfolding of this process continued even in that difficult period after the French Revolution, with holy founders such as the Venerable William Joseph Chaminade (1761–1850) who incorporated total consecration to Mary into the Society of Mary, which he founded as the object of a special perpetual religious vow,[96] and the Venerable Francis Mary Paul Libermann (1802–1852), Jewish convert and "second founder" of the Holy Ghost Fathers, who characterized his fledgling institute in these terms:

> What distinguishes us from all other workers in the Lord's vineyard is a quite special consecration which we make of all our society, of each of its members, of all their works and enterprises to the most holy Heart of Mary, a heart eminently apostolic and all inflamed with desires for the glory of God and the salvation of souls.[97]

[95] *Inseg* X:3 (1987), 1436–37; *ORE* 1022:11.

[96] Cf. Henri Lebon, S.M., "Chaminade (Guillaume-Joseph)", in *DSp*, 2:454–59; Peter A. Resch, S.M., "Filial Piety", in *Mariology*, 3:165.

[97] *Theotokos*, 219; cf. Michael O'Carroll, C.S.Sp., *Veni Creator Spiritus: A Theological Encyclopedia of the Holy Spirit* (Collegeville, Minn.: Liturgical Press, "A Michael Glazier Book", 1990), 136–38; Paul Sigrist, "Libermann (François-Marie-Paul)", in *DSp*, 9:764–80.

It would take us beyond our immediate scope to detail all the modern congregations in the Church in which Marian consecration constitutes an integral part of their charism. Instead we will simply note here the impetus for Marian consecration among the faithful which spread almost like wildfire from the courageous response of the Abbé Desgenettes to the interior words which he heard telling him to consecrate his parish to the Immaculate Heart of Mary on December 3, 1836.[98] The moribund parish of Notre-Dame des Victoires became almost overnight a vibrant center of Christian faith and worship and, through the establishment of the Archconfraternity of the Most Holy and Immaculate Heart of Mary, a catalyst for thousands of conversions.[99]

Interestingly, in the ways of Providence, the happenings at the Parisian church of Notre-Dame des Victoires would come to be known within nine years to Anthony Mary Claret (1807–1870), who already had a deep and tender filial devotion to Mary. So impressed was he with what he read in the *Annals* of the Archconfraternity that he renamed a secular institute which he had founded "Daughters of the Most Holy and Immaculate Heart of Mary".[100] Eventually, under the same inspiration, he would also found a congregation of missionaries whom he would call "Sons of the Immaculate Heart of Mary" and would give the name as well to a congregation for Christian doctrine which he founded in Cuba.[101] Early in his priestly life he had written:

[98] Interestingly, the Curé of Ars had already consecrated his parish to Mary conceived without sin on May 1, 1836, cf. Francis Trochu, *The Curé of Ars: St. Jean-Marie-Baptiste Vianney*, trans. Dom Ernest Graf, O.S.B. (Rockford, Ill.: Tan Books and Publishers, 1977), 306, n. 4, and Pope John Paul II's allusion to this act, *Inseg* IX:2 (1986), 904; *ORE* 962:9.

[99] Jean Letourneur, "Dufriche-Desgenettes", in *DSp*, 3:1757–59.

[100] Juan María Lozano, C.M.F., *Mystic and Man of Action: Saint Anthony Mary Claret*, trans. Joseph Daries, C.M.F. (Chicago: Claretian Publications, 1977), 141; cf. Julio Aramendia, C.F.M., "Claret (Bienheureux Antoine-Marie)", in *DSp*, 2:932–37.

[101] Lozano, 144.

"I entrust myself totally to Mary, as her son and priest. . . . Everything I do or suffer in my ministry will be done for her." [102] Later he made the consecration to the Immaculate Heart of Mary part of the ceremony of joining his missionary congregation.[103] For him, according to Father Lozano, being a Son of the Immaculate Heart of Mary meant being an instrument of the Virgin in her struggle against Satan.[104] For him, consecration to Mary has a definitely apostolic thrust because

> the mystery of Mary Immaculate, as he sees it, is not so much a mystery of beauty as it is of power. In his view, the Immaculate Virgin is the Lady of Victories, the Strong Woman, who, because she was never bitten by the serpent, has kept all her forces intact to crush his head. The Saint moves, then, within a perspective drawn from the "protoevangelium" of Genesis 3:15 and the twelfth chapter of the *Apocalypse*.[105]
>
> But just as the devil avails himself of his "seed," the wicked, so the Blessed Virgin makes use of apostles whom she has chosen and formed especially to combat him. He demonstrated this historically in his very first sermon on the Heart of Mary, showing how, throughout the history of the Church, the Blessed Virgin has answered each new heresy with a special intervention of her own. The last such interventions, he remarks, were the manifestation of her Heart at the Church of Notre-Dame des Victoires, in Paris, and in the foundation of her Congregation.[106]

[102] Lozano, 141.

[103] Ibid., 142.

[104] Ibid., 140.

[105] This perspective is also notable in the thought of John Paul II. Three times in the course of his encyclical *Redemptoris Mater* he links Genesis 3:15 to Revelation 12, speaking of Mary as "the woman" of the *Protoevangelium* and of the Apocalypse who symbolizes and "incarnates" in herself the struggle against evil and the victory over it. Cf. nos. 11, 24, 47 (*Inseg* X:1 [1987], 689–90; 706–7; 738); cf. also Angelus address and Prayer at the Piazza di Spagna on the Feast of the Immaculate Conception, 1991, *OR*, 131, no. 284:4–5; *ORE* 1220:5.

[106] Lozano, 135.

The notion of Marian consecration as equipping one to be a soldier of Christ in the battle with the powers of darkness (cf. Eph 6:12) becomes ever stronger in the twentieth century. We just heard it sounded above in Saint Anthony Mary Claret and know that it had been prophesied by Saint Louis-Marie Grignion de Montfort that Mary would have a special role to play in the latter times (*les derniers temps*)[107] and that those especially consecrated to her would have a decisive role to play in the battle waged by the enemy.[108] A striking figure who incarnates these ideals is Saint Maximilian-Maria Kolbe (1894–1941), the founder of the *Militia Immaculatae*.

The saint would later relate that as a young minor seminarian he felt so impelled to enter into battle in the service of Our Lady that

> bowing his face to the floor before the altar of the Immaculata during Mass one day he promised her that he would fight for her. Although at that time he did not know how he was to do this, he thought of his "battle" as a material and bloody one. The military life and career, for which he had an obvious inclination, appeared to him to be in perfect harmony with that of a knight devoted to his Lady.[109]

On October 16, 1917, three days after the final apparition of Our Lady in Fatima and a few months before his priestly ordination, Maximilian, together with six other Conventual Franciscan colleagues, founded the *Militia Immaculatae*. It was a direct response to Masonic demonstrations which had been held in Saint Peter's Square in which banners were carried depicting Saint Michael the Archangel being crushed by Lucifer with slogans on them such as, "The devil will govern in the Vatican, and the Pope will act as Swiss Guard for

[107] *True Devotion*, nos. 49–59.

[108] Ibid., nos. 56–57.

[109] Antonio Ricciardi, O.F.M. Conv., *St. Maximilian Kolbe: Apostle of Our Difficult Age*, trans. Daughters of St. Paul (Boston: St. Paul Editions, 1982), 27.

him."[110] By this time Maximilian had discovered how he would engage in the battle as Our Lady's "knight".

His ideal was chivalrous, but eminently practical: he and his companions would consecrate themselves totally to Our Lady in order to be instruments in her hands for the extension of the Kingdom of the Heart of Jesus. Here is how he explained the rationale for the Militia and its consecration to one of his confrères a few years after its foundation, distinguishing it from the Confraternity of the Miraculous Medal headquartered in Paris:

> In regard to the confraternity from Paris, it limits itself to prayer alone, while the M.I., although it employs prayer as its main weapon, nevertheless immerses itself in action with all the means that circumstances permit. . . . Moreover, we consecrate ourselves to the Immaculate without reserve and that constitutes the essence of the M.I.; the Parisian Association doesn't have this. *All our sufferings, deeds, thoughts, words, action, life, death, eternity and all of us are always the irrevocable possession (what a delight!) of the Immaculate Queen of heaven and earth. So even when we are not thinking of it (as we like to reflect on it) she directs every one of our actions, prearranges all the circumstances, repairs the damage from our falls and leads us lovingly toward heaven, and through us she is pleased to implant good ideas, sentiments and examples everywhere in order to save souls and lead them to the good Jesus.* There is, therefore, a beautiful difference.[111]

Maximilian, who was familiar with de Montfort and saw the movement which he founded as a means of fulfilling his prophecy on the latter times,[112] was also conscious of standing in the great tradition of Marian slavery. Although he did not employ the word with the frequency of de Montfort,

[110] Cf. St. Maximilian Kolbe, O.F.M. Conv., *Gli scritti di Massimiliano Kolbe: eroe di Oświeçim e Beato della Chiesa*, 3 vols., trans. Cristoforo Zambelli (Florence: Città di Vita, 1975–1978), no. 1277 (3:664–65), no. 1278 (3:669), no. 1328 (3:771–72).

[111] Kolbe, *Scritti*, no. 56 (1:113); trans. in Anselm W. Romb, O.F.M. Conv., ed., *The Kolbe Reader* (Libertyville, Ill.: Franciscan Marytown Press, 1987), 15 (my emphasis).

[112] Kolbe, *Scritti*, no. 1129 (3:291–93); Romb, 36–39.

he leaves no doubt about its implications in the following text:

> You belong to her as her own property. Let her do with you what she wishes. Do not let her feel herself bound by any restrictions following from the obligations a mother has towards her own son. *Be hers, her property; let her make free use of you and dispose of you without any limits, for whatever purpose she wishes.*
>
> Let her be your owner, your Lady and absolute Queen. A servant sells his labor; you, on the contrary, offer yours as a gift: your fatigue, your suffering, all that is yours. Beg her not to pay attention to your free will, but to act towards you always and in full liberty as she desires.
>
> Be her son, her servant, her slave of love, in every way and under whatever formulation yet devised or which can be devised now or in the future. In a word, be all hers.
>
> Be her soldier so that others may become ever more perfectly hers, like you yourself, and even more than you; so that all those who live and will live all over the world may work together with her in her struggle against the infernal serpent.
>
> Belong to the Immaculate so that your conscience, becoming ever purer, may be purified still more, become immaculate as she is for Jesus, so that you too may become a mother and conqueror of hearts for her.[113]

Standing in the great tradition which we have been sketching, Maximilian brings a note of urgency about the battle, Mary's "struggle against the infernal serpent" (cf. Gen 3:15) and, hence, the all-consuming goal of his life was to mobilize an army, a militia completely at her disposal. This is clearly illustrated in the official Act of Consecration for the Militia Immaculatae:

> If it pleases you, use all that I am and have without reserve, wholly to accomplish what was said of you: "She will crush your head", and, "You alone have destroyed all heresies in the whole world." *Let me be a fit instrument in your immaculate and merciful hands for intro-*

[113] Kolbe, *Scritti*, no. 1334 (3:797–98); Romb, 194 (my emphasis).

> *ducing and increasing your glory to the maximum in all the many strayed and indifferent souls, and thus help extend as far as possible the blessed kingdom of the most Sacred Heart of Jesus.* For wherever you enter you obtain the grace of conversion and growth in holiness, since it is through your hands that all graces come to us from the most Sacred Heart of Jesus.[114]

Standing in this great spiritual tradition of Marian consecration as equipping one for active service in the Church Militant was Frank Duff (1889–1980).[115] In 1918 after being challenged to a rereading of de Montfort's *True Devotion*, which he had initially considered as "wildly extravagant", Duff tells us:

> The sudden realization came to me that the book was true, a complete conviction that what I had been regarding as exaggerated and unreal was fully justified. The excesses which I thought I found in the book were really deficiencies in myself, wide gaps of knowledge and comprehension.[116]

In the wake of a discussion of that book by a Dublin conference of the Saint Vincent de Paul Society four years later, on September 7, 1921, the Legion of Mary was born,[117] and Duff insisted that "the starting of the Legion was divinely held up for several years until de Montfort had provided the soil or atmosphere in which the Legion could take life."[118] The apostolate of the Legion, which has been responsible for remarkable works of charity and evangelization since its foundation, is built on a promise addressed to the Holy Spirit in which the legionary declares himself to be the "soldier and child" of Mary and prays:

[114] Kolbe, *Scritti*, no. 37 (1:71); no. 1329 (3:778); no. 1331 (3:785); Romb, 159–60 (my emphasis).

[115] Cf. *Theotokos*, 125; O'Carroll, *Veni Creator Spiritus*, 73–74.

[116] Robert Bradshaw, *Frank Duff: Founder of the Legion of Mary* (Bay Shore, N.Y.: Montfort Publications, 1985), 55.

[117] Bradshaw, 67–68.

[118] Frank Duff, *The Woman of Genesis* (Dublin: Praedicanda Publications, 1976), 73; cf. also 75.

> Let thy power overshadow me, and come into my soul with fire and love. And make it one with Mary's love and Mary's will to save the world; So that I may be pure in her who was made Immaculate by Thee; So that Christ my Lord may likewise grow in me through Thee; So that I with her, His Mother, may bring Him to the world and to the souls who need Him; So that they and I, the battle won, may reign with her for ever in the glory of the Blessed Trinity.[119]

In this same spirit the 1961 edition of *The Official Handbook of the Legion of Mary* devotes an entire section to "the duty of legionaries towards Mary" [120] and commends in particular the consecration of Saint Louis de Montfort.[121]

These historical considerations, far from being exhaustive or constituting a definitive study of Marian consecration in the life of the Church, nonetheless illustrate a remarkable consistency and convergence in the practice of placing one's life, one's work, and the apostolate itself in the hands of Mary.[122] Apart from the pontifical acts of consecration which we will study next, the Church's cumulative wisdom on Marian consecration in the spiritual journey of the Church might be seen as summarized in two magisterial texts. The first is the laconic but nonetheless lapidary statement made in the Second Vatican Council's Decree on the Apostolate of the Laity: "Everyone should have a genuine devotion to her [Mary] and entrust his life to her motherly care." [123] The second is

[119] *The Official Handbook of the Legion of Mary* (Dublin: Concilium Legionis Mariae, 1961), 52–53.

[120] Ibid., 128–47.

[121] Ibid., 142–47.

[122] Besides the articles on the subject in *Theotokos* and *NDM*, further helpful summaries of the history of Marian consecration may be found in J. Laurenceau, O.P., "Aperçus sur l'histoire de la consécration à Marie", *Cahiers Marials*, no. 137 (1983), 66–84, and W. G. Most, "Marian Consecration as Service: Historical, Theological and Spiritual Reflections", *Miles Immaculatae* 24 (1988): 443–45.

[123] *"Hanc devotissime colant omnes suamque vitam atque apostolatum eius maternae curae commendent"* (*Apostolicam Actuositatem* [Vatican II Decree on Apostolate of Lay People], no. 4 [hereafter cited as *AA*]).

contained in John Paul II's Marian Year encyclical, *Redemptoris Mater*, number 48:

> Marian *spirituality*, like its corresponding *devotion*, finds a very rich source in the historical experience of individuals and of the various Christian communities present among the different peoples and nations of the world. In this regard, I would like to recall, among the many witnesses and teachers of this spirituality, the figure of Saint Louis Marie Grignion de Montfort, who proposes consecration to Christ through the hands of Mary, as an effective means for Christians to live faithfully their baptismal commitments. I am pleased to note that in our own time too new manifestations of this spirituality and devotion are not lacking.[124]

As one thoroughly formed in the tradition of this spirituality of Marian consecration, we should not be surprised to see John Paul continue to deepen and develop its major lines.

[124] *Inseg* X:1 (1987), 739; St. Paul ed., 68.

2

THE PAPAL MAGISTERIUM AND PAPAL ACTS OF CONSECRATION

If, as we have just seen, Pope John Paul II is the heir of the great ecclesial tradition of Marian consecration, manifested in various ways in the course of the Church's almost two millennia of history, he might be said to be even more explicitly the inheritor of the legacy of papal consecration to the Hearts of Jesus and Mary.[1] In his handling of the history of "devotional" consecration, Jungmann rightly sees the necessity of reckoning with the phenomenon of consecration to the Sacred Heart of Jesus as intimately related to the consecration to Mary and her Immaculate Heart.[2] Of necessity this leads us to a brief consideration here of the meaning of the term "heart" as the object of consecration[3] and the historical background of these pontifical acts of consecration.

It might be fairly said that the impetus for consecration to the Hearts of Jesus and Mary stems from Saint John Eudes and is expressed in his prayer, *Ave Cor Sanctissimum*, which

[1] Cf. Arthur Burton Calkins, "The Cultus of the Hearts of Jesus and Mary in the Papal Magisterium from Pius IX to Pius XII", to be published in the *Acta* of the Tenth International Mariological Congress, held in Kevelaer, Germany, from September 11 to 17, 1987.

[2] Cf. Jungmann, 307–14. While I find Jungmann's enumeration of the principal facts helpful, I cannot say the same for his grasp of their theological import.

[3] The history and theology of the Hearts of Jesus and Mary and the Pope's own contributions in this area will be treated at greater length in the concluding chapter of this work.

he addressed jointly to the Hearts of Jesus and Mary as *Cor amantissimum Jesu et Mariae.* He conceived of the two as "one heart" in terms of the text in the Acts of the Apostles 4:32 and thus prayed: "To you we offer, we give, we consecrate, we immolate our heart [*Tibi cor nostrum offerimus, donamus, consecramus, immolamus*]."[4] Clearly the saint and the subsequent ecclesial tradition understood the heart as the most apt symbol of the love of Jesus and of Mary[5] so that the heart is ultimately equivalent to the person, a theological application of the figure of speech known as synecdoche.[6]

The human heart as a natural symbol—and, indeed, there is much to be said in favor of seeing it as the preeminent symbol of the person[7]—evokes many levels of meaning; these become immeasurably enriched from the supernatural perspective. Let us listen to what Pope John Paul II refers to as "the richness of anthropological resonance . . . which the word 'heart' awakens." In a remarkable homily given on June 28, 1984, at the Gemelli Polyclinic[8] and Faculty of Medicine in Rome he said:

> This word [heart] evokes not only sentiments proper to the affective sphere, but also all those memories, thoughts, reasonings, plans, that make up man's innermost world. The heart in biblical culture, and also in a large part of other cultures, is that essential

[4] St. John Eudes, *The Sacred Heart of Jesus*, trans. Richard Flower, O.S.B. (New York: P. J. Kenedy & Sons, 1946), 173–74. For a discussion of the "conjoint" cultus of the Hearts of Jesus and Mary, cf. Arthur Burton Calkins, "The Union of the Hearts of Jesus and Mary in St. Francis de Sales and St. John Eudes", *Miles Immaculatae* 25 (1989): 472–512.

[5] On the heart as the natural symbol of the person and the application of this symbolism to the Hearts of Jesus and Mary, cf. Arthur Burton Calkins, "Why the Heart?" *Homiletic & Pastoral Review* 89, no. 9 (1989): 18–23.

[6] Cf. Louis Verheylezoon, S.J., *Devotion to the Sacred Heart: Object, Ends, Practice, Motives* (Westminster, Md.: Newman Press, 1955; reprint, Rockford, Ill.: Tan Books and Publishers, 1978), 29.

[7] Cf. *Études Carmélitaines: Le Cœur* (Paris: Desclée de Brouwer, 1950).

[8] It was in this hospital that the Pope recuperated from the attempt made on his life.

center of the personality in which man stands before God as the totality of body and soul, as I who am thinking, willing and loving, as the center in which the memory of the past opens up to the planning of the future.

Certainly, the human heart that interests the anatomist, the physiologist, the cardiologist, the surgeon, etc., and their scientific contribution—I am happy to acknowledge in such a place as this—takes on great importance for the serene and harmonious development of man in the course of his earthly existence. But the significance, according to which we now refer to the heart, transcends these partial considerations to reach the sanctuary of personal self-awareness in which is summarized and, so to speak, condensed the concrete essence of man, the center in which the individual decides on himself in the face of others, the world, and God himself.

Only of man can it be properly said that *he has a heart.* It cannot be said, obviously, of a pure spirit, nor even of an animal. The *redire ad cor* ("returning to the heart") from the scattering of multiple external experiences is a possibility reserved uniquely to man.[9]

This brief consideration of the "anthropological resonance" of the word *heart* provides an appropriate preamble to considering the Sacred Heart of Jesus as a symbol. In what is perhaps the single most important passage in his monumental encyclical letter *Haurietis Aquas*, the Servant of God Pope Pius XII taught authoritatively about the aptness of the Heart of Jesus as a symbol and the various levels of its symbolism:

The Heart of the Incarnate Word is deservedly and rightly considered the chief sign and symbol of that threefold love with which the divine Redeemer unceasingly loves His eternal Father and all mankind.

It is a symbol of that *divine love* which He shares with the Father and the Holy Spirit but which He, the Word made flesh, alone manifests through a weak and perishable body, since "in Him dwells the fullness of the Godhead bodily" (Col. 2:9).

[9] *Inseg* VII:1 (1984), 1974–75; *ORE* 843:9.

It is, besides, the symbol of that *burning love which, infused into His soul*, enriches the human will of Christ and enlightens and governs its acts by the most perfect knowledge derived both from the beatific vision and that which is directly infused.

And finally—and this in a more natural and direct way—it is the symbol also of *sensible love*, since the body of Jesus Christ, formed by the Holy Spirit, in the womb of the Virgin Mary, possesses full powers of feelings and perception, in fact, more so than any other human body.[10]

Pope John Paul II, standing within the dogmatic tradition so carefully developed and consolidated by the magisterial teaching of Pius XII, presents the Heart of Jesus as a symbol in terms of his own unique anthropological insights:

From our faith we know that at a determined time in history, "the Word became flesh and made his dwelling among us" (Jn. 1:14). From that moment *God began to love with a human heart*, a true heart capable of beating in an intense, tender and impassioned way. The Heart of Jesus has truly experienced feelings of joy before the splendor of nature, the candor of children, the glance of a pure young man; feelings of friendship toward the Apostles, Lazarus, the disciples; feelings of compassion for the sick, the poor, the many persons tried by struggle, by loneliness, by sin, feelings of anguish before the prospect of suffering and the mystery of death. There is no authentically human feeling that the Heart of Jesus did not experience . . .

Of the infinite power that is proper to God, the Heart of Christ kept only the defenceless power of the love that forgives. And in the radical loneliness of the Cross, he accepted being pierced by the centurion's lance so that from the open wound there might pour out upon the world's ugly deeds the inexhaustible torrent of a mercy that washes, purifies and renews.

In the Heart of Christ, therefore, there meet divine richness and human poverty, the power of grace and the frailty of nature, an appeal from God and a response from man. In the Heart of Christ

[10] *AAS* 48 (1956): 327–28; Francis Larkin, SS.CC., ed., *Haurietis Aquas: The Sacred Heart Encyclical of Pope Pius XII* (Orlando, Fl.: Sacred Heart Publications Center, 1974), 23–24 (my emphasis).

the history of mankind has its definitive place of arrival, because "the Father has assigned all judgment to the Son" (Jn. 5:22). *Therefore, willing or not, every human heart must refer to the Heart of Christ.*[11]

The texts which we have just cited on the Heart of Jesus cannot simply be predicated of the Heart of Mary without any further qualification. This is so because the Heart of Jesus is a human symbol of a Divine Person, whereas the Heart of Mary is the symbol of a human creature. Nonetheless, in an analogous way which keeps this distinction in mind, Mary's Immaculate Heart is also a uniquely appropriate symbol of her person. Hence the decree of the Sacred Congregation of Rites establishing the Feast of the Immaculate Heart of Mary states:

> With this devotion the Church renders the honor due to the Immaculate Heart of the Blessed Virgin Mary, since under the symbol of this heart she venerates with reverence the eminent and singular holiness of the Mother of God and especially her most ardent love for God and Jesus her Son and moreover her maternal compassion for all those redeemed by the divine Blood.[12]

If, then, the Heart of Jesus evokes the whole mystery of the God-Man, the Heart of Mary likewise calls to mind her Motherhood of Christ and the Church.

Movements in favor of consecration to the Hearts of Jesus and Mary

From about the time of the beatification of Margaret Mary Alacoque in 1864, a groundswell in favor of the consecration of the world to the Sacred Heart of Jesus and the consecration of the world to the Immaculate Heart of Mary began to gain momentum. Each initiative seems to have been independent, even if complementary. As far as I have

[11] *Inseg* VII:1 (1984), 1975–76; *ORE* 843:9 (final emphasis my own).

[12] Decree of May 4, 1944, *AAS* 37 (1945): 50; English trans. in *ORE* 959:12.

been able to determine, the earliest would appear to have been that promoting the consecration of the world to the Immaculate Heart of Mary. It was in the form of a petition presented to the Venerable Pope Pius IX in 1864 by Cardinal Gousset of Rheims and supported by Archbishop de la Tour-d'Auvergne of Bourges, Bishop Mermillod, and other bishops of France and Spain.[13]

Both movements surfaced in the course of the First Vatican Council (1869–1870). The archbishop of Bourges strove to win the support of all the Council Fathers for the consecration to Mary's Heart first requested six years earlier and for the establishment of a feast in honor of her Queenship.[14] During the same period Père Henri Ramière, S.J. (1821–1884), the great animator of the Apostleship of Prayer[15] who was serving as *peritus* to the archbishop of Beauvais,

> submitted to the Bishops present in Rome a request whereby the Holy Father was asked . . . to consecrate the whole Church to the Sacred Heart [of Jesus]. The request was already supported by two hundred and seventy-two Bishops when the Franco-German war broke out and the Council was adjourned.[16]

Notwithstanding the volatile political situation in much of Western Europe after the constrained adjournment of the council, the drive for the consecration to the Sacred Heart of Jesus gained momentum with the approach of the second centenary of the "great revelation" of the Lord made to

[13] Cf. G. Geenen, O.P., "Les Antécédents Doctrinaux et Historiques de la Consécration du Monde au Cœur Immaculé de Marie", in *Maria*, 1:863; Gabriele Roschini, O.S.M., "La Consacrazione del Mondo al Cuore Immacolato di Maria", in *Il Cuore Immacolato di Maria, Settimana di Studi Mariani* (Rome: Edizioni Marianum, 1946), 56.

[14] Geenen, 863.

[15] Cf. Gérald de Becker, SS.CC., *Lexique Pour la Théologie du Cœur du Christ* (Paris: Editions Téqui, 1975), 295–96; Pierre Vallin, "Ramière (Henri)", in *DSp*, 13:63–70.

[16] Verheylezoon, 143.

Saint Margaret Mary in 1675. Cardinal Desprez, the archbishop of Toulouse, addressed a letter to all the Catholic bishops in the world in 1874, to which a new petition was attached, and in April of 1875, Père Ramière presented the petition to Pius IX together with the names of the 534 bishops and 23 superiors general who subscribed to it.[17]

Consecration of the human race to the Sacred Heart of Jesus

In response to Père Ramière the Pope said, "I shall do what you want, but in my own way." [18] He then instructed the Sacred Congregation of Rites to prepare a formula of consecration which he himself approved and had published along with an invitation to Catholics throughout the world to consecrate themselves together to the Sacred Heart of Jesus.[19] The Holy Father invited all to choose for this special act of consecration June 16, 1875, the second centenary of the best known and arguably most important of the apparitions of Christ to Saint Margaret Mary at Paray-le-Monial.[20] The consecration was solemnly made in churches throughout the world on that date; the Pope himself made it in his private chapel,[21] but not publicly in the Vatican Basilica as the petition had asked.[22]

In 1891, during the pontificate of Leo XIII, a vast movement surfaced in Italy, led by the cardinal archbishops of Milan and Turin, in favor of the consecration of the dio-

[17] Arthur R. McGratty, S.J., *The Sacred Heart Yesterday and Today* (New York: Benziger Brothers, 1951), 222–24.

[18] Verheylezoon, 143.

[19] The Latin decree and the Act of Consecration in Italian are published in *Acta Sanctae Sedis* 8 (1874–1875): 402–4 (hereafter cited as *ASS*). An English translation of the prayer is found in *The Treasury of the Sacred Heart* (New York: D. & J. Sadlier & Co., 1879), 330–34.

[20] McGratty, 224; on the "great revelation", see 93.

[21] Verheylezoon, 144.

[22] McGratty, 223.

ceses of Italy to the Most Holy Heart of Mary.[23] It was at the Marian Congress of Turin in September of 1898 that this desideratum was given concrete form, and that was due, it appears, primarily to the initiative of the Pope himself in his brief of August 2, 1898.[24] The project of the archbishop of Turin was unanimously approved by the congress which petitioned the Holy Father for the consecration of Italy to the Immaculate Heart of Mary by means of a formula adopted at the congress.[25] By a rescript of December 12, 1898, the Sacred Congregation of Rites approved the proposed formula not only for those dioceses which had requested it, but also for those who would do so in the future.[26]

Earlier in that same year, on June 10, 1898, Mother Mary of the Divine Heart Droste zu Vischering (1863–1899),[27] a spiritual daughter of Saint John Eudes, had written to Pope Leo XIII that the Lord desired him to consecrate the entire human race to the Heart of Jesus. Although deeply touched, he did not immediately act upon the letter. It seems that his first intention was to wait to make the consecration in the Jubilee Year of 1900.[28] The nun began a second letter on the Feast of the Immaculate Conception that year which her confessor allowed to be dispatched only on the Feast of

[23] Roschini, "Consacrazione del Mondo", 56.

[24] Geenen, 864. For the text of the brief see Santino Epis, "La Consacrazione dell'Italia a Maria: Un Capitolo di Storia e un Impegno Permanente", in *La Consacrazione dell'Italia a Maria*, De Fiores, Epis, Amorth, eds., (Rome: Edizioni Paoline, 1983), 67–68.

[25] Epis, 75–77.

[26] *ASS* 31 (1898–1899): 538–40.

[27] Beatified by Pope Paul VI on November 1, 1975. Cf. de Becker, *Lexique*, 116–17; Constantin Becker, "Marie du Divin Cœur", in *DSp*, 10:485–86; Louis Chasle, *Sister Mary of the Divine Heart*, trans. by a member of the order (London: Burns & Oates, 1906); Pierre Cras, "Mother Mary of the Divine Heart: A Divine Messenger", in *Divine Masterpieces*, ed. and trans. John J. Sullivan, S.J. (Paterson, N.J.: St. Anthony Guild Press, 1960), 161–84.

[28] Chasle, 365–66.

Epiphany in 1899.[29] He was even more deeply moved by this second letter. Then there was a further intervention of Divine Providence. On March 1, 1899, the Pope had to undergo major surgery for a tumor,[30] which, given the fact that he was almost ninety and that a general anesthetic could not be used, was most successful.

In gratitude to God, he decided to delay the consecration no longer. He had the question of the theological aspects of the proposed consecration and his authority to consecrate the unbaptized carefully studied.[31] Evidently the principal agent of the study was the Jesuit Cardinal Camillo Mazzella (1833–1900), a noted exponent of the neoscholastic revival and prefect of the Congregation of Rites.[32] Abbé Chasle, commissioned by the superior general of the Sisters of the Good Shepherd to write the first biography of Blessed Mary of the Divine Heart, benefited from consulting some of the major protagonists involved in this fascinating episode in the Church's history and shared his researches three years after Blessed Mary's death with Leo XIII himself.[33] Here is part of his account of the role of the cardinal prefect in this matter:

> No one could have given a more favourable testimony than Cardinal Mazzella, S.J., Prefect of the Sacred Congregation of Rites, who knew everything [regarding Mother Mary of the Divine Heart's request for the consecration of the human race to the

[29] Although she was German, she wrote the letter in French. The original text is given in Charles Lebrun, C.J.M., *Le Bienheureux Jean Eudes et le Culte Public du Cœur de Jésus*, 2nd ed. (Paris: P. Lethielleux, 1918), 232–36; an English translation is supplied in McGratty, 228–30.

[30] Cras, 182.

[31] McGratty, 230–31; Cras, 181–82.

[32] See J. Flynn, "Mazzella, Camillo", in *New Catholic Encyclopedia*, vol. 9 (New York: McGraw-Hill Book Co., 1967), 523–24 (hereafter cited as *NCE*); on the cardinal's role in the formulation of the theology of the consecration, see also Francesco Degli Esposti, *La Teologia del Sacro Cuore di Gesù da Leone XIII a Pio XII* (Rome: Casa Editrice Herder, 1967), 26–27; 47–48.

[33] Chasle, xxx–xxxi.

> Sacred Heart of Jesus]; he says: "This is a very touching letter, and certainly appears to have been dictated by Our Lord." At the same time it was agreed that the proofs needed to justify this proposed act should be sought elsewhere. "My Lord Cardinal," Leo XIII said, "take this letter and lay it aside; at the present moment it must not be taken into account." It was therefore resolved that the consecration of the human race to the Sacred Heart should be brought forward, as the consequence of an application of the principles of theology, and of Catholic tradition, and not as the result of any private revelation. The Cardinal left the Vatican commissioned to examine the question *in se*, that is to say, from the point of tradition only, putting aside the supernatural information of the person who had petitioned Leo XIII to take up the matter.[34]

The Cardinal's reply was positive and on Easter Sunday, April 2, 1899, as prefect of the Sacred Congregation of Rites, he signed a decree announcing the Pope's intention to consecrate the entire world to the Sacred Heart of Jesus.[35] In passing one might note the rather striking parallel between the successful recovery of Leo XIII and the consecration of the world to the Heart of Jesus in 1899 and the recovery of John Paul II and the consecration of the world to the Immaculate Heart of Mary on the first anniversary of the attempt on his life in 1982.

[34] Ibid., 368–69. It should be noted that Pius XII took the same position vis-à-vis the revelations to St. Margaret Mary Alacoque in *Haurietis Aquas*: "It must not be said that this devotion has taken its origin from some private revelation of God and has suddenly appeared in the Church; rather, it has blossomed forth of its own accord as a result of that lively faith and burning devotion of men who were endowed with heavenly gifts, and who were drawn towards the adorable Redeemer and His glorious wounds which they saw as irresistible proofs of that unbounded love. Consequently, it is clear that the revelations made to St. Margaret Mary brought nothing new into Catholic doctrine. Their importance lay in this that Christ Our Lord, exposing His Sacred Heart, wished in a quite extraordinary way to invite the minds of men to a contemplation of, and a devotion to, the mystery of God's merciful love for the human race" (*AAS* 48 [1956]: 340; Larkin trans., 35–36).

[35] *ASS* 31 (1898–1899): 701–2; cf. also Chasle, 370–71; Gérald de Becker, SS.CC., *Les Sacrés-Cœurs de Jésus et de Marie: Étude Doctrinale* (Rome: Études Picpuciennes no. 5, 1959), 142.

Thus it was that Pope Leo XIII issued his great encyclical letter on consecration to the Sacred Heart of Jesus, *Annum Sacrum*, explaining the rationale of this act and directing a triduum [36] to be held in the principal church of every town and village, concluding on June 11, 1899, with the recitation of the Act of Consecration of the Human Race to the Sacred Heart of Jesus (published with the encyclical).[37] Because of the significance of this act, which Leo referred to as "the greatest of my pontificate",[38] and of the encyclical which carefully developed its rationale, it will be advantageous for us to note some of the underlying theological principles made explicit in it. They will shed considerable light on subsequent papal acts relating to Marian consecration.

The encyclical carefully outlines the twofold basis for Christ's Kingship over all creatures: His natural right as Son of God and His acquired right as Redeemer of the human race:

> This world-wide and solemn testimony of allegiance and piety is especially appropriate to Jesus Christ, who is the Head and supreme Lord of the race. His empire extends not only over Catholic nations and those who, having been duly washed in the waters of holy Baptism, belong of right to the Church, although erroneous opinions keep them astray, or dissent from her teaching cuts them off from her care; it comprises also all those who are deprived of the Christian faith, so that the whole human race is most truly under the power of Jesus Christ. For He who is the Only-begotten Son of God the Father, having the same substance with Him and being the brightness of His glory and the figure of His substance (Heb. 1:3), necessarily has everything in common with the Father, and therefore sovereign power over all things. . . .

[36] Mother Maria Droste zu Vischering died on June 8, 1899, at the hour of first Vespers of the Feast of the Sacred Heart of Jesus, just before the beginning of the triduum. Cf. Cras, 183.

[37] *ASS* 31 (1898–1899): 651–52.

[38] McGratty, 232.

> But this is not all. *Christ reigns not only by natural right as the Son of God, but also by a right that He has acquired.* For He it was who snatched us "from the power of darkness" (Col. 1:13) and "gave Himself for the redemption of all" (1 Tim. 2:6). Therefore not only Catholics, and those who have duly received Christian Baptism, but also all men, individually and collectively, have become to Him "a purchased people" (1 Pt. 2:9).[39]

Since the sovereignty of Christ is already established over us by nature and conquest, why should there be an explicit consecration? Leo answers thus:

> To this twofold ground of His power and domination He graciously allows us, if we think fit, to add voluntary consecration [*devotio voluntaria*]. Jesus Christ, our God and our Redeemer, is rich in the fullest and perfect possession of all things: we, on the other hand, are so poor and needy that we have nothing of our own to offer Him as a gift. But yet, in His infinite goodness and love, *He in no way objects to our giving and consecrating* [*demus, addicamus*] to Him what is already His, as if it were really our own; nay, far from refusing such an offering, He positively desires it and asks for it: "My son, give me thy heart." We are, therefore, able to be pleasing to Him by the good will and the affection of our soul. *For by consecrating ourselves to Him we not only declare our open and free acknowledgment and acceptance of His authority over us* [*Nam ipsi devovendo nos, non modo et agnoscimus et accipimus imperium eius aperte ac libenter*], but we also testify that if what we offer as a gift were really our own, we would still offer it with our whole heart. We also beg of Him that He would vouchsafe to receive it from us, though clearly His own.[40]

Having established the reason for making an explicit act of consecration, the Pontiff next answers the question: "Why make this consecration to the Heart of Jesus?"

[39] *ASS* 31 (1898–1899): 647, 648; Claudia Carlen, I.H.M., *The Papal Encyclicals, 1878–1903* (Raleigh, N.C.: McGrath Publishing Co., 1981), 452–53 (hereafter cited as Carlen 2), (my emphasis). On this point cf. the excellent commentary of Degli Esposti, 24.

[40] *ASS* 31 (1898–1899): 648–49; Carlen 2:452–53 (my emphasis). Cf. Degli Esposti, 25.

> Since there is in the Sacred Heart a symbol and a sensible image of the infinite love of Jesus Christ [*Quoniamque inest in Sacro Corde symbolum atque expressa imago infinitae Iesu Christi caritatis*] which moves us to love one another, therefore is it fit and proper that we should consecrate ourselves to His most Sacred Heart—an act which is nothing else than an offering and a binding of oneself to Jesus Christ, seeing that whatever honor, veneration and love is given to this divine Heart is really and truly given to Christ Himself [*ideo consentaneum est dicare se Cordi eius augustissimo: quod tamen nihil est aliud quam dedere atque obligare se Iesu Christo, quia quidquid honoris, obsequii, pietatis divino Cordi tribuitur, vere et proprie Christo tribuitur ipsi*].[41]

Here in specifying the Heart of Jesus as the "symbol and sensible image of the infinite love of Jesus Christ", Leo is at once recognizing the symbolic value of the heart in this *cultus* and also declaring its equivalence with the person of Jesus Christ.[42] In other words he is defining the formal object of the consecration.

Since he had been asked to consecrate the entire human race to the Sacred Heart of Jesus, and had had the matter studied as we have seen above,[43] he also deals with his authority to do this.

> We hold the place of Him who came to save that which was lost, and who shed His blood for the salvation of the whole human race. And so We greatly desire to bring to the true life those who sit in the shadow of death. As We have already sent messengers of Christ over the earth to instruct them, so now, in pity for their lot with all Our soul We commend them, and as far as in Us lies We consecrate them to the Sacred Heart of Jesus [*Sacratissimo Cordi Iesu commendamus maiorem in modo et, quantum in Nobis est, dedicamus*].[44]

Let us note the precision of the Pope here with his careful use of language as signaled by Monsignor John F. Murphy:

[41] *ASS* 31 (1898–1899): 649; Carlen 2:453.
[42] Cf. Degli Esposti, 25, 31–32.
[43] Cf. above, 82–83.
[44] *ASS* 31 (1898–1899): 649; Carlen 2:453.

> We note in the consecration of Leo XIII the use of two words, *commendamus* and *dedicamus*. These terms are not here employed as synonyms. Thus the Holy Father would commend *all*; and inasmuch as was in his power [*quantum in Nobis*] would consecrate in a less perfect manner those over whom his influence was less direct.[45]

It would seem that this distinction was based on Cardinal Mazzella's appreciation of a

> celebrated page of the *Summa* [*Theologiae* III, q. 59, a. 4], where the angelic Doctor, in speaking of Our Lord's kingdom, distinguishes between those who submit themselves to Him, *quantum ad executionem potestatis*, that is to say, who obey His laws; or those who submit only *quantum ad potestatem*; that is to say, who without knowing Him and remaining outside His fold are yet His subjects, and whether they will or not, cannot divest themselves of the strict obligation of coming back to Him.[46]

It is also of interest to note that in the official Latin text of *Annum Sacrum* and in the act of consecration the word *consecrare* does not occur. The words of the act which are usually rendered into English as "behold, each one of us freely consecrates himself today to Thy Most Sacred Heart" are: *en hodie Sacratissimo Cordi tuo se quisque nostrum sponte dedicat.*[47] Only the act itself is mentioned once in the encyclical as *formula Consecrationis*[48] and this designation appears as the heading of the act as well. Although the word *consecrate* has become a "consecrated" term in English and many other modern languages with the meaning of "offering or

[45] John F. Murphy, *Mary's Immaculate Heart: The Meaning of the Devotion to the Immaculate Heart of Mary* (Milwaukee: Bruce Publishing Company, 1951), 99; cf. also Roschini, "Consacrazione del Mondo", 67–70.

[46] Chasle, 369–70. This text from the *Summa* was in fact specifically cited in *Annum Sacrum*, see *ASS* 31 (1898–1899): 648; Carlen 2:452.

[47] *ASS* 31 (1898–1899): 651.

[48] Ibid.

binding" oneself to Jesus or His Mother, it is not so in Latin.[49]

The consecration of the human race to the Sacred Heart of Jesus, Father O'Carroll tells us, "gave a certain stimulus to the practice of consecration to the Immaculate Heart."[50] This should not be surprising because the *cultus* of the two Hearts had developed side by side from the time of Saint John Eudes[51] and, while maintaining the necessary distinction between "devotion" to the Sacred Heart of Jesus as an act of *latria* and that to the Immaculate Heart of Mary as an act of *hyperdulia*, the two "acts of religion" are obviously complementary and not mutually exclusive.[52] Consequently we find that at the national Marian Congress held at Lyons in 1900 the following *vota* were adopted:

1. that after the consecration of the human race to the Sacred Heart should come the consecration of the universe to the Most Holy Virgin under the title of Queen of the universe;
2. that a feast called the feast of the universal royalty of Mary be instituted and celebrated yearly with a proper office;
3. that the Holy Father would deign to add to the Litany of Loreto the invocation "Queen of the universe, pray for us."[53]

[49] We have seen above on page 54 that, according to Fr. Jungmann, the first usage of the word *consecrare* in this context was in Spinelli's *Hortulus Marianus* of 1622. Papal Latinists have obviously and consistently opted for a more classical vocaulary.

[50] *Theotokos*, 108.

[51] The saint was described by St. Pius X at the time of his beatification as "the father, doctor and apostle of the [liturgical] devotion to the Most Holy Hearts of Jesus and Mary", see *AAS* 1 (1909): 480. Pius XI used the same titles in the Decree of Canonization, see *AAS* 17 (1925): 490 (errata corrected, 727).

[52] This important distinction between *latria* and *hyperdulia* will be dealt with in the second part of this work.

[53] Geenen, 864 (my trans.).

In that same year following Leo's Act of Consecration, Father Alfred Deschamps launched a movement in Toulouse in favor of the consecration of individuals, families, parishes, dioceses, and the whole human race to the Immaculate Heart of Mary.[54]

The impetus in favor of consecration to the Sacred Heart of Jesus continued during the pontificates of his immediate successors, Saint Pius X and Pope Benedict XV.[55] On August 22, 1906, Pius X prescribed that an annual renewal of the consecration to the Sacred Heart of Jesus should take place each year on the Feast of the Sacred Heart according to the Leonine formula.[56] Petitions for a consecration to the Immaculate Heart of Mary, similar to that of Leo XIII to the Sacred Heart of Jesus, continued to pour into Rome representing millions of supporters. There were those of Father Dechamps' "Marian Crusade" and those of the Archconfraternity of Notre-Dame des Victoires in 1906; those of the Montfortian Father Gebhard, in the name of the archbishop of Ottawa in 1907; those of Father Le Doré, superior general of the Eudists, in 1908 and 1912; those of Father Lintelo, a Belgian Jesuit, in 1914.[57] On one occasion in 1907, the Pope indicated that he was favorably disposed to the initiative,[58] and in 1914, on the occasion of the Eucharistic Congress in Lourdes, which was also a Marian Congress, the saint indicated that he awaited the right moment, a celebration which would be strictly Marian.[59] In 1907 the same Pontiff also approved and indulgenced Saint Louis-Marie de Montfort's Act of Consecration to Our Lady and

[54] Geenen, 865; Roschini, "Consacrazione del Mondo", 56–57.

[55] Degli Esposti, 66.

[56] *ASS* 39 (1906): 569–70.

[57] Geenen, 865.

[58] Roschini, "Consacrazione del Mondo", 57; Geenen, 865.

[59] Roschini, "Consacrazione del Mondo", 58; Geenen, 866.

another addressed to the Immaculate Heart of Mary for use by groups.[60]

Benedict XV would provide further stimulus that the consecration to the Sacred Heart of Jesus become ever more rooted among the faithful in *Libenter Tuas*, his letter to Father Mateo Crawley-Boevey, SS.CC. (1875–1960)[61] of April 27, 1915, on the consecration of families,[62] and in his letter to the bishops of Poland on the occasion of the consecration of their nation to the Heart of Jesus.[63] And evidently as a response to petitions addressed to him by Berthe Petit[64] to consecrate the world to the Sorrowful and Immaculate Heart of Mary, Benedict concluded his letter to the dean of the Sacred College of Cardinals on May 31, 1915, eight days after Italy had entered World War I, with an exhortation to invoke Mary's Sorrowful and Immaculate Heart.[65]

During the pontificate of Pius XI there were further refinements of the magisterium on the matter of consecration to the Most Sacred Heart of Jesus. The first of these occurred in the encyclical *Quas Primas* of December 11, 1925, by which he instituted the liturgical feast of Christ the King. In accord with the teaching of his predecessor Leo XIII in *Annum Sacrum*, Pius XI taught that Christ deserves the title "King" not only in a metaphorical but also in a

60 *Theotokos*, 108.

61 Cf. Francis Larkin, SS.CC., "Crawley-Boevey, Mateo", in *NCE*, 4:16; Gérald de Becker, SS.CC., "Intronisation", in *Lexique*, 171–73.

62 *AAS* 7 (1915): 203–5; English trans. in Timothy Terrance O'Donnell, *Heart of the Redeemer: An Apologia for the Contemporary and Perennial Value of the Devotion to the Sacred Heart of Jesus* (Manassas, Va.: Trinity Communications, 1989), 167–69; Degli Esposti, 69–70.

63 *AAS* 13 (1921): 11.

64 Cf. Joseph A. Pelletier, A.A., *The Immaculate Heart of Mary* (Worcester, Mass.: An Assumption Publication, 1976), 125–47; *The Sorrowful and Immaculate Heart of Mary: Message of Berthe Petit, Franciscan Tertiary (1870–1943)*, trans. Kylemore Abbey nun (Kenosha, Wis.: Franciscan Marytown Press, 1974).

65 *Sorrowful and Immaculate Heart*, 33.

strict sense,[66] that He is King by natural as well as by acquired right [*iure non tantum nativo sed etiam quaesito*].[67] Conscious of the theological principles already established, he noted:

> The kingship and empire of Christ have been recognized in the pious custom, practiced by many families, of dedicating themselves [*se dedicarent ac dederent*] to the Sacred Heart of Jesus; not only families have performed this act of dedication, but nations, too, and kingdoms. In fact, the whole of the human race was at the instance of Pope Leo XIII, in the Holy Year of 1900, consecrated to the Divine Heart [*consecrata est*].[68]

Finally, he concluded:

> Therefore by Our Apostolic Authority We institute the Feast of the Kingship of Our Lord Jesus Christ to be observed yearly throughout the whole world on the last Sunday of the month of October—the Sunday, that is, which immediately precedes the Feast of All Saints. We further ordain that the dedication of mankind to the Sacred Heart of Jesus [*generis humani Sacratissimo Cordi Iesu dedicatio*], which Our predecessor of saintly memory, Pope Pius X, commanded to be renewed yearly, be made annually on that day.[69]

About this mandate and its basis Father Degli Esposti comments:

> It is commonly accepted by the commentators that Pius XI placed the last stone in the doctrine of the consecration to the Sacred Heart with the connection which he made on the dogmatic, historical, social, and liturgical plane between the *cultus* to the Sacred Heart and the Kingship of Christ.[70]

[66] *AAS* 17 (1925): 595–96.

[67] *AAS* 17 (1925): 599.

[68] Ibid., 606; Claudia Carlen, *The Papal Encyclicals 1903–1939* (Raleigh, N.C.: McGrath Publishing Co., 1981), 276–77 (hereafter cited as Carlen 3).

[69] *AAS* 17 (1925): 607; Carlen 3:277.

[70] Degli Esposti, 136 (my trans.).

The second of these refinements was presented in the course of his great encyclical on reparation to the Sacred Heart of Jesus, *Miserentissimus Redemptor,* of May 8, 1928. The fundamental argument of the encyclical is that the two greatest acts of worship which can be offered to the Sacred Heart of Jesus are consecration and reparation; while the objective of the encyclical is to present authoritative teaching on reparation, the meaning of consecration is also expounded authoritatively.

Consecration, the Pope insists, is the greatest homage which we can offer to the Lord.

> Assuredly among those things which properly pertain to the worship of the Most Sacred Heart, a special place must be given to that Consecration [*consecratio*], whereby we devote [*devovemus*] ourselves and all things that are ours to the Divine Heart of Jesus, acknowledging that we have received all things from the everlasting love of God. When Our Saviour had taught Margaret Mary, the most innocent disciple of His Heart, how much He desired that this duty of devotion [*devotionis officium*] should be rendered to him by men, moved in this not so much by His own right as by His immense charity for us; she herself, with her spiritual father, Claude de la Colombière, rendered it the first of all.[71]

It will be noted that he derives the exigency for this consecration from the revelations of Paray-le-Monial. These had already been given the maximum approbation of the Church in the bull *Ecclesiae Consuetudo* of May 13, 1920, issued by Benedict XV for the canonization of Saint Margaret Mary Alacoque.[72]

Pius XI sees the consecration to the Sacred Heart not merely as a "pious devotion", but as an act that will have significant consequences.

> Now these things so auspiciously and happily begun as we taught in Our Encyclical Letter "Quas primas," we Ourselves, consenting

[71] *AAS* 20 (1928): 167–168; Carlen 3:322.

[72] *AAS* 12 (1920): 486–513; Degli Esposti, 74.

> to very many long-continued desires and prayers of Bishops and people, brought to completion and perfected, by God's grace, when at the close of the Jubilee Year, We instituted the Feast of Christ the King of All, to be solemnly celebrated throughout the whole Christian world. Now when we did this, not only did we set in a clear light that supreme sovereignty which Christ holds over the whole universe, over civil and domestic society, and over individual men, but at the same time *we anticipated the joys of that most auspicious day, whereon the whole world will gladly and willingly render obedience to the most sweet lordship of Christ the King.* For this reason, We decreed at the same time that this same Consecration should be renewed every year on the occasion of that appointed festal day, *so that the fruit of this same Consecration might be obtained more certainly and more abundantly, and all peoples might be joined together in Christian charity and in the reconciliation of peace, in the Heart of the King of kings and Lord of lords.*[73]

Clearly, according to Pius, consecration to the Sacred Heart, when taken seriously, will bring about the reign of Christ the King.

Two further precisions about consecration are made in the course of the development of this magisterial teaching on reparation. The first is that: "The first and foremost thing in Consecration is this, that the creature's love should be given in return for the love of the Creator [*Nam, . . . illud est in consecratione primum ac praecipuum ut amori Creatoris creaturae amor rependatur*]." [74] In other words consecration to the Sacred Heart of Jesus is an act of latreutic worship (an exercise of the virtue of religion) and an act of love (the theological virtue of charity).

The second precision is based explicitly on the teaching of Saint Thomas Aquinas on the virtue of religion, the moral virtue which excels all others because it pertains to our duties toward God. In the corpus of article 8, question 81, of the *Secunda secundae* of the *Summa Theologiae*, the

[73] *AAS* 20 (1928): 168–69; Carlen 3:323 (my emphasis).
[74] *AAS* 20 (1928): 169; Carlen 3:323.

Common Doctor holds that the second signification of the word holiness [*sanctitas*] denotes firmness [*firmitas*]. Pius XI says:

> To Consecration, therefore, whereby we are devoted to God and are called holy to God, by that holiness and stability which, as the Angelic Doctor teaches, is proper to consecration (*ST* II–II. q. 81, a. 8 c), there must be added expiation [*Consecrationi igitur, qua Deo devovemur et sancti Deo vocamur, ea sanctitate ac firmitate quae, ut docet Angelicus, consecrationis est propria, addenda est expiatio*].[75]

The reason, then, that Pius expects abundant fruit from this consecration is precisely because it implies a permanent, stable relationship with Jesus Christ. How could members of the Church live their consecration to Christ without making the Church and the world more holy?

Consecration of the world to the Immaculate Heart of Mary

It should also be noted that during the reign of Pius XI the decree permitting the *cultus* or veneration of Our Lady of Fatima was issued by the bishop of Leiria on October 13, 1930, and that on May 13, 1931, the bishops of Portugal consecrated their dioceses and their country to the Immaculate Heart of Mary. In 1934, in his letter *Ex officiosis litteris*, the Pope congratulated Portugal "on the extraordinary favors which the Blessed Virgin and Mother of God has just heaped upon the country." [76]

The impetus toward consecration to the Immaculate Heart of Mary also continued to gain momentum. The French Marian Congresses of Lourdes (1930), Liesse (1934), and Boulogne-sur-Mer (1938) petitioned the Holy Father to make an official consecration of the human race to the

[75] *AAS* 20 (1928): 169; Carlen 3:323.

[76] *AAS* 26 (1934): 628 (my trans.). Cf. also Geenen, 867; Roschini, "Consacrazione del Mondo", 59.

Immaculate Heart of Mary.[77] But the impetus came not only from the ranks of theologians and signers of petitions, it came also from what may be called the "charismatic order".[78] Just as the *cultus* of the Sacred Heart of Jesus developed notably after the revelations to Saint Margaret Mary, even though as Pope John Paul II pointed out in his letter to Peter-Hans Kolvenbach, S.J., of October 5, 1986, "the elements of this devotion belong in a permanent fashion to the spirituality of the Church throughout her history",[79] and as the decisive spur toward the consecration of the human race to the Sacred Heart came from Blessed Mary of the Divine Heart, so we should not be surprised at the interventions from the "charismatic order" in favor of the parallel and analogous consecration to the Immaculate Heart of Mary. We have already made reference to the role Berthe Petit would play in this regard until her death in 1943.[80] Another protagonist, apparently directed by the Lord in this regard, was the Servant of God Alexandrina Maria da Costa.[81]

Of these "charismatic agents" promoting consecration to the Immaculate Heart of Mary, surely the one whose efforts are best known is Lúcia dos Santos, Sister Lúcia of the Immaculate Heart of Mary, O.C.D., the surviving seer of Fatima.[82] She tells us in her memoirs that on July 13, 1917,

[77] Geenen, 868; *Theotokos*, 108.

[78] Cf. Joseph de Sainte-Marie, O.C.D., *Reflections on the Act of Consecration at Fatima of Pope John Paul II on 13th May 1982*, trans. William Lawson, S.J. (Chulmleigh, Devon.: Augustine Publishing Co., 1983), 8–9. This booklet had originally appeared in French as an article in *Marianum* 44 (1982): 88–142.

[79] *Inseg* IX:2 (1986), 843; *ORE* 960:7.

[80] Cf. above, 91.

[81] Cf. Francis Johnston, *Alexandrina: The Agony and the Glory* (Rockford, Ill.: Tan Books and Publishers, 1982), 40–41.

[82] On May 15, 1991, just after his return to Rome from his second pilgrimage to Fatima, Pope John Paul II said, "During our century the Church's experience of Fatima has developed *in connection with a special entrustment to the Heart of the Mother of the Redeemer*", *ORE* 1191:11.

Our Lady said that she would return to ask for the consecration of Russia to her Immaculate Heart.[83] She testifies that those words of Our Lady were fulfilled on June 13, 1929, in Tuy, Spain.[84] Twice, in fact, she spoke of the "consecration of Russia to the Sacred Hearts of Jesus and Mary",[85] while on the majority of occasions she spoke of the consecration as only to the Immaculate Heart of Mary. But on May 18, 1936, she added that the Lord wills this consecration to Mary's Heart "because I want my whole Church to acknowledge that consecration as a triumph of the Immaculate Heart of Mary, so that it may extend its veneration later on, and put the devotion to this Immaculate Heart beside the devotion to My Sacred Heart." [86]

On May 13, 1938, the bishops of Portugal consecrated their country again, this time in thanksgiving, to the Immaculate Heart of Mary.[87] In June of that year, prompted by Father Pinho, S.J., spiritual director of Alexandrina Maria da Costa, they wrote to Pius XI asking him to consecrate the world to the Immaculate Heart of Mary.[88] Pope Pius XI died on February 10, 1939, and was succeeded on March 2 of that same year by his secretary of state, Cardinal Pacelli, who took the name of Pius XII. It was evidently at this point that the matter became somewhat complex as the Portuguese hierarchy strove to amalgamate the different requests of Lúcia and Alexandrina. Here is the result of the

[83] Cf. Antonio Maria Martins, S.J., ed. and trans., *Memórias e Cartas da Irmã Lúcia* (Porto, Portugal: Simão Guimarães, Filhos, Lda., 1973), 219, 227, 341; Louis Kondor, S.V.D., ed., *Fatima in Lucia's Own Words,* trans. Dominican Nuns of Perpetual Rosary (Fatima, Portugal: Postulation Centre, 1976), 104, 108, 162.

[84] Martins, 465; Kondor, 200.

[85] Letter of May 29, 1930, to Fr. Gonzalves, Martins, 405; letter of June 12, 1930, to the same, Martins, 411.

[86] Martins, 415. I substituted the word "veneration" for "cult", which is used in the Martins translation, because of the unhappy associations of this word in the English-speaking world.

[87] Geenen, 867; Roschini, "Consacrazione del Mondo", 59.

[88] Joseph de Sainte-Marie, *Reflections*, 16.

late Father Joseph de Sainte-Marie's efforts to sort out the issues:

> In October, 1940, they [the bishops of Portugal] sought to combine the testimony of Sister Lúcia with that of Alexandrina, and they ordered her [Lúcia] to write herself to the Holy Father, asking him to consecrate the world to the Heart of the Blessed Virgin. But Lúcia, until then, had received from Heaven requests bearing only on the consecration of Russia, not on that of the world. When she received the order from her bishop she took to prayer, on October 22nd, asking for light on what she should do. She received from Our Lord, not from Our Lady, the following answer (remember that the war was raging at the time): "Tribulation will grow. I shall punish the nations for their crimes with war, famine, persecution of My Church, persecution which will fall especially on him who is My Vicar on earth. His Holiness will obtain the shortening of these days of tribulation if he meets My wishes and makes the act of consecration to the Immaculate Heart of Mary of the entire world with special mention of Russia." [89]

The response to this cumulative impulse for consecration to the Immaculate Heart of Mary came from the Servant of God Pope Pius XII on October 31, 1942 in the course of a radio broadcast to pilgrims at Fatima celebrating the Silver Jubilee of the last of the 1917 apparitions.[90] Concluding the broadcast, he prayed:

> To you and to your Immaculate Heart, We, the common father of the vast Christian family, We, the Vicar of Him to whom was given "all power in heaven and on earth," and from whom we have received the care of so many souls redeemed by His Blood;

[89] Joseph de Sainte-Marie, *Reflections,* 17. Martins has published two letters of Lúcia to Pope Pius XII carrying out the orders of the Portuguese hierarchy: that of October 24, 1940 (which was not sent), 431–33; and that of December 2, 1940 (which was sent), 437–39.

[90] He himself had been consecrated a bishop on May 13, 1917, the day of the first of the six apparitions of Our Lady to the three little shepherds of Fatima. John Paul II called attention to this fact in his homily at Fatima on May 13, 1982, see *Inseg* V:2 (1982), 1574; *Portugal,* 81.

to you and to your Immaculate Heart in this tragic hour of human history, We commit, We entrust, We consecrate [*affidiamo, rimettiamo, consacriamo*], not only the Holy Church, the mystical body of your Jesus, which suffers and bleeds in so many places and is afflicted in so many ways, but also the entire world torn by violent discord, scorched in a fire of hate, victim of its own iniquities. . . . Finally, just as the Church and the entire human race were consecrated to the Heart of your Jesus, because by placing in Him every hope, it may be for them a token and pledge of victory and salvation; so, henceforth, may they be perpetually consecrated to you, to your Immaculate Heart [*così parimenti da oggi siano essi in perpetuo consacrati anche a Voi, al vostro Cuore Immacolato*], O Our Mother and Queen of the world, in order that your love and protection may hasten the triumph of the Kingdom of God.[91]

The act of consecration, originally made in Portuguese, was renewed in Italian in Saint Peter's Basilica on the Feast of the Immaculate Conception 1942.[92] It has been referred to many times by Pope John Paul II, especially in his own major consecrations to the Immaculate Heart of Mary of May 13, 1982, and March 25, 1984.[93] Such a significant text requires a careful analysis.

1. The Pope was careful to indicate the equivalence of the Immaculate Heart of Mary with her person by saying twice: "To you and to your Immaculate Heart". In this he was not only following the common teaching of theologians, but he was also consciously following the line taken by Leo XIII in

[91] *AAS* 34 (1942): 318–19, 324–25; *OL,* no. 374, 380 (slightly altered). Cf. *AAS* 34 (1942): 313–25 for the text of the radio message and the act of consecration in both Portuguese and Italian.

[92] Geenen, 869. Père Laurenceau comments on the slight differences between the Portuguese text of October 31 and the Italian text used on this occasion, see Laurenceau, 76.

[93] December 8, 1981, *Inseg* IV:2 (1981), 869, 873; *ORE* 714:2, 12; May 13, 1982, *Inseg* V:2 (1982), 1574–75, 1586; *Portugal,* 81; *ORE* 735:5; May 19, 1982, *Inseg* V:2 (1982), 1759; *Portugal,* 200; March 25, 1984, *Inseg* VII:1 (1984), 775; *ORE* 828:9; December 31, 1984, *Inseg* VII:2 (1984), 1684; *ORE* 869:4; September 22, 1986, *Inseg* IX:2 (1986), 699; October 16, 1988, *Inseg* XI:3 (1988), 1240; *ORE* 1061:1.

Annum Sacrum, where his predecessor had said that consecration to the Sacred Heart of Jesus is "an act which is nothing else than an offering and a binding of oneself to Jesus Christ".[94]

With the publication of the Mass of the Immaculate Heart of Mary mandated by Pius XII for the entire Latin Rite on May 4, 1944, as a memorial of this consecration, the formal object of the *cultus* was further clarified by the decree of the Sacred Congregation of Rites which stated that the Church under the symbol of the Immaculate Heart of Mary "venerates with reverence the eminent and singular holiness of the Mother of God and especially her most ardent love for God and Jesus, her Son, and moreover her maternal compassion for all those redeemed by the divine Blood." [95]

2. Likewise following the precedent set by Leo, Pius XII referred to himself as "the common father of the vast Christian family" and "the Vicar of Him to whom was given 'all power in heaven and on earth' ", thus supplying the rationale for his consecration of the whole human race as well as the Church. On this basis he prayed for separated Christians, "the peoples separated by error or discord",[96] and he also explicitly included those without Christian faith: "Extend your protection to unbelievers and to them who still stand in the shadow of death. Grant them peace. May the Sun of truth dawn in their lives." [97] By using the words *confiamos, entregamos, consagramos* in Portuguese and *affidiamo, rimettiamo, consacriamo* in Italian he seemed to signal the groups whom he had in mind: unbelievers, separated Christians, and Roman Catholics with the verbs becoming stronger as his immediate authority reached its maximum.[98]

[94] *ASS* 31 (1898–1899): 649; Carlen 2:453.

[95] *AAS* 37 (1945): 50; *ORE* 959:12. Cf. above, 79.

[96] *AAS* 34 (1942): 318, 325; *OL*, no. 378.

[97] *AAS* 34 (1942): 318, 324; *OL*, no. 377.

[98] The English translation appears a bit less nuanced here.

3. It is clear that the analogy with Leo's earlier consecration to the Sacred Heart of Jesus is quite deliberate. Pius finds no conflict between the two acts, but rather sees them as complementary and evidently intended in the divine plan. This is made manifest in the conclusion of the prayer of consecration itself, in the establishment of the Feast of the Immaculate Heart of Mary,[99] in any number of references[100] which link his act of consecration and Leo's together, and most explicitly in the conclusion of Pius' monumental Sacred Heart encyclical, *Haurietis Aquas*:

> That graces for the Christian family and for the whole human race may flow more abundantly from devotion to the Sacred Heart, let the faithful strive to join it closely with devotion to the Immaculate Heart of the Mother of God. By the will of God, the Most Blessed Virgin was inseparably joined with Christ in accomplishing the work of man's redemption so that our salvation flows from the love of Jesus Christ and His suffering, intimately united with the love and sorrows of His mother [*ex Iesu Christi caritate eiusque cruciatibus cum amore doloribusque ipsius Matris intime consociatis sit nostra salus profecta*]. It is, then, highly fitting that after due homage has been paid to the Most Sacred Heart of Jesus, Christian people who have obtained divine life from Christ through Mary, manifest similar piety and the love of their grateful souls for the most loving heart of our heavenly Mother.
>
> The memorable act of consecration [*consecrationis ritus*] by which We Ourselves, in the most wise and loving dispositions of Divine Providence, solemnly dedicated [*dicavimus ac devovimus*] the Church and the whole world to the Immaculate Heart of the Blessed Virgin Mary, is in perfect accord with devotion to the Sacred Heart.[101]

4. In this consecration Pius, mindful of the request of Sister Lúcia, made implicit allusion to Russia with these words:

[99] *AAS* 37 (1945): 51

[100] Cf. the letter *Ex officiosis litteris* to the bishop of Autun of February 15, 1948, *AAS* 40 (1948): 107; *OL*, no. 443; and the encyclical *Auspicia quaedam* of May 1, 1948, *AAS* 40 (1948): 171; *OL*, no. 451.

[101] *AAS* 48 (1956): 352; *OL*, no. 778.

> To the peoples separated by error or discord, and especially to those who profess special devotion to you and among whom there was once not a home where your venerated icon was not honored (today perhaps hidden and awaiting better days), grant peace and lead them back to the one fold of Christ under the one and true Shepherd.[102]

But on July 7, 1952, in his apostolic letter *Sacro Vergente Anno*, Pius made his reference explicit: "Just as not many years ago We consecrated the entire world to the Immaculate Heart of the Virgin Mother of God, in a most special way, so now We dedicate and consecrate all the peoples of Russia to that same Immaculate Heart." [103]

One stone remained to be placed in the doctrinal structure of the consecration to the Immaculate Heart of Mary, however, in order to establish the basis of that act beyond any shadow of a doubt. Leo XIII had grounded the consecration to the Sacred Heart of Jesus on the Kingship of Christ by nature and by acquired right,[104] and Pius XI had further corroborated this theologoumenon in his encyclical *Quas Primas*.[105] It was really a matter of making explicit what was already implicit in the 1942 consecration itself since the act had begun with the words "Queen of the most holy Rosary".[106]

This final stone was supplied in another radio address to Fatima on the occasion of the coronation of the statue of Our Lady in the Cova da Iría on May 13, 1946. In that notable allocution Pius said:

> [Mary] is mysteriously related in the order of the hypostatic union with the most Blessed Trinity, with Him Who alone, by essence, is Infinite Majesty, King of kings and Lord of lords, being firstborn

[102] *AAS* 34 (1942): 318, 325; *OL*, no. 378.

[103] *AAS* 44 (1952): 511; *OL*, no. 576.

[104] Cf. above, 85–86.

[105] Cf. above, 91–92.

[106] *AAS* 34 (1942): 317, 324; *OL*, no. 373.

Daughter of the Father, pure Mother of the Word, beloved Spouse of the Holy Spirit. She is the Mother of the Divine King to Whom from the maternal womb the Lord God gave the throne of David and enduring royalty in the House of Jacob, Who proclaimed that all power had been given to Him in heaven and on earth. *He, the Son of God, decrees for His heavenly Mother the glory, the majesty, the power of His own kingdom.* Associated as Mother and Helper with the King of Martyrs in the ineffable work of the redemption of mankind, she is forever most powerfully associated in the distribution of graces and divine redemption.

Jesus is King of the eternal ages by nature and by conquest. *Through Him, with Him, and under Him, Mary is Queen by grace, by divine relationship, by conquest, by singular election. Her kingdom is as vast as that of her divine Son from Whose dominion nothing is excluded.*[107]

With a wonderful clarity and conciseness Pius XII lays out the reasons for Mary's Queenship: it is totally subservient to the Kingship of Christ, derived from it, and at the same time united to it. Father William G. Most comments:

We should not think of her dominion as something as it were separate from that of her Son: no, in royal rule as in all else, she forms a sort of unitary principle with Him. Just as her offering melted together with His on Calvary, so as to form the one great price of Redemption, so her Queenship and His Kingship are one authority, inseparable.

We can easily see then, that we can, with theological exactness, say much the same of consecration to her as Pope Leo XIII said of consecration to Christ the King. We recognize by our consecra-

[107] *AAS* 38 (1946): 266; Br. Stanley G. Mathews, S.M., ed., *Queen of the Universe: An Anthology on the Assumption and Queenship of Mary* (Saint Meinrad, Ind.: Grail Publications, 1957), 233–34 (my emphasis). Interestingly, St. Louis-Marie Grignion de Montfort had used virtually the same terminology in his *True Devotion to the Blessed Virgin Mary*, no. 38, where he wrote that "Mary is Queen of heaven and earth by grace as Jesus is king by nature and conquest."

tion that she, as Queen of the Universe with Him, already has fullest rights to our service.[108]

On October 11, 1954, toward the conclusion of the first Marian Year in the Church's life, the Servant of God issued his encyclical letter *Ad Caeli Reginam* on the Queenship of Mary. In that document he not only reaffirmed what he had said in the 1946 radio broadcast on Mary's Queenship, but he also explicitly underscored the role of analogy[109] in arriving at a correct understanding of Mary's Queenship:

> We may certainly conclude that just as Christ, the new Adam, must be called King, not only because He is the Son of God, but also because He is our Redeemer; so, by a certain kind of analogy [*quodam analogiae modo*], the most Blessed Virgin is Queen, not only because she is the Mother of God, but also because, as the new Eve, she was associated with the new Adam.
>
> And so it is that Jesus Christ, alone, God and man, is King in the full, proper, and absolute sense of the term. Yet Mary also, although in a restricted way and only by analogy [*quamvis temperato modo et analogiae ratione*], shares in the royal dignity as the Mother of Christ who is God, as His associate in the labors of the Divine redemption, and in His struggle against His enemies and in the victory He won over them all. From this association with Christ the King she obtains a splendor and eminence surpassing the excellence of all created things.[110]

Finally, in that same Marian Year encyclical which commemorated the 100th anniversary of the proclamation of the Dogma of the Immaculate Conception by Pius IX and declared the Queenship of Mary in a solemn manner, the

[108] William G. Most, *Vatican II—Marian Council* (Athlone, Ireland: St. Paul Publications, 1972), 136. Cf. also his commentary on the text of Pius XII's radio message in *Mary in Our Life: Our Lady in Doctrine and Devotion* (New York: P. J. Kenedy & Sons, 1955), 51–55.

[109] The theological understanding of analogy and its specific application to the question of Marian consecration will be studied in detail in the second part of this work.

[110] *AAS* 46 (1954): 635; Mathews, 245.

Pope mandated the annual renewal of the consecration to the Immaculate Heart of Mary on the newly established Feast of her Queenship.[111] In this way he confirmed that consecration to Mary is related to her Queenship, just as Pius XI had linked consecration to the Sacred Heart with the Kingship of Christ in *Quas Primas*.[112] Now the correlation was not only theologically, but also liturgically, established.

It remains to be noted that the theology and devotion to the Hearts of Jesus and Mary reached a remarkable culmination during the pontificate of Pius XII. No doubt his crowning magisterial achievement in this field was his great Sacred Heart encyclical *Haurietis Aquas*. It was a brilliant summary of all that had preceded it, continuing the work of Leo XIII, Pius XI, and even his own while presenting the biblical, patristic, and theological foundations of the *cultus* with great precision "so that the faithful, better instructed, could practice it with greater fervor".[113] In the course of this extremely rich document the Pope mentions that

> this devotion is an act of religion of high order; it demands of us a complete and unreserved determination to devote and consecrate ourselves to the love of the divine Redeemer [*quatenus plenam et absolutissimam se devovendi et consecrandi voluntatem a nobis postulet Divini Redemptoris amori*], Whose wounded Heart is its living token and symbol.[114]

In effect he says that consecration is the only really appropriate response to the love of Christ, and he concludes the document by exhorting the faithful to unite to this devotion

[111] *AAS* 46 (1954): 638; *OL*, no. 714.

[112] Cf. Firmin M. Schmidt, O.F.M. Cap., "Our Lady's Queenship in the Light of *Quas Primas*", *Marian Studies* 4 (1953): 118–33, and above, 91.

[113] Degli Esposti, 240 (my trans.). Cf. also the excellent overview of the encyclical in Mario Luigi Cardinal Ciappi, O.P., *The Heart of Christ, the Centre of the Mystery of Salvation,* trans. Leslie Wearne and Andrew Wade (Rome: Cuore di Cristo Publishers, 1983), 87–94.

[114] *AAS* 48 (1956): 311; Larkin, *Haurietis Aquas*, 9.

that of the Immaculate Heart of Mary.[115] The consecration to her Heart he sees as a Divinely intended complement to the consecration to His Heart.[116] His teaching on Marian consecration as well is so remarkably thorough that the American Montfort Fathers were able to compile a sizeable anthology of Pius XII's teaching on consecration to Mary.[117]

After the great momentum for Marian consecration which peaked in the pontificate of Pius XII, the initiatives of his two immediate successors are seen as less dramatic, but both build on the foundation laid by Pius. So close to the era of Pius, the Servant of God Pope John XXIII did not have to overstress his legacy. In his first encyclical, *Ad Petri Cathedram*, Pope John alluded approvingly to his predecessor's act of consecration to the Immaculate Heart of Mary,[118] and again a few months later in a radio message broadcast to the Italian National Eucharistic Congress in Catania, Sicily, he spoke of the good results to be sought from the consecration of Italy to the Immaculate Heart of Mary, carried out by the bishops of Italy earlier that same day, September 13, 1959.[119]

At the conclusion of the third session of the Second Vatican Council on November 21, 1964, Pope Paul VI alluded to the consecration performed by his predecessor, Pope Pius XII, and announced that he had decided to send a special mission to Fatima to present the Golden Rose, the sign of special papal favor.

[115] Cf. above, 101.

[116] Cf. his letter to the chaplain of the Grand Retour, July 2, 1948. *Le Grand Retour* 16 (August-September 1948): 1, quoted in Hubert M. Pocock, S.M.M., ed., *Pius XII on Consecration to Mary* (Bay Shore, N.Y.: Montfort Publications, 1956), 16.

[117] Cf. Pocock, 51–55, which contains a helpful appendix on the consecrations to the Sacred Heart of Jesus and the Immaculate Heart of Mary according to Pius XII.

[118] *AAS* 51 (1959): 518; *The Pope Speaks* 5:374 (hereafter cited as *TPS*).

[119] *AAS* 51 (1959): 712–13; *TPS* 6:94.

The world to which this Ecumenical Council intends to devote great and loving consideration and care . . . Our predecessor, Pius XII, not without heavenly inspiration, solemnly dedicated to the Immaculate Heart of the Virgin Mary. We have decided that it is only right for Us to commemorate [*commemorari*] this very holy act of devotion in a special way here today. And so with this in mind, We have decided to send a special mission in the near future to bring the Golden Rose to the church at Fatima. . . . In this way We commit [*committimus*] the human race, its difficulties and anxieties, its just aspirations and ardent hopes, to the protection of our heavenly Mother.

O Virgin Mother of God, most august Mother of the Church, We commend [*commendamus*] the whole Church and the Ecumenical Council to you. . . . We commend [*commendamus*] the whole human race to your Immaculate Heart, O Virgin Mother of God.[120]

This reaffirmation of the consecration of Pius XII, together with the proclamation of Mary as "Mother of the Church" which immediately preceded it, needs to be assessed in the light of the complex situation which had built up to a *crescendo* during the last week of the Council's third session.[121] Father Wiltgen, acknowledged as an impartial historian of the Council, says of these initiatives of Paul VI that they were to be

. . . considered a partial reply to 510 heads of dioceses, archdioceses and patriarchates from seventy-six countries who had petitioned Pope Paul to consecrate the entire world during the Council to the Immaculate Heart of Mary, as requested by Our Lady of Fatima. The signatures of these prelates had been delivered to the Holy Father on February 3, 1964, by Archbishop Sigaud of Diamantina, Brazil. But the bishops of Germany and France, as

[120] *AAS* 56 (1964): 1017–18; *TPS* 10:140–41. Léon Vandergheynst in his study *Le Pape et la Consécration du Monde à Marie* (Brussels: La Pensée Catholique; Paris: Office Général de Livre, 1968) argues forcefully that this act was a "consecration" in the strict sense.

[121] Cf. Ralph M. Wiltgen, S.V.D., *The Rhine Flows into the Tiber: A History of Vatican II* (Rockford, Ill.: Tan Books and Publishers, 1985), 234–43.

well as Cardinal Bea, were known to be opposed to such a consecration, and it did not take place.[122]

Given the cross-currents in the Council at the time, these actions of Paul VI are seen to be quite bold. Even if this reaffirmation was not all that certain of the Council Fathers wished, the Pope clearly expressed his will on this matter. Another factor which is almost never alluded to by commentators is that the Council Fathers did go on record in favor of Marian consecration in the Decree on the Apostolate of the Laity. We have already made reference to this above,[123] but it is worth noting again because it is a text which uses one of the classic terms for consecration, *commendare*, and yet its import has thus far been virtually ignored:

> Perfect model of this apostolic spiritual life is the Blessed Virgin Mary, Queen of Apostles. While on earth her life was like that of any other, filled with labors and the cares of the home; always, however, she remained intimately united to her Son and cooperated in an entirely unique way in the Saviour's work. And now, assumed into heaven, "her motherly love keeps her attentive to her Son's brothers, still on pilgrimage amid the dangers and difficulties of life, until they arrive at the happiness of the fatherland." Everyone should have a genuine devotion to her and entrust his life to her motherly care. [*Hanc devotissime colant omnes suamque vitam atque apostolatum eius maternae curae commendent.*][124]

Further, although Marian consecration is not explicitly referred to in the following text, given the powerful magis-

[122] Wiltgen, 241. On the distinction between the request for the consecration of Russia to the Immaculate Heart of Mary and the consecration of the whole world, see Joseph de Sainte-Marie, *Reflections*, 16–18.

[123] Cf. above, 73.

[124] *AA,* no. 4; Sacrosanctum Oecumenicum Concilium Vaticanum II, *Constitutiones, Decreta, Declarationes* (Vatican City: Typis Polyglottis Vaticanis, 1974), 468; Austin Flannery, O.P., ed., *Vatican Council II: The Conciliar and Post Conciliar Documents* (Collegeville, Minn.: Liturgical Press, 1975), 771–72 (hereafter cited as Flan.).

terial endorsement we have already seen for it, it must be recognized as included:

> The Sacred Synod . . . admonishes all the Church's children generously to foster the cult toward the Most Blessed Virgin, particularly the liturgical cult. Moreover, they should esteem highly practices and pious exercises toward her which have in the course of centuries been commended by the Magisterium.[125]

Father Most argues convincingly that "the greatest of these recommended practices is Marian consecration." [126]

On May 22, 1966, Pope Paul VI addressed a radio message to those assembled for the dedication of the national votive church erected on Mount Grisa near Trieste in commemoration of the consecration of Italy to the Immaculate Heart of Mary, and he used the occasion to comment on the significance of this national act.[127] Even more significantly, on May 13, 1967, he issued his apostolic exhortation *Signum Magnum* to coincide with the fiftieth anniversary of the first apparition of Mary to the children of Fatima and his own pilgrimage to that shrine. Recalling the great Act of Consecration of Pius XII in 1942 and his own reaffirmation of it in 1964, he went on to make this appeal:

> So now We urge all members of the Church to consecrate [*consecrent*] themselves once again to the Immaculate Heart of Mary, to translate this pious act into concrete action in their daily lives. In this way they will comply ever more closely with God's will and as imitators of their heavenly Queen, they will truly be recognized as her offspring.[128]

[125] *LG,* no. 67; Dominic J. Unger, O.F.M. Cap., ed. and trans., *Mary, Christ and the Church* (Bay Shore, N.Y.: Montfort Publications, 1979), 17.

[126] Most, *Vatican II,* 160; cf. also 52 and 134–37.

[127] Cf. *Insegnamenti di Paolo VI,* IV (Vatican City: Libreria Editrice Vaticana, 1966), 255–57.

[128] *AAS* 59 (1967): 475; *TPS* 12:286.

In other significant documents and allocutions of the pontificate of Paul VI as well, references to entrustment to Mary are not wanting. Thus in the apostolic letter *Apostolorum Limina* of May 23, 1974, he entrusted the Holy Year to Mary,[129] and in his apostolic exhortation *Paterna Cum Benevolentia* of December 8, 1974, he entrusted the reconciliation which he so ardently desired as the fruit of the Holy Year observance to Mary's intercession.[130] We find him making the same kinds of statements in his semiannual addresses to his collaborators in the central government of the Church.[131] Perhaps the most heartfelt and poignant of these acts of entrustment came on the Feast of the Immaculate Conception in 1975:

> Listen, O Mary, to our filial voice, echoing the sentiments of the whole Church on this tenth anniversary of the Second Vatican Council, and at the happy conclusion of this Holy Year, and we earnestly implore your special heavenly assistance in this critical hour for the spiritual and civil destiny of the world.
>
> To you, spiritual Mother of the Mystical Body of Christ, which is the Church, we entrust the deliberate Christian commitment which we assumed with holy Baptism, and we confirm it in the spirit of renewal, which has marked the sacred Jubilee that we have just celebrated, and which must mark our witness as living members of the Catholic Church in the years to come.
>
> To you, the Mother of the Church, we therefore entrust our commitment to reconciliation, which has likewise been strengthened during the Holy Year: reconciliation with God, reconciliation with all men our brethren, the longed-for complete reconciliation with all those who believe in our one Teacher and Redeemer, your Son Jesus Christ, ever increasing reconciliation through justice, liberty, cooperation among the different social

[129] *AAS* 66 (1974): 307; *TPS* 19:161.

[130] *AAS* 67 (1975): 23; *TPS* 19:332.

[131] Cf. Address of June 22, 1974, *Insegnamenti di Paolo VI*, XII (1974), 738–39; *TPS* 19:126; Address of December 22, 1976, *AAS* 69 (1977): 46; *TPS* 22:21.

groups, and finally reconciliation between the peoples and nations in a watchful and sincere spirit of security, collaboration, and peace.[132]

Significantly, but not surprisingly, the appositeness of this very act of entrustment was singled out by the then Cardinal Wojtyła at the end of the retreat which he preached to Pope Paul VI and his coworkers just three months later. Here are his words:

Both holy scripture, so rich in metaphor as we have just found, and the experience of the faithful see the Mother of God as the one who in a very special way is united with the Church at the most difficult moments in her history, when the attacks on her become most threatening. And this is in full accord with the vision of the woman revealed in Genesis and Revelation. Precisely in periods when Christ, and therefore his Church, Pope, bishops, priests, religious and all the faithful become the sign which provokes the most implacable and premeditated contradiction, Mary appears particularly close to the Church, because the Church is always in a way her Christ, first the Christ-child and then the crucified and risen Christ.

If in such periods, such times in history, *there arises a particular need to entrust oneself to Mary*—as the Holy Father did on 8th December 1975, the 10th anniversary of the end of the Council—that need flows directly from the integral logic of the faith, from rediscovery of the whole divine economy and from understanding of its mysteries.

The Father in heaven demonstrated the greatest trust in mankind by giving mankind his Son (cf. Jn 3:16). The human creature to whom he first entrusted him was Mary, the woman of the *proto-*

[132] The Italian text may be found in *Marianum* 38 (1976); 397–98; the English text is in *ORE* 403:12 and Paul VI, *Mary—God's Mother and Ours* (Boston: St. Paul Editions, 1979), 218–19.

evangelium (cf. Gen. 3:15), then Mary of Nazareth and Bethlehem. *And until the end of time she will remain the one to whom God entrusts the whole of his mystery of salvation.*[133]

[133] Karol Wojtyła, *Sign of Contradiction* (New York: Crossroad-Seabury, 1979), 205 (my emphasis). Perhaps one of the most striking instances of the notion of God's "entrusting" of Himself to Mary in his papal magisterium occurs in *Redemptoris Mater,* no. 39: "For it must be recognized that before anyone else it was God himself, the Eternal Father, who *entrusted himself to the Virgin of Nazareth,* giving her his own Son in the mystery of the Incarnation" [*Etenim oportet agnoscere Deum ipsum, aeternum Patrem, imprimis se credidisse Virgini Nazarethanae, dando ei suum Filium in Incarnationis mysterio*] (*Inseg* X:1 [1987], 726; St. Paul ed., 55). In the Latin text the verb *credere* is used in the sense of entrusting or committing something to someone.

3

THE POLISH CONTEXT

Having considered at least some of the high points of the history of Marian consecration in the spiritual journey of the Church and the authoritative acts of the papal magisterium fostering this deliberate relationship of belonging to Mary, we will now consider yet another set of circumstances which provide further context for understanding the Pope's "program of consecration and entrustment to Mary".

National Marian piety

The deep Marian piety of his native Poland and its inherent exigency to express itself in consecration has surely penetrated Karol Wojtyła to his very core.[1] This can be seen in his very first papal utterance from the central loggia of Saint Peter's on the evening of Monday, October 16, 1978, which we have already noted.[2] If I cite it again, I do so because I am convinced that such spontaneous remarks at such a significant moment in his life and that of the Church cannot and should not be undervalued:

> I was afraid to accept this nomination, but I did it in the spirit of obedience to our Lord Jesus Christ and of total confidence in His Mother, the most holy Madonna. . . . And so I present myself to

[1] Cf. Edward D. O'Connor, C.S.C., "The Roots of Pope John Paul II's Devotion to Mary", *Marian Studies* 39 (1988): 83–85.

[2] Cf. above, 27.

> you all to confess our common faith, our hope, our confidence in the Mother of Christ and of the Church. . . .[3]

We will discover that this theme of "confidence in the Mother of Christ and of the Church" figures profoundly in his theology of entrustment [*affidamento*].

In introducing an Italian translation of the Marian homilies of the former Cardinal Wojtyła, the late primate of Poland, Stefan Cardinal Wyszyński, said, "We are profoundly convinced that the election of this 'Polish Pope' to the Apostolic See is due above all to the work of the Madonna, Our Lady of Jasna Góra; before [whom] our own Polish Pope, at that time Cardinal Wojtyła, Archbishop of Krakow, loved often to kneel in fervent prayer."[4] Indeed, Jasna Góra, the Bright Mountain, for over 600 years the privileged sanctuary of Mary's special presence in the life of the Polish nation through her miraculous icon of Częstochowa, is at the heart not only of Polish Marian devotion, but also of Polish Catholicism, culture, and national identity. Its rich history is well recorded and carefully reflected upon in Father Marian Załęcki's *Theology of a Marian Shrine, Our Lady of Częstochowa*.[5] Together with another Marian shrine closer to his native Wadowice and his episcopal see of Krakow, Kalwaria Zebrzydowska,[6] it figures prominently in all the stages of the life of Karol

[3] *Inseg* I (1978), 3; *Talks*, 48–49. In effect this first public statement quite evidently follows very closely what he tells us of his response to the canonical question put to him in the conclave after his election as Pope in *The Redeemer of Man* [*Redemptor Hominis*] (Boston: St. Paul Editions, 1979), no. 2; *Inseg* II:1 (1979), 552, 611; *Messages of John Paul II: Servant of Truth* (Boston: St. Paul Editions, 1979), 501 (hereafter cited as *Messages*).

[4] Karol Wojtyła, *Maria: Omelie*, preface by Stefan Cardinal Wyszyński, trans. Janina Korzeniewska (Vatican City: Libreria Editrice Vaticana, 1982), 5 (hereafter cited as *Omelie*).

[5] *Marian Library Studies*, n.s., 8 (Dayton, Oh.: University of Dayton, 1976).

[6] Cf. the Pope's moving description of this shrine to André Frossard as "a sanctuary which is so dear to me and which I visited so often in my youth, and later as

Wojtyła up to the time of his election as Pope and, indeed, throughout his pontificate.[7]

National consecrations

Above I spoke of the exigency of Poland's unique relationship with the Mother of God to express itself in consecration. In fact on his first return to Poland as Pope, the Holy Father himself enumerated these great acts of dedication in Polish history during his pilgrimage to Jasna Góra, the Bright Mountain of Częstochowa.[8] The first and, indeed, the archetype of these acts was constituted by the famous vows of Jan Kazimierz (John Casimir), king of Poland, which he made in 1656. Here is Dr. Williams' account of the circumstances which led up to it:

> Near the outset of the Swedish Flood [*Potop*], 1655–1660, during which almost all of the Commonwealth was invaded by the Lutheran king Charles X Vasa (1654–1660) of Sweden, Jasna Góra was, along with Lwow, one of the few strongholds to turn back the Protestant foe. Early in the war, King John II Casimir Vasa, had had to escape by way of Cracow into exile in Silesia, which was at that time under the crown of Bohemia. Because of the valor of the peasants, who fought the Protestants after their lords and marshals had surrendered, John Casimir, quickened by the miraculous defense of Jasna Góra under the protection of the Virgin, returned to the stricken Commonwealth by way of the Carpath-

priest and bishop. I can tell you that, in the manner of devotion shown by the people to whom I belong, I found there what I had discovered in the treatise [of Saint Louis de Montfort on *True Devotion to the Blessed Virgin*]", Frossard, 127. Likewise his address there on June 7, 1979, is a testimony to his deep attachment to this Marian holy place, see *Inseg* II:1 (1979), 1476–79; *Poland,* 197–201.

[7] Cf. Williams, 38–42. He has visited Jasna Góra as Pope in 1979, 1983, 1987, and 1991. After the first visit he has prepared each time by yearlong cycles of prayers to Our Lady in Polish at the end of his Wednesday general audiences.

[8] The entire homily and Act of Consecration of June 4, 1979, is a moving testimony to the Pope's and his nation's Marian devotion; see *Inseg* II:1 (1979), 1410–19; *Poland,* 99–115.

> ians and entered Lwow, which was still in the hands of a palatine and a captain loyal to the Polish Crown. In the Catholic Cathedral of Lwow in 1656, in the presence of his own Queen, John Casimir committed himself in a kind of heavenly nuptial covenant to the Virgin of Częstochowa, declaring her Queen of Poland.[9]

He further promised to seek permission from the Holy See to celebrate an annual feast of Mary, Queen of Poland.[10] This was eventually conceded for the third of May. An interesting link between John Paul II and the vows of Jan Kazimierz was forged when on his second trip to Poland he crowned the image of the Mother of God before which the famous vows of April 1, 1656, were made.[11]

But there are many others as well. He referred, quite deliberately, to these vows in the discourse to the Polish bishops of the Wrocław region during their "ad limina" visit on December 17, 1987.[12] On receiving Lech Wałęsa on February 5, 1991, on his first state visit to the Vatican as president of the Third Republic of Poland, he referred to Poland as a "bulwark of Christianity" in terms of its strategic geographical position and said:

> Against this background we are not surprised at the prophetic gesture of King John Casimir who, when entrusting our nation and its people to the patronage of Our Lady, proclaimed her the Queen of Poland. His example and intuition of faith have had specific results in our times.[13]

Further in that same year he quoted the beginning of Jan Kazimierz' vow formula in his Jasna Góra cycle prayer of

[9] Williams, 39. Not only was this an instance of putting himself and his kingdom under the *patrocinium* of Mary, but it even antecedes the "Contract of Holy Matrimony with the Most Blessed Virgin Mary, Mother of God" made in the same spirit by St. John Eudes twelve years later, cf. above, 60.

[10] Cf. Załęcki, 127–28 for the text of the vows in Latin and English.

[11] *Inseg* VI:1 (1983), 1582; *ORE* 791:6–7.

[12] *Inseg* X:3 (1987), 1439; *ORE* 1022:11.

[13] *ORE* 1177:3.

May 1,[14] referred devotedly to the icon before which the vows were made in his visit to the pro-cathedral of Lubaczów on June 2,[15] and commented at length on this action of the Polish king the next day at a Mass in the sports stadium of the same city.[16]

Maria Winowska, in her article "Le Culte Marial en Pologne", makes the point that while Poland cannot claim a monopoly on Mary's Queenship and France, for instance, had been consecrated to her 18 years earlier, nonetheless there are unique features in the consecration of Poland and Mary's Queenly reign in that country. She singles out three characteristics of that reign in Poland. It is (1) social, (2) apostolic, and (3) missionary in nature.[17] With regard to the first characteristic, the very text of Jan Kazimierz' vows is expiatory in nature; he recognizes that he and his nobles have abused the peasants.

> As I clearly see, too, with stricken heart, because of the cries and anguish of the peasants, that thy Son, equitable judge, lashed my kingdom during the past seven years with plagues, wars and other disasters, then I do vow that on the restoration of peace, I will, with all the other estates, utilize every means to avert further misfortunes, and I will strive that all people of my kingdom shall be freed from all unjust burdens and oppression. May this be so, O most merciful Lady and Queen. Obtain the grace of thy Son, that I succeed in executing these vows.[18]

About this social aspect, Williams remarks, "Although his promise was frustrated by the magnates and the gentry after

[14] *ORE* 1189:3.

[15] *ORE* 1194:8.

[16] *ORE* 1194:9.

[17] *Maria* 4:690. Fr. Jan Pach, O.S.P.P.E., also attaches great significance to the social dimension of Marian consecration in Poland vis-à-vis the tradition in France; cf. his *Maria nell' Insegnamento del Cardinal Stefan Wyszyński*, Dissertationes ad Lauream in Pontificia Facultate Theologica "Marianum", no. 49 (Rome, 1989), 94, 256.

[18] Załęcki, 127–28.

the Treaty of Oliwa of 1660, the peasants and their priests still regarded the Queen of Heaven as their ultimate recourse." [19]

Concerning the apostolic and missionary characteristics of Poland's fealty to Mary, Winowska says, "Hemmed in between schism, heresy, and Islam, Poland has had to defend its territory over the centuries in order to defend its faith." [20] Even during the partition of the country between Russia, Prussia, and Austria,[21] the great principle of unity was "the Queen of Poland", especially in her shrine on the Bright Mountain. Rallying around their Queen, Poles retained both their faith and their national identity against overwhelming odds, even to the point of sending missionaries to evangelize in other countries. Even prior to the dissolution of the Communist ascendancy, the exceptional strength of the Church in Poland was unique in the countries of the Eastern bloc and of the world. How could its vitality be explained? In his homily at Jasna Góra on June 4, 1979, John Paul II put it thus:

> During the great novena [of years before the celebration of the millennium of Christianity in Poland in 1966], the Cardinal Primate [Wyszński] expressed himself as follows with regard to the significance of the shrine of Częstochowa for the life of the Church: "What has happened at Jasna Góra? We are still unable to give an adequate answer. Something has happened that is beyond our powers of imagining. . . . Jasna Góra has shown itself an inward bond in Polish life, a force that touches the depths of our hearts and holds the entire nation in the humble yet strong attitude of fidelity to God, to the Church and to her Hierarchy. . . . For many of us it was a great surprise to see the power of the Queen of Poland display itself so magnificently."
>
> It is no wonder then that I too should come here today. I have, in fact, taken with me from Poland to the chair of St. Peter in

[19] Williams, 39.

[20] Winowska, 694 (my trans.).

[21] Cf. Williams, 22–23.

> Rome this "holy habit" of the heart, which has been built up by the faith of so many generations, has been tested by the Christian experience of so many centuries, and is deeply rooted in my soul.[22]

Jan Kazimierz was not the initiator of this fealty of the Polish people to Mary, but he did give it concrete expression. Says Winowska, "In deciding to consecrate his kingdom to Mary officially, King Jan Kazimierz was only obeying a passionate desire of his people. It could be said without exaggeration that in those years of liberation, Mary was more the Queen of Poland than he was its king."[23]

When, after 123 years of subjugation by other governments, Poland became independent and launched its Second Republic (1918–1939), it was only natural that the Polish bishops would rededicate their country to its Queen. This was done at Jasna Góra on July 27, 1920, just two months after the birth of Karol Wojtyła, in these words:

> Most Holy Virgin Mary! Behold, we Polish bishops, in the name of all our dioceses, on behalf of all faithful sons and daughters of Poland, we pay you our deepest respect and our humble homage. Once again, we choose you for our queen, our sovereign, and we flee to your powerful protection. . . . Weed out from our hearts the seeds of discord; cleanse our souls from sins and from the national vices that we may praise and serve God and you in the purity of our hearts, queen of the Polish crown! We dedicate and consecrate ourselves to you today. Therefore, defend us, watch over us as your property.[24]

This act of the Polish bishops "on behalf of all faithful sons and daughters of Poland" was to launch a phenomenon of public corporate Marian consecration most probably unique in the annals of any nation in any century. Poland's "day in the sun" as an independent and sovereign nation was short-

[22] *Inseg* II:1 (1979), 1411; *Poland,* 101.

[23] Winowska, 691 (my trans.).

[24] Polish text and English translation given in Załęcki, 133.

lived, only twenty-one years. And yet as the smoke of World War II cleared away and Poland burrowed out from under the devastation and carnage of the holocaust,[25] its bishops regrouped again at Jasna Góra on September 8, 1946, under the primate of Poland, Cardinal August Hlond, together with 700,000 of the faithful to reconsecrate the nation to Mary, this time particularly to her Immaculate Heart.

> Immaculate Virgin, most pure Mother of God! As King Jan Kazimierz once, after the Swedish invasion, elected Thee patroness and queen of the nation and commended to thy special care and defense the republic, so do we the children of the Polish nation at this historic moment stand before thy throne with tributes of love, worship, and thankfulness. To Thee and to thy Immaculate Heart[26] we dedicate ourselves in the entire nation and the resurrected republic. . . . To thy Son and our Redeemer we pledge to preserve faith in his teachings and his law, to defend his gospel and his Church and to work for his Kingdom on earth. Our Lady and Queen! To Thee we flee for protection. Surround with thy maternal care the Polish family and guard its holiness. . . . Unite the nation in harmony and brotherly love. Give to this Polish land, soaked with blood and tears, peaceful and praiseworthy existence in truth, justice, and freedom. Be the Polish republic's queen, guide, light, and patroness.
>
> Powerful aid of the faithful! Enfold the Pope and the Holy Church with thy protecting cloak; be their shield in days of oppression. Give to the Church freedom and effective action. Obtain for her leaders apostolic and holy zeal. Withhold the flood of atheism. Show to those who have strayed from the Church the way to the unity of Christ's sheepflock. Lead them to the truth with the tenderness of thy Immaculate Heart. . . .
>
> Mother of God and our Mother, accept our offering and our vows. Gather all of us to thy Immaculate Heart and unite us forever with Christ and his holy kingdom.[27]

[25] Cf. Polish understanding of this term in Williams, 23.

[26] The repetition of the phraseology of Pius XII's Act of Consecration of October 31, 1942, is obviously deliberate.

[27] The entire text in Polish and English is given in Załęcki, 134.

This act is significant also in that it was influenced by the message of Fatima [28] and followed in the wake of the great consecratory prayer of Pius XII on October 31, 1942, by less than four years. It was duly noted by that Pontiff not only once but twice in his letters to the Polish episcopate: *Flagranti semper animi* [29] of January 18, 1948, and *Cum iam lustri abeat* [30] of September 1, 1951. Also of moment is the fact that this collegial act of the Polish bishops preceded by less than two months the ordination of Karol Wojtyła to the priesthood.

Correlation with the thought of Cardinal Wyszyński

A further note might be added here about Cardinal Hlond. Polish by birth, but educated in Turin as a Salesian of Saint John Bosco and then later in Rome, he was named primate of Poland by Pius XI whom he had first met when he was superior of a Salesian house in Vienna.[31] He had inherited the deep Marian piety of his native Poland and that of Don Bosco. Having suffered with Poland through the Second World War and having been arrested by the Gestapo, he maintained a boundless confidence in the Mother of God until the end of his life. The spiritual testament which he left read: "Keep working under the protection of Our Blessed Mother. Victory, when it comes, will be the victory of the Most Blessed Virgin. *Nil desperandum!*" [32] Evidently he spoke virtually the same words

[28] Załęcki, 133.

[29] *AAS* 40 (1948): 324–28; *OL*, no. 442.

[30] *AAS* 43 (1951): 775–78; *OL*, no. 541–46.

[31] Cf. B. Stasiewski, "Hlond, Augustyn", in *NCE*, 7:41; Robin Anderson, *Between Two Wars: The Story of Pope Pius XI* (Chicago: Franciscan Herald Press, 1977), 28.

[32] Andrzej Micewski, *Cardinal Wyszyński: A Biography*, trans. William R. Brand and Katarzyna Mroczkowska-Brand (New York: Harcourt Brace Jovanovich, 1984), 42.

on his deathbed.[33] John Paul II has quoted them on several occasions: shortly after his elevation to the cardinalate on October 30, 1967,[34] and as Pope on May 10, 1979, to Frank Duff;[35] on June 19, 1983, during his second papal visit to Poland;[36] and on December 17, 1987, to the bishops of the province of Wrocław on their "ad limina" visit.[37]

Cardinal Hlond was succeeded as primate of Poland by Stefan Wyszyński, whom the Pope referred to on the occasion of his funeral as "the Primate of the Millennium"[38] which means, opines one of his biographers, "not only that he created the program in celebration of the Millennium, but also that he was one of the greatest Polish church figures of ten centuries."[39] Created cardinal by Pope Pius XII in 1953, he was unable to attend the consistory in Rome for the conferral of the red hat (which he would receive only on May 14, 1957) and in fact was arrested by Polish authorities on September 25 of that same year and sent into "forced isolation" until September 28, 1956.[40] Providentially, it was during this difficult period in Wyszyński's life that his "program of entrustment" to Mary was born.[41] Here are some of the pertinent facts as supplied by Andrzej

[33] These words are sometimes quoted in two different ways: "The victory, *when* it comes, will come through Mary" and "The victory, *if* it comes, will come through Mary".

[34] *Omelie,* 127.

[35] Bradshaw, 233.

[36] *Inseg* VI:1 (1983), 1600; *ORE* 791:10.

[37] *Inseg* X:3 (1987), 1436; *ORE* 1022:11. On this occasion the quote of Cardinal Hlond is given: "Victory, if it comes, will be victory through Mary." Cardinal Wyszyński supplies the citation in Italian with the conjunction *se* (if) as well, see *Omelie,* 5.

[38] *Inseg* IV:1 (1981), 1219; *ORE* 687:8.

[39] Micewski, 455.

[40] Cf. "Biography of Card. Stefan Wyszynski: 1901–1981", *ORE* 687:2, 12 (hereafter cited as "Biography".)

[41] Cf. Pach, 71.

Micewski, a recent biographer of the cardinal:

> Maria Okońska and Janina Michalska obtained permits and visited Komańcza [where Wyszyński was being detained at the time] on March 25, 1956, which was the Feast of the Annunciation as well as the anniversary of Stefan Wyszyński's consecration as bishop. On that day, the Primate disclosed his Marian program, telling the two women that on December 8, 1953, while imprisoned in Stoczek, after deep reflection, *he had made his act of submission to the Blessed Virgin for the freedom of the Church and Poland.*[42]
>
> The Primate's main idea was to defend the faith of the nation against militant atheism by means of the power of the Virgin Mary. *Having dedicated himself personally in submission to her motherhood for the sake of the Church and the nation, he had slowly been forming the idea that the tormented homeland ought to dedicate itself in submission to Mary, as a national community, for the freedom of its own Church and of the Church throughout the world.*[43]

Hence in the course of his confinement an expansive plan of pastoral action was conceived which would embrace not only the Church in Poland, but the Church Universal as well, and which would eventually issue in four collective acts of consecration to Mary. The first of these acts would be in commemoration of the 300th anniversary of the vows of King Jan Kazimierz in 1656. The year 1956 was proclaimed a special "Marian Year" for Poland and its culminating point was the celebration which took place at Jasna Góra on August 26, 1956, the Feast of Our Lady of Częstochowa. It featured an updated renewal of the king's vows which the primate himself composed. He would later say about this particular inspiration:

[42] So significant does John Paul II consider this personal act of Wyszyński of December 8, 1953, that in crowning a famous image of Our Lady and the Divine Child from Stoczek Warminski during his second visit to Poland he mentioned this place as the site where Stefan Wyszyński composed and made this consecration which would have such a powerful impact on the subsequent history of the nation. Cf. *Inseg* VI:1 (1983), 1583; *ORE* 791:7.

[43] Micewski, 154 (my emphasis).

> The thought of renewing the Vows of Kazimierz on their three hundredth anniversary sprang up in my spirit there in Prudnik, not far from Głogówek, where three hundred years ago the king and the Primate thought about how to free the nation from its twin subjugations: to foreign power and to social misery. When, later in my imprisonment, I followed almost the same track, from Prudnik to the southeast [to Komańcza], to the mountains, I went with the thought: There must be new Vows of Renewal! And it was precisely there that they sprang up, in the southeast, among the mountains. They were written and transferred from there to Jasna Góra.[44]

The circumstances surrounding the renewal of these vows were undoubtedly even more poignant than those which had prevailed ten years earlier because of the absence of the cardinal primate, Stefan Wyszński. One of the sobering focal points of the ceremony that day on the Virgin's Bright Mountain was the empty episcopal chair surmounted by his coat of arms. Part of the deeply moving text reads:

> We, Polish bishops and *the royal priesthood, the people acquired by the redeeming Blood of thy Son,* are again coming to thy throne, O Mary, mediatrix of all graces, mother of mercy and of all consolation. . . . We stand before thee with hearts filled with gratitude that in the time of glory and in the days of frightening disaster thou wert for us the ever assisting Virgin. We stand before thee also with contrite and guilty hearts because we have not yet fulfilled the promises made by our fathers. Look upon us with the eyes of thy mercy and listen to the voices of millions dedicated to thee, as the people of God.
>
> Queen of Poland! Today, we renew the vows of our ancestors and recognize thee anew as our patroness and queen of our Polish nation. To [thy] special protection and defense we commit ourselves and our possessions as well. We appeal humbly to thy aid and mercy in the struggle to remain faithful to God, to the Holy Cross, to the Gospel, to the Holy Church and its shepherds, to our fatherland, the vanguard of Christendom, consecrated to thy

[44] Micewski, 156.

Immaculate Heart and to the Sacred Heart of thy Son. Remember us, O Virgin Mother, before the throne of God; be mindful of the people dedicated to [thee], who still want to be thy kingdom under the care of the best Father of all nations on the earth.

Queen of Poland! We promise thee to do what lies in our power that Poland may in truth be the kingdom of thy Son and thine, subjected to thee entirely in its social and national life. . . .

In the fulfillment of these vows we see the living "votum" of the nation which pleases thee more than those of granite and bronze. May this total dedication impel us to a worthy preparation of our great anniversary of a thousand years of Christianity. On the eve of Poland's 1000th anniversary of baptism we recall that thou wert the first who sang the hymn of liberation from sin; that thou wert the first who stood in defense of the little ones and showed to the world the Sun of Justice, Christ our God. We want to remember that thou art the Mother of our way, truth and life, that in thy holy face we easily recognize thy Son to whom thou wilt surely lead us.

O Queen of Poland! Accept our promises, strengthen them in our hearts and bring them before the throne of the Almighty God. Into thy hands we entrust our past and future, our national and social life, the Church of thy Son and all that we love in God. Therefore, lead us throughout this Polish land to the gates of the heavenly country and through the door of the new life in Jesus, the Blessed Fruit of thy womb.[45]

The act itself had been led by Bishop Michał Klepacz of Łódź who functioned as head of the council of bishops. Approximately a million of the faithful stood before the monastery of Jasna Góra, "repeating loudly and full of emotion after each of the verses read by the bishop: 'Queen of Poland, we promise!' "[46] It had been decided that the Primate would pronounce the vows ten minutes before they were recited at Jasna Góra, but later it was discovered that both recitations took place virtually simultaneously.[47]

[45] The entire text in Polish and English is given in Załęcki, 139–44.

[46] Micewski, 158–59.

[47] Ibid., 157–58.

As Father Marian Załęcki, O.S.P., points out, this renewal of the "vows of the nation", also called "the vow of Jasna Góra", in effect inaugurated the "Great Novena" (1957–1966) in preparation for the solemn celebration of the Millennium of Christianity in Poland.[48] The pastoral plan for this "Great Novena" was to be an important phase of the "program of entrustment" drawn up by Cardinal Wyszyński during his imprisonment and presented to Bishops Klepacz and Choromański three days after the renewal of the Vows of Jan Kazimierz.[49] The official inauguration of this ambitious program of the "renewal of Polish society in the Catholic spirit" took place on May 3, 1957, and was to reach its apex exactly nine years later at Jasna Góra on May 3, 1966, with the solemn proclamation of the "act of complete servitude to the Mother of God for the freedom of the Church in Poland and in the whole world".[50] One of the features of this nine-year period would be the peregrination of a copy of the famous icon of Our Lady of Częstochowa, blessed by Pope Pius XII, to all the dioceses and parishes of Poland.[51]

On March 1, 1961, the Cardinal gave an address to the priests of the capital in the Warsaw Major Seminary Chapel in which he revealed some of his rationale for this program of the "Great Novena" by speaking of a "fortunate Divine atavism":

> My dearest Brothers! In the tragic disturbance of the human catastrophe in the garden, God Himself revealed the delicate hand of a Maiden. Prophetic dreams and visions longed for her. *Ecce Virgo*

[48] Załęcki, 145; Pach, 75–82.

[49] Micewski, 156; "Biography", 2.

[50] "Biography", 2, 12. It should be noted that there are two explicitly national Marian feasts celebrated in Poland with Jasna Góra as focal point: the Feast of Mary, Queen of Poland (May 3), which harks back to the vows of Jan Kasimierz, and the Feast of Our Lady of Częstochowa (August 26).

[51] Micewski, 174–75.

concipiet et pariet. . . . There will be Emmanuel! . . . There will be "God with us"! . . . And they believed! Esther entreated the king, as the mother of the sons of Zebedee entreated Christ, as Mary entreated at Cana, and later prayed for the disciples of Jesus beneath the Cross, on Calvary. There must be someone of a delicate, motherly soul, for it is necessary to give birth . . . birth! . . .

At the moment set by God, God the Heavenly Father Himself gave his Word Everlasting, His Son begotten before all ages—to a Woman. Why did He not give Him to the Sanhedrin, or the Synagogue? Why did He not give Him to Zion, to the temple? After all, generations prayed there. He gave Him to Mary, a maid from Nazareth!

A sort of Divine atavism is repeated here, the giving of everything to a Woman. Even on Calvary God did the same! His Apostles, the Church born from the side of Christ on the Cross, He gave again to a Woman. He gave Her the Apostle, and in him—all of humanity. "Behold your Son"! Let us call this a happy, Divine atavism. From Eden to Calvary! [52]

Convinced that this "atavism" was a fundamental dimension of God's providential plan, Cardinal Wyszyński carried this same conviction about the necessity of consecration to Mary with him to the Second Vatican Council. On the Council floor he spoke of the tradition of "Marian slavery" or the "slavery of love" taught by Saint Louis-Marie Grignion de Montfort and how this had been lived in Poland from times past. He proposed that all the bishops, united with the Pope, should consecrate the Church to Mary in the Council hall. Then, on returning home, they should repeat the act in all the dioceses of the world and finally it should be performed in every parish.[53] Ultimately, the rationale behind such an act was detailed in a *Memoriale* sub-

[52] "Oddanie Się Matce Boga Zywego", trans. Rev. Seraphim Michalenko, M.I.C., typescript, 7–8.

[53] Salient passages from the Latin text of this intervention are provided in Karol Wojtyła, "Znaczenie Kardynała Stefana Wyszyńskiego dla Współczesnego Kościoła", *Zeszyty Naukowe* 3 (1971): 34. Interestingly he used the word *committerent* for his proposal and then spoke of its repetition in the dioceses and parishes

mitted in the name of the Polish hierarchy. It would be a profession of faith in the unique intercession of Mary as Mother of God and a means of beseeching her for (1) the freedom to practice the faith and live according to Christian principles; (2) the unity of all Christians as "one flock under one shepherd"; and (3) peace among all the nations on earth.[54] The proposal was not accepted by the Council Fathers as such, but as we have seen above Pope Paul VI did entrust the Church to Mary in the presence of the Council Fathers on November 21, 1964.[55]

This "act of servitude" would be deeply engraved on the consciousness of Karol Wojtyla. As archbishop of Krakow he entered wholeheartedly into the spirit of the "Great Novena". He led a renewal of the consecration of the priests of the archdiocese of Krakow to Our Lady at Jasna Góra on April 23, 1963, a year after this had been done by his predecessor, Archbishop Eugeniusz Baziak.[56] He consecrated the entire archdiocese of Krakow to Our Lady in the Royal Metropolitan Cathedral of the Wawel on September 5, 1965, before the concluding session of the Second Vatican Council.[57] He wrote a brief analysis of the solemn national "act" in advance of the event for the benefit of his clergy[58] and addressed the faithful of the archdiocese during

---

of the world as an *actus consecrationis*. One wonders if it was due to this speech of Cardinal Wyszyński and the influence of the Polish hierarchy that the already cited text of *Apostolicam Actuositatem*, no. 4, recommended entrustment to Mary.

[54] Cf. *Acta Synodalia Sacrosancti Concilii Oecumenici Vaticani II,* vol. 3, Periodus 3a, Pars 1, 441–44; Wojtyła, "Znaczenie", 34. The complete text of the *Memoriale* (summarized in the *Acta*) was published in *Marianum* 28 (1966): 41–51.

[55] Cf. above, 106–8.

[56] Cf. the homily he delivered on that occasion in Karol Wojtyła, *Il Buon Pastore: Scritti, Discorsi e Lettere Pastorali,* trans. Elzbieta Cywiak and Renzo Panzone (Rome: Edizioni Logos, 1978), 31–41.

[57] The text of this act is also to be found in *Il Buon Pastore,* 109–11.

[58] "Tysiacleci chrztu a oddanie Matce Boskiej", *Notificationes e Curia Metropolitana Cracoviensi (*1965): 189–95.

the "Great Novena"[59] and even after its official conclusion,[60] reflecting on the significance of renewing the vows of baptism in the hands of Mary.[61]

He preached one of the principal homilies at Jasna Góra on that occasion, one which already shows some of the main contours of his own "program of entrustment".[62] Later he wrote commentaries on it[63] and frequently referred to it in his preaching.[64] As archbishop of Krakow, his was the third signature on the document, after that of the primate and the once-imprisoned archbishop of Poznan.

While the text of this "act of servitude" for such a solemn moment in the life of a nation is of necessity rather lengthy, nevertheless because of its importance as a landmark and point of reference in the Pope's spirituality and theology, it deserves to be presented substantially.

> Our Father, who art in heaven, Father of Our Lord Jesus Christ, whom you gave to the world by the power of the Holy Spirit, through Mary your servant, the Virgin Mother of God and mother of the Church! Father of all God's children, of all nations and races, and from whom all fatherhood comes in heaven and on earth! We beseech you today, through Our Lord Jesus Christ,

[59] Cf. letters of July 10, 1963, and August 21, 1965 (*Il Buon Pastore,* 49–52, 81–85) and his discourse of August 1965 (ibid., 93–102).

[60] Cf. his homily preceding the leave-taking of the copy of the national "pilgrim" icon of Częstochowa from the Cathedral of the Wawel on May 8, 1966 (Karol Wojtyła, *Chiamati all' Amore: Itinerari di Santità* [Rome: Edizioni Logos, 1980], 61–64), the text of an "act of consecration" dating from a few days after the great "act of servitude" at Jasna Góra (ibid., 67–70), and his pastoral letter of January 25, 1967 (*Il Buon Pastore,* 137–42).

[61] Cf. his pastoral letter of February 14, 1966 (*Il Buon Pastore,* 122) and his act of consecration of May 1966 made a short time after the "act of servitude" made at Jasna Góra (*Chiamati all' Amore,* 70).

[62] *Omelie,* 71–81.

[63] "Komentarz teologiczno-diszpasterski do aktu dokonanego na Jansnej Gorze dnia 3 maja 1966 R", *Ateneum Kaplanskie* 79 (1972): 5–21; "Oddanie Bogurodzicy w świetle nauki Soboru", *Przewodnnik Katolicki,* no. 26 (1972): 228.

[64] Cf. *Omelie,* 32, 58–59, 127–28.

Mediator between heaven and earth, through the intercession of the mother of Christ and our mother, and through the intercession of all the holy patrons of Poland! . . .

Today, after completing our examination of conscience throughout the nine year novena, which prepared us for the celebration of the Millennium, and after renewing our baptismal vows, in this jubilee year, called the *Te Deum of the Polish nation*, we cry unto you with grateful hearts: "Blessed be the Holy Trinity and undivided Unity. Let us give glory to God because He has shown mercy to us." . . .

Today, we want to lay the foundation for the preservation of the gift of faith for the future generations of Poland for at least another thousand years. We will accomplish this through the reliable hands of our Blessed Mother, whose protection and aid we experienced throughout the ages. Full of gratitude to the Mother of Christ, whom your Son gave to his Holy Church, we recall her comforting presence in the Church's history and in our native land. She was the one who persevered at the foot of the Cross of Christ on Calvary. With gratitude in our hearts we recall her maternal protection in years gone by and we are confident that thanks to her alone the faith in Poland was preserved. Therefore, Father, we are eager to place our beloved native land in the hands of Mary for another thousand years. Virgin Mother, mother of the Church, queen of Poland and our Lady of Częstochowa, you are given to us, as our strength in the defense of the Polish nation! . . .

On this day, with hopeful hearts we place under your eternal and maternal yoke of love, all the baptized children of God of the Polish nation, and all that Poland stands for, for freedom of the Church in the entire world and in our native land, for the spread of Christ's kingdom on earth.

Therefore, we place all our people in Poland and outside, in a slavery of love for the intention of the Church. From this day on, our beloved mother and queen of Poland, look upon us Poles, your nation, as on your possession, as an instrument in your hands for the good of the Church, to which we are most grateful for the light of faith, for the power of the Cross, for the spiritual unity of love and peace. . . .

Having offered ourselves for the intention of the Church, which is the living Christ in our times, we believe, that through you, we are placing ourselves in slavery towards Christ himself and his salvific work on earth. O blessed and glorious Virgin, we trust that by this act of deep faith and confidence we will obtain freedom for the Church, and your protection for our native land for another thousand years of faith. Please accept our confidence and strengthen it in our hearts and place it at the throne of the Triune God. Amen.[65]

We have already noted the emergence of the terminology of "Marian servitude" or "slavery" at the end of the sixteenth century in Spain and the defense of this terminology given by Pope John Paul II.[66] Here is how the then cardinal archbishop of Krakow contextualized this conception the day of this act of consecration:

From the height of the Cross He who was our Redeemer, He who made us sons of God, entrusts the disciple to the Mother. One could say that from the height of the Cross He consigned him to the "slavery" of Mary. This peculiar link which unites the disciples of Christ and the apostles to the Mother of the Son of God was called from the seventeenth century "the holy slavery". But in His entrustment of the disciple to the Mother one finds a great directive of the history of the whole Church, of all Christianity. Not only was the first disciple, John, entrusted to her, but all the disciples are entrusted to "her holy slavery", all the apostles and all who have received baptism.[67]

Wojtyła showed his awareness of the historical provenance of the concept of "holy slavery" in the seventeenth century. For now it is sufficient to note Father Załęcki's comment on the link between the 1966 "act of servitude" and Grignion de Montfort:

The consecration bears a great resemblance with the consecration used by St. Louis de Montfort. His idea of the personal consecration into slavery to Mary found its full expression in the "col-

[65] The entire text in Polish and in English is given in Załęcki, 153–57.

[66] Cf. above, 55–56, 64–66.

[67] *Omelie,* 79 (my trans.).

> lective" consecration of Poland. To be a slave of Christ through Mary makes a man truly free. Mary does not hold anything for herself but perfects and offers it to Christ. Then it is obvious that the "personal" consecration of St. Louis de Montfort was imitated in the Polish "collective" consecration to express the desire of Christian freedom as a suffering people—servant of the Lord. Filled with a deep gratitude to the Mother of Christ for her special and most blessed presence in the Christian history of Poland, the bishops headed by the Primate Stefan Cardinal Wyszyński consecrated their people and land into the slavery of Mary to ensure the freedom and success of the Church in the second millennium of Poland's history.[68]

In a homily at Jasna Góra for the Feast of Our Lady of Częstochowa in 1977, Cardinal Wojtyła said about being "slaves of Mary": "We are not ashamed of this because this means the fullness of our liberty and our dignity."[69]

There were yet two more national acts of consecration of the Polish nation after the great "act of servitude" of the Millennium in which the Pope as archbishop of Krakow played a part. On September 5, 1971, the Polish episcopate made an "act of consecration to Holy Mary, Mother of the Church" at Jasna Góra. It will be recalled that the title "Mother of the Church" was proclaimed by Pope Paul VI on November 21, 1964, at the conclusion of the third session of the Council.[70]

There was contestation within the Council about this title for a variety of reasons, including fear of ecumenical offense, and it had been dropped from the chapter on Mary in the schema on the Church without ever having been put to a vote, by the action of the Theological Commission.[71] But, on the other hand, there was some strong support for it

[68] Załęcki, 292.

[69] *Omelie*, 58 (my trans.).

[70] Cf. *AAS* 56 (1964): 1014–18; *TPS* 10:137–40.

[71] Cf. Wiltgen, 240–41; *Theotokos*, 251–53; Gerard Philips, "La Vierge au IIe Concile du Vatican et L'Avenir de la Mariologie", in *Maria*, 8:63.

which, in effect, was vindicated by the action of Paul VI and subsequent history. Not surprisingly, some of the strongest support came from Cardinal Wyszyński and the bishops of Poland.[72] Further, the same year as the consecration to Mary, Mother of the Church, a special Mass formulary for the *Festum Beatae Mariae Virginis Matris Ecclesiae*, to be celebrated on Pentecost Monday, was approved by the Holy See for use in Poland on October 11, 1971.[73] And again that same year Cardinal Wojtyła would write an article in praise of the primate of Poland noting "the role that Polish millennial devotion (966–1966), centered in Jasna Góra, played in that proclamation" of the title of "Mary, Mother of the Church".[74]

Here are salient excerpts of the text:

> We come to you, O Mother, for help. We desire to commit to you the Church of Christ and the entire world. We feel ourselves to be a small, living part of the Church of your Son. It is our Church, therefore, we have a right to offer it to you. At the same time we are a small living part of the human family, which is our family, hence we can also offer it to you.
>
> The Second Vatican Council called us to responsibility for the Church and the moral face of the world. But above all, you yourself sensitized our hearts to the sorrows of all peoples and of the universal Church. You yourself inspired us to dedicate the whole nation to you, both those living in the homeland and those beyond its borders, with the Millennial Act of Jasna Góra, to the slavery of your maternal love for the freedom of the Church in Poland and in the world. In the spirit of that act we feel ourselves urged by you with an obligation to urgency for supernatural help for the Church and the world.
>
> We do this in most intimate union with the intentions of the Holy Father Pope Paul VI who, proclaiming you Mother of the Church, in the presence of all the Fathers of the Council,

[72] Wiltgen, 154, 240.

[73] Cf. Ignazio M. Calabuig Adan, O.S.M., "Tre Messe in onore della Beata Vergine *Madre della Chiesa*", *Marianum* 36 (1974): 70–78.

[74] Williams, 175, 375; Wojtyła, "Znaczenie", 33–35.

entrusted the whole Church of Christ and the human family to your maternal heart.[75]

Here, as well as in the consecration of 1966, we may note what might be called the "vicarious" dimension of the act. It is performed not just for Poland, but on behalf of the entire Church. Cardinal Wojtyła had already alluded to this in commenting on the millennial act of consecration:

And so, thanks to the connection in time which occurred between the preparation for the millennium of Baptism and the subsequent sessions of Vatican Council II, there it took form as though a fuller expression of our millennium. The Church in Poland entered anew into the consciousness of the universal Church and at the same time, it itself gained anew the consciousness of its own deep bond with the whole Christian *Universitas*. . . . And Cardinal Stefan Wyszyński, bringing as it were to conclusion the idea of this gift which the Church in Poland, part of the Christian *Universitas*, desired to offer "to other parts and to the whole Church" carried out on the 3rd of May 1966 at Jasna Góra the Millennial Act of handing over to the maternal slavery of Mary: " . . . that the whole and individual parts experience growth."[76]

Bringing this concept of Poland's self-consecration to Mary as its gift to the Universal Church to a high point of culmination, the Polish episcopate took the bold initiative on June 7, 1976, whereby, acting vicariously, they consecrated mankind to Mary.[77] Here is the Pope's own description:

On June 7, 1976, they consecrated to you *all of humanity*, all the nations and peoples of the modern world, and their brothers and sisters who are close to them by faith, by language and by the

[75] *"O Matce i Krolewej Polakow"—Refleksje, modlitwy, piesni* (Jasna Góra, Rome: Paulini, 1982), 263–66. English translation by Dr. John Grondelski and Fr. Ignatius Kuziemski.

[76] Wojtyła, "Znaczenie", 32–33. English trans. by Fr. Seraphim Michalenko, M.I.C.

[77] The text used on this occasion was that of the Act of Consecration which Pope Paul VI had made on December 8, 1975. Cf. above, 110–11.

> destinies they share in history, extending this consecration to the furthest limits of love as is demanded by your heart, the heart of a Mother who embraces each and every person, always and everywhere.[78]

In his own "Act of Consecration to the Mother of God" made on his first return to Poland as Pope on June 4, 1979, he summed up all of these previous acts by the Polish episcopal body and ratified them:

> By the inscrutable designs of divine Providence I am today present here at Jasna Góra, in my earthly homeland, Poland, and I wish first of all to confirm the acts of consecration and of trust that at various times—"in many and various ways"—were pronounced by the Cardinal Primate and the Polish Episcopate. In a very special way I wish to confirm and renew the act of consecration pronounced at Jasna Góra on May 3, 1966, on the occasion of the millennium of Poland. With this act the Polish bishops wished, by giving themselves to you, Mother of God, "in your maternal slavery of love," to serve the great cause of *the freedom of the Church* not only in their own homeland but in the whole world. . . .
>
> Today I come to Jasna Góra as its first pilgrim Pope, and I wish to renew the entire heritage of trust, of consecration and of hope that has been accumulated here with such magnanimity by my Brothers in the Episcopate and my fellow-countrymen.[79]

Thus does John Paul pay tribute to the collective episcopal consecrations to Mary, Queen of Poland, which have set such a remarkable precedent and unparalleled example in twentieth century Catholicism and which have contributed so much to his own perspective and theology. Cardinal Stefan Wyszyński, for his part, considered the Pope's act of June 4, 1979, as an "official recognition of the Polish Marian path", which he himself had been so instrumental in charting, and as a stage of the systematic preparation of

[78] *Inseg* II:1 (1979), 1417; *Poland,* 111.

[79] *Inseg* II:1 (1979), 1417; *Poland,* 111.

Catholic opinion for a future act of consecration of the Church and the world to Our Lady.[80]

The influence of the "Primate of the Millennium" on Pope John Paul II's program of Marian consecration and entrustment can hardly be underestimated. We might say that Wojtyła inherited a double portion of his spirit (cf. 2 Kgs 2:9–12). Before the assembled episcopate of Poland on June 19, 1983, John Paul said:

> My first steps during my pilgrimage this year in the homeland were directed to the Warsaw Cathedral, to the tomb of Cardinal Stefan Wyszyński of holy memory, the Primate of the Millennium. I celebrated the first Holy Mass for him, recommending to God his immortal soul and also giving thanks for the service he rendered to the Church in Poland for over thirty years as Bishop and as Primate.
>
> It is indeed difficult to express the importance of this service, not only with regard to the Church in Poland, but also with regard to the universal Church. . . .
>
> In this meeting of the Polish Episcopal Conference I wish to render homage one more time, after his death, to the memory of the great Primate, to whom the Church, Poland, and all of us—I in particular—owe so much.[81]

The Pope had already acknowledged the stature of the primate while he was still living on his first return to Poland:

> The Cardinal Primate has become a . . . keystone. . . . The keystone is that which forms the arch, which reflects the strength of the foundations of the building. The Cardinal Primate *shows the strength of the foundation of the Church, which is Jesus Christ.* This is what his strength consists of. The Cardinal Primate has been teaching for over thirty years that *he owes his strength to Mary,* the Mother of Christ. We all know well that it is possible, thanks to Mary, to make the strength of the foundation that is Christ shine out, and effectively to become a keystone of the Church.[82]

[80] Pach, 87–88.

[81] *Inseg* VI:1 (1983), 1585–86; *ORE* 791:7.

[82] *Inseg* II:1 (1979), 1376; *Poland,* 50–51.

Recuperating in the Gemelli Polyclinic from the attempt on his life, he would repeat the same words in his letter to the Polish nation on the occasion of the death of the "Primate of the Millennium".[83]

[83] *Inseg* IV:1 (1981), 1218; *ORE* 687:8.

4

Marian Consecration in Contemporary Theological Reflection

Now it remains for us to consider some representative contemporary theological reflection on this phenomenon of Marian consecration which we have been tracing in the spiritual journey of the Church.

The postconciliar context

The first thing to be noted is that after the cresting of what might be described as the "Marian Era" which flourished under Pius XII, the impetus for consecration to Our Lady declined in much of the Catholic Church along with other Marian devotions. Consequently little was written in the conciliar and immediate postconciliar period by theologians about the foundations of this practice. Two notable exceptions were the publication of essays produced on the occasion of the fourth centenary of the Jesuit Marian Congregations in 1963[1] and the papers produced for a study week on this topic which was promoted by the Italian *Collegamento Mariano Nazionale* in 1968 in the light of the Second Vatican Council.[2]

[1] *La consacrazione nella Congregazione Mariana,* trans. of *Quatrième Centenaire des Congrégations Mariales. Documents du Congrès Européen,* Rome, September 8–12, 1963 (Rome: Edizioni Stella Matutina, 1963).

[2] *Teologia e Pastorale della Consacrazione a Maria* (Padua: Edizioni Messagero, 1969).

We have already noted that this was not the case in Poland during that same period where the Marian theology of chapter eight of *Lumen Gentium*, commented upon at length by Cardinal Wojtyła,[3] blended harmoniously with Cardinal Primate Wyszyński's ambitious "program of Marian entrustment".[4] Within the first eleven years following the Second Vatican Council, Poland's bishops consecrated the nation three times to the Madonna on her Bright Mountain of Częstochowa. With the accession to the papacy of Karol Wojtyła, this tradition, dormant in many areas of the Western Church in the immediate postconciliar period, was brought to the fore in a striking way.

John Paul's "program of entrustment" was soon noted by theologians and faithful and became a stimulus for pastoral practice and theological reflection.[5] Hence, not surprisingly, the bulk of contemporary theological deliberation on this subject has been occasioned by the praxis and magisterium of John Paul II. Before taking note of these developments, however, it would be apposite to take into consideration those which developed in the immediate wake of Vatican II.

A good illustration of the application of the Council's orientations to the theology of Marian consecration may be found in the French Montfort journal, *Cahiers Marials*, number 86, of January 15, 1973. Its first article by the Sulpician exegete, Henri Cazelles, was devoted to a study of the consecration of Christ and the consecration of man.[6] It sought

[3] Besides the articles already cited, he produced a commentary on all the documents of the Council in which this chapter featured prominently: *Sources of Renewal: The Implementation of the Second Vatican Council,* trans. P. S. Falla (San Francisco: Harper & Row, 1980).

[4] Cf. above, 122–37.

[5] Appropriately one of the first collections of essays to be published on Marian consecration in his pontificate took his motto as its title: *Totus Tuus: attualità e significato della consacrazione a Maria* (Rome: Santuario Madonna del Divino Amore, 1978). It, too, was sponsored by the Italian *Collegamento Mariano Nazionale.*

[6] H. Cazelles, P.S.S., "Consécration du Christ et consécration de l'homme", *Cahiers Marials,* no. 86 (1973): 5–13.

to ground the practice of Marian consecration, particularly as recommended by Saint Louis-Marie Grignion de Montfort, on a solid biblical and Christological foundation. In it Père Cazelles reviewed the difference between the sacred and the profane, God's calling of His people to holiness (cf. Lev 19:2), the holiness and consecration of Christ as Priest by the Holy Spirit and his own self-consecration (cf. Jn 17:19), the consecration of the Christian in baptism and the renewal of one's baptismal commitment "through the hands of Mary" as proposed by de Montfort.

The second article by Canadian Montfort Father J. P. Michaud attempted to describe Marian consecration from the perspective of being at the service of the mystery of God's dwelling among men.[7] It considered Mary at the time of the Annunciation as giving herself freely to this mystery by her response "Be it done to me according to your word" (Lk 1:38), the consecration of her virginity to God, her service to the revelation of Christ at Cana (Jn 2:1–11), her collaboration in the great price of our salvation on Calvary and her acceptance of spiritual motherhood on our behalf (Jn 19:25–27), her presence in the Cenacle as Mother (Acts 1:14), and her continued service of intercession on behalf of her children even in glory (*LG*, no. 62). The thrust of the presentation was to indicate that as Mary, by virtue of her consecration, "devoted herself totally [*totaliter devovit*] to the Person and work of her Son" (*LG*, no. 56), so the Christian who follows her example must do no less.

A further article, by the editor Father Alphonse Bossard, expatiated at length on the nature of the total gift (consecration) to Christ through Mary according to de Montfort.[8] In it he underscored de Montfort's insistence on this consecra-

[7] J. P. Michaud, S.M.M., "Au service du Mystère de Dieu avec les Hommes", *Cahiers Marials*, no. 86 (1973): 15–22.

[8] A. Bossard, S.M.M., "Le don total au Christ par Marie selon Montfort", *Cahiers Marials*, no. 86 (1973): 29–48.

tion as the perfect renewal of the promises of baptism and the Christocentrism of de Montfort's vision.

This brief synopsis may serve to underscore the point that, especially since the Second Vatican Council, there has been a strong motivation to illustrate the Trinitarian, Christological, ecclesial, biblical, liturgical, and anthropological dimensions of the practice of Marian consecration.[9] These, in turn, may provide further bases for ecumenical dialogue by demonstrating that the entrusting of oneself, of groups, and of the entire Church to the Mother of God is not an unhealthy accretion, but an organic element in the development of the Catholic tradition.[10] Particularly since the Council, theologians have been concerned above all to show that the "total gift of oneself [to Mary] for life and for eternity"[11] has a thoroughly Christological perspective in that it flows from the will of Christ and is ultimately oriented to Him. Theological research in this area, then, as in all other areas of Mariology and Marian spirituality, aims at illuminating the fact that "in the Virgin Mary everything is relative to Christ and dependent upon Him."[12]

We have already noted that the word "consecration" as a description of the giving of oneself to Mary, while its first use dates at least from Saint John of Damascus[13] and it has held a certain "pride of place" for the past three hundred

[9] These are listed among the characteristics of genuine Marian devotion outlined by Paul VI in his apostolic exhortation *Marialis Cultus,* nos. 25–37, *AAS* 66 (1974): 135–49; Paul VI, *Mary—God's Mother and Ours,* 122–38.

[10] Cf. Congregation for Catholic Education, *The Virgin Mary in Intellectual and Spiritual Formation* (March 25, 1988), no. 14; *Marianum* 50 (1988): 40–41; *ORE* 1043:20.

[11] This is the description of Marian consecration made by Pius XII in his allocution to representatives of the Marian Congregations on January 21, 1945, which has since become a classic definition. Cf. Domenico Bertetto, S.D.B., *Il Magistero Mariano di Pio XII* (Rome: Edizioni Paoline, 1956), no. 136; *OL,* no. 389.

[12] *Marialis Cultus,* no. 25, *AAS* 66 (1974): 135; Paul VI, *Mary—God's Mother and Ours,* 122–23.

[13] Cf. above, 47–48.

fifty years,[14] is surely not the only term used to delineate the relationship of "belonging" to Mary. Nonetheless, it has provided a helpful point of departure for analyzing the theological content of this consistent phenomenon in the life of the Church. Père Henri Cazelles, whose study on the consecration of Christ we have already noted, undertook a further biblical investigation ten years later on the Holy Spirit as the agent in the consecration of Christ, Mary, and the Church.[15] Such essays have had the merit of highlighting the primary initiative of God in consecrating, the mission of the Christ as the "consecrated" of the Father, Mary as the consecrated creature *par excellence*, and baptism as the fundamental Christian consecration.

Discussion of the meaning of "entrustment" vis-à-vis "consecration"

Pope John Paul II's own "program of Marian consecration and entrustment", launched from the first months of his pontificate, has also introduced a further consideration into the contemporary theological discussion of Marian consecration. After detailing some of his most important and solemn acts of consecration to Our Lady,[16] Father Stefano De Fiores, S.M.M., the well-known Italian Mariologist, points out:

> Regarding the expressive language of these acts, the Pope is not bound by a stereotyped formula, but has recourse to various terms, which take into account the pastoral context: to entrust, to consecrate, to dedicate, to offer, to commend, to serve [*affidare, consacrare, dedicare, offrire, raccomandare, servire*]. . . . His preference is for

[14] Cf. above, 54; F. M. Franzi, "Per un orientamento sul tema della 'consacrazione a Maria' ", in *Teologia e Pastorale della Consacrazione a Maria*, 8.

[15] H. Cazelles, P.S.S., "L'Esprit qui consacre le Christ, Marie, L'Eglise", *Cahiers Marials,* no. 133 (1982): 131–45.

[16] Cf. above, 31–37.

> the binomial: *affidare-consacrare*, with the noticeable preeminence of the first verb. Thus from June 7, 1981, the neologism entrustment [*affidamento*] enters into the texts, arousing interest and some theological interpretations.[17]

One of the principal considerations of theologians, then, in the course of this pontificate, has been the discussion of the meaning of entrustment [*affidamento*] and whether this word is an exact synonym for consecration or in what sense it differs. First, it may be helpful to point out that the word does not express a new concept in the context of acts of offering to Our Lady, even if John Paul II has made much more extensive use of it than popes before him. It should be pointed out that the Servant of God Pius XII used the words *affidiamo* and *consacriamo* in his consecration of the world to the Immaculate Heart of Mary on October 31, 1942,[18] and that Paul VI chose the word *affidiamo* together with synonyms like *confidiamo* and *consegniamo* to describe the entrustment of our Christian commitment to Our Lady in his Prayer on the Feast of the Immaculate Conception 1975.[19] Further, the history of Marian consecration illustrates that the Latin equivalents of this term, such as *committere* and *commendare*, are well attested in the tradition and find their context especially in the medieval *patrocinium*.[20]

Nevertheless it is quite legitimate to inquire about the nuances conveyed by the words entrust/entrustment (*affidare/affidamento*) and whether these signal a shift in direction or a further precision in the meaning of the "gift of oneself to Mary". Monsignor Francesco Franzi, auxiliary bishop of Novara, one of the first to note the papal preference for this term, underscores in the first instance its appro-

[17] Stefano De Fiores, S.M.M., *Maria nella Teologia Contemporanea,* 2nd ed. (Rome: Centro di Cultura Mariana "Mater Ecclesiae", 1987), 331 (my trans.).

[18] Cf. above, 98–99, 100.

[19] Cf. above, 110.

[20] Cf. above, 48–49, 52.

priateness vis-à-vis the very theologically weighty word *consecration.*

> It is known that not a few objections have been made to "consecration to Mary". The term "consecration" summons to mind a religious content so profound that it seems to correspond uniquely to the relationship which we have with God. It refers us instinctively, in fact, to the ontological state of consecration accomplished in us by baptism which truly "grafts" us into Christ and makes us "His", participants in Him. . . .
>
> It is clear that we cannot use the term "consecration" in a univocal sense—when we speak of our relationship with Mary whether in our "being" or in our "moral conduct". True, we have bonds with her—those which we express by affirming that Mary is Mother to us and that we are her children—, but certainly these are not identical to those which bind us to Christ. . . . [21]
>
> In comparison the term "entrustment" seems more suitable. It is simpler; it refers to normal relationships among men and does not immediately express a religious content which reminds us of God. Given today's mentality, suspicious of unduly enlarging the area of the "religious", it can prove to be more welcome.
>
> We must beware, however, of the risk of impoverishing the significance of "entrustment" by not paying sufficient attention to that particular category of relations with Mary to which the term refers and is meant to confirm, constituting an act of faith in such relations and a coherent commitment of life.
>
> Thus it is very important to consider with care the significance which such "entrustment" acquires in the discourse of the Holy Father [particularly of the morning of June 7, 1981].[22]

After analyzing the text of the "consecration" of Pentecost, 1981, which became the paradigm of the "acts of consecration" of May 13, 1982, and March 25, 1984,[23] Bishop

[21] The bishop is obviously referring to the necessity of invoking the principle of analogy which we will treat in part two of this work.

[22] Francesco Maria Franzi, " 'Consacrazione' o 'affidamento'? " *Miles Immaculatae* 17 (1981): 218–19 (my trans.).

[23] Cf. above, 32–35.

Franzi makes a number of helpful theological precisions and then draws this conclusion:

> Those who speak of "entrustment to Our Lady" and those who speak of "consecration to Our Lady", in substance wish to express the same reality, a relationship which one acknowledges having with the Holy Virgin and which he wishes to reaffirm.
>
> I perceive that the Holy Father himself uses the one and the other term indiscriminately, almost as if they were two synonyms, without any difference of content between the two expressions. . . .[24]
>
> When we speak of "entrustment to Mary" and of "consecration to Her", in substance we intend to recognize who Mary is for us; what she does for us; who we are for her; what we, consequently, ought to do toward her.[25]

Ultimately, then, he sees the two terms as equivalent and proposes that it is a matter of pastoral sensitivity as to which word, "consecration" or "entrustment", is more appropriate on a particular occasion.[26]

Father Stefano De Fiores also sees the word *entrustment* as bringing an enrichment to the discussion of this topic in that it implies a special confidence in Mary. Interestingly the root *trust* is clearly present in the English word *entrust* even as the root *fid* (from *fiducia*) is equally apparent in the Italian word *affidamento*. Hence he says of the word *entrustment* that

[24] This would seem to be verified especially in the Consecration of Ireland to Mary where five times the Holy Father repeated the phrase "We entrust and consecrate to you" (cf. *Inseg* II:2 [1979], 469; *Ireland "In the Footsteps of St. Patrick"* [Boston: St. Paul Editions, 1979], 89–90 [hereafter cited as *Ireland*]) and in the letter to the bishops of the Church dated December 8, 1983, in which he presented the text of "the Act of consecration and entrustment" which he asked them to make on March 24 or 25, 1984, in union with him (cf. *Inseg* VII:1 (1984), 417; *ORE* 823:2). In his consecration of Brazil to Our Lady on October 19, 1991, he prayed: "O Virgin of the Cliff, we come before your beautiful image . . . to consecrate our lives to you and entrust to you the new evangelization" (*ORE* 1214:3), using the word "consecrate" for persons while retaining "entrust" for projects.

[25] Franzi, " 'Consacrazione' o 'affidamento' ? ", 225–26 (my trans.).

[26] Ibid., 227–28.

> it includes an attitude of interior trust which expresses itself in a corresponding act. In order to make an act of entrustment it is then necessary to have trust [the Italian word also implies confidence, reliance, even assurance] in the person to whom one entrusts himself or hands something over, even his own life.[27]

While recognizing the advantages of both words in terms of their connotations and the difficulties which they seek to resolve, he says that the discussion remains open.[28]

There are others who have taken a more decisive position. Canon René Laurentin, for instance, believes that the word *consecration* is not suitable to express our relationship to Mary. He forthrightly states that:

> In the strict sense of the word there is no consecration except to God. But in current language we speak of "to consecrate oneself" [sic] to a project, to one's affairs, to one's family. This has a meaning that is quite banal: not to neglect, to attend to.
>
> No doubt, one can use this banal sense to say: "I consecrate myself to Mary." Unfortunately this language obscures what is essential. We say: "I consecrate myself", while forgetting that it is God who consecrates, according to the proper sense of the word.
>
> The consecration is made to Mary, or to her Heart, while to a certain extent implicitly forgetting God whom we just guess at, as in a mist. Its priority, its gratuitousness becomes hazy or disappears. What is essential becomes marginal.[29]

Because he feels that the analogical use of the term *consecration* confuses the theological task unnecessarily[30] and

[27] De Fiores, *Maria nella Teologia Contemporanea,* 335 (my trans.).

[28] Ibid., 336.

[29] René Laurentin, "Consecration and Entrustment: A Commitment to the Hearts of Jesus and Mary—Its Meaning for Our Personal Lives and the Life of Our People", trans. Srs. Edita Telan, M.I.C., and Rachel de Mars, M.I.C., in *The Alliance of the Hearts of Jesus and Mary: The International Theological/Pastoral Conference, Manila, Philippines, 30 November–3 December 1987, Texts and Documents* (Manila: Bahay Maria, 1988), 242.

[30] Cf. ibid., 238–40; also his *A Year of Grace with Mary*, 126–31.

constitutes "a scandal for the ecumenical dialogue",[31] Laurentin prefers rather to speak of Mary's role in our consecration to God[32] and concludes that "if we can only, in this proper sense, be consecrated to God, it is worth entrusting ourselves to Mary for that purpose. Whoever is entrusted to this very loving mother, beloved of God, is not lost and those who have done so have never been disappointed."[33] In saying this the canon obviously prefers to distance himself from the tradition represented by Saint Louis-Marie Grignion de Montfort[34] who holds that the consecration to God [Christ] through Mary also includes a consecration to Mary: "It follows that we consecrate ourselves at one and the same time to Mary and to Jesus. We give ourselves to Mary because Jesus chose her as the perfect means to unite himself to us and unite us to him. We give ourselves to Jesus because he is our last end."[35]

On the other side of the consecration/entrustment issue is the position espoused by the late Père Joseph de Sainte-Marie, O.C.D. (d. 1985). After a lengthy excursus on the complementarity of the terms "consecration" and "sanctification",[36] and with the understanding that sanctification is the final end of consecration,[37] he defines consecration to Mary as the covenant we make with her in order to permit

[31] Laurentin, "Consecration", 239.

[32] Laurentin, *A Year of Grace,* 11, 131–34.

[33] Ibid., 134.

[34] Strangely at one point in his Manila presentation on the question of consecration he compared St. Maximilian Kolbe with St. Louis de Montfort and said of the latter that he "was no less intensely apostolic and missionary, not without a megalomania similar to that of Kolbe, when he built, with a shovel and a wheelbarrow, the mountain of Pontchateau to the glory of the Cross", Laurentin, "Consecration", 249.

[35] *True Devotion,* no. 125; cf. also Alphonse Bossard, S.M.M., "Se consacrer à Marie", *Cahiers Marials,* no. 137 (1983): 100–101.

[36] Joseph de Sainte-Marie, *Teologia,* III:2–III:59.

[37] Ibid., III:7.

her to exercise fully in us her maternal function, consecrating, sanctifying, and enlivening us.[38] Again he says that

> to consecrate oneself to Mary, as we have said, is to make a covenant with her which allows us to live more deeply that which we made with Christ in our baptism. We see clearly now the two complementary dimensions, or better, the double movement: *to give oneself to Mary in order to receive from her, through her, with her and in her the life of Christ*; and to receive from Mary the life of Christ in order to give her the glory which Christ himself wishes through her, or rather which he wishes to receive through himself in her.[39]

Hence, from Père Joseph de Sainte-Marie's perspective the act performed by Pope John Paul II on May 13, 1982, in Fatima "was an act of 'affidamento' of entrusting, not a consecration properly so called" [40] because "to consecrate humanity or a particular people to God is to entrust it to Him; but it is to do something more—it is to undertake at the same time to sanctify that humanity and to start it at once on the road to conversion and sanctification." [41] While Laurentin argues that the word *consecration* says too much, Joseph de Sainte-Marie argues that the word *entrustment* doesn't say enough.

Another factor that may be well considered at this point is the Pope's own intention in his use of the cognate terms *entrust* and *entrustment* and their meaning in his own mother tongue. Father George Domanski, O.F.M. Conv., points out that in the writings of Saint Maximilian Kolbe one meets the interchangeable use of two terms: consecration (in Polish: *poswiecenie*) and self-giving/abandonment[42] (in

[38] Ibid., III:58–III:59.

[39] Ibid., V:11–V:12 (my trans.).

[40] Joseph de Sainte-Marie, *Reflections,* 19.

[41] Ibid., 29.

[42] This second term suggests all the richness of meaning associated with the French word *abandon* as used by the writers of the seventeenth-century French School, especially by Jean-Pierre de Caussade, S.J. Cf. J. Neville Ward, "Abandon", in *The Westminster Dictionary of Christian Spirituality*, ed. Gordon S.

Polish: *oddanie*).[43] Father George Kosicki, C.S.B., has considered at some length the meaning of the Polish word most frequently used by John Paul II, translated into Italian as "*affidare*" and into English as "entrust". The word is *zawierzać*, the same word employed in Cardinal Wyszyński's various consecrations of Poland.[44]

Let us allow Father Kosicki to share some of his discoveries about this word:

> I continued to wonder about the word "entrust" until I met a priest from Poland, a colleague of the present Pope while at the University of Lublin where Karol Wojtyła taught as Bishop of Krakow. I asked him about the word "entrust" and its Polish meaning, mentioning that I was disappointed that he didn't use the word "consecrate" to Mary in his *Letter to all Priests* [of April 8, 1979].[45] His response was very clear and reassuring. He pointed out that the Polish word "zawierzać" (translated as "entrust") is a strong word and is used for what we call in English "consecration" to Mary. He went on to say that the Polish word which is the equivalent root word to the English "consecration" (viz. "konsekracia") is usually reserved for the consecration at Mass. He went further to point out that the word "entrust" was a special word for John Paul II because of the way he has used it in his Polish writings. He added that the motto of John Paul, "Totus Tuus", (I am) all yours (Mary), means, "I consecrate myself to you, Mary" and is what Pope John Paul has in mind when he uses "zawierzać" (translated into English as "entrust"). In short the Polish "to entrust" means "to consecrate".[46]
>
> Let us consider the word that would best describe our relationship to Mary. Recently, a priest pointed out to me that for him the word "entrust" was a strong word because it was a general word

Wakefield (Philadelphia: Westminster Press, 1983), 1–2; P. Pourrat, "Abandon", *in DSp*, 1:1–49.

[43] Cited in Franzi, " 'Consacrazione' o 'affidamento' ? ", 227.

[44] Cf. Kosicki, 64.

[45] *Inseg* II:1 (1979), 860–61; *ORE* 577:9.

[46] Kosicki, 66–67.

and it can be used in a variety of ways in applying the word to Mary. The word "consecrate", however, is so strong a word that when it is applied to Mary it needs to be nuanced. It is something like the word "homage" where a distinction has to be made between *cultus latriae* (worship of God) and *cultus hyperduliae* (the homage we pay to Mary). This priest went on to point out that in translating a word from another language, the strong word usually becomes a weaker one. This seems to be the case with the word "entrust" when used as a translation for the Polish word used by John Paul II. The word "entrust", however, has the strength of describing what the Father did in his relationship to Mary (entrusting the Word to her) and what Jesus did in his own relationship to Mary and further what he did in his relationship to us on the Cross (Jn. 19:25–27). On the other hand we cannot dismiss the word "consecration" in regard to Mary after Vatican II. In choosing a proper word for this relationship the main point must be kept before us, namely, the reality that Mary is our mother and that, even more, she is charged with the role of preparing us, the Bride, the disciples, and this by way of the Cross. This is the role of Mary in spiritual warfare. Our part in this warfare means more than just a relationship with her as mother; it also means a relationship with her as queen-mother, standing with her at the cross of Jesus. It seems that the word "entrust" could be used on two levels: first of all a confiding of our lives to Mary as mother and then, secondly, a confiding of our lives to Mary as queen, our leader in this spiritual warfare. The word "consecrate", however, is a word that makes clear this second aspect of our relationship to Mary as our leader in spiritual warfare, leading us to the Cross and so on to the Cenacle to be fully Church.[47]

I believe that I have now sufficiently illustrated the principal issues involved in the contemporary discussion of "consecration or entrustment" in order to justify my own usage of both words in the title of this work and in describing Pope John Paul II's program as one of "consecration *and* entrustment" to Mary. I believe that each word can be justified and offer shades of meaning not conveyed by the

[47] Ibid., 74–75.

other. From the foregoing exposition, as well, one may surmise the wisdom of Father De Fiores' declaration that the discussion remains open.[48]

Recovery of the biblical concept of welcoming/receiving Mary

Another helpful insight of Stefano De Fiores regarding the question of the Christian's relationship to Mary revolves around the seemingly simple statement made in John 19:27: "And from that hour the disciple took her to his own home." The rich biblical theme of receiving/welcoming Mary provides a scriptural way of describing further this relationship of the disciple with Mary.

> To receive (*lambanein*) in the Johannine vocabulary is the verb of faith: it indicates a spiritual attitude, "it implies an availability and participation by the subject" and an interior disposition of openness. When it is concerned with the person of Jesus, as in John 1:12, "it is practically synonymous with *pistéuein*" (to believe)—says I. de la Potterie—concluding that "to receive Jesus and to receive his Mother" are, definitively, two equivalent attitudes.[49]
>
> If I must express a preference, this would be for the biblical expression put in evidence in our time in the exegesis of John 19:27: the *welcome* of Mary on the part of the disciple whom Jesus loved. To welcome Mary with all the richness of spiritual attitudes which the Johannine term allows, is a realistic and simple proposal, which has the advantage of being biblical and therefore potentially also ecumenical. To receive Mary signifies being open to her and her maternal mission, bringing her into one's own spiritual inwardness where Christ is already welcomed as also his other gifts in faith: it is an expression which evokes all Christian and Marian spirituality

[48] Cf. De Fiores, *Maria nella Teologia Contemporanea,* 336.

[49] Ibid., 327 (my trans.). It might be noted that the word translated here as "receive" has the sense of "to receive graciously" or "to welcome". Cf. I. de la Potterie, S.J., "La parole de Jésus 'Voici ta Mère' et l'accueil du Disciple (Jn. 19, 27b)", *Marianum* 36 (1974): 33–35.

(although at different levels) of the New Testament. From the cultural point of view the welcome of the other is a categorical imperative if one wishes to construct a society which is truly a communion.[50]

Monsignor Franzi presents the matter in this way:

How shall we describe this gesture of the apostle? Is he "entrusted" to Mary? Is he "consecrated" to her?

It seems to us, in fact, that neither the one expression nor the other succeeds in saying all.

The Gospel is more simple and more profound: it states the fact: "he received her"—that is the response to a reality in that case joyously known: "she is your mother".[51]

Here the bishop's remark is a good reminder that no one word, neither *entrustment* nor *consecration*, nor even *welcome* can exhaust the richness of the disciple's relationship with Mary. Being a biblical term, however, which occurs in that capital text, John 19:27, the concept of "welcoming Mary into one's life" as John Paul II will put it, brings out yet further dimensions in the Christian's relationship with Mary.

Traditional elements of the theology of Marian consecration largely absent from contemporary discussion

Finally, it might be noted that two themes traditionally related to the question of Marian consecration seem to be largely absent from the contemporary discussion. The first is that of Our Lady's Queenship.[52] It might be noted that this emphasis is at least implicitly present in the prayers of Saints Ildephonsus of Toledo and John of Damascus who both

[50] De Fiores, *Maria nella Teologia Contemporanea,* 328 (my trans.).

[51] Franzi, " 'Consacrazione' o 'affidamento' ? ", 226.

[52] Cf. the helpful bibliography on this topic and the treatment of the relationship between Mary's Queenship and consecration to her in Most, "Marian Consecration", 441–51.

address Mary as "Lady" or "My Lady"[53] and in the whole tradition of "Marian slavery".[54] Furthermore, the papal magisterium of the Servant of God Pope Pius XII solemnly proposed Our Lady's Queenship as the doctrinal basis for the public acts of consecration to the Immaculate Heart of Mary and mandated the annual renewal of the consecration of the world to the Immaculate Heart every year on the Feast of the Queenship which he instituted.[55]

The second theme is that of Mary's mediation. The two principal and most consistent proponents of Marian consecration among the canonized saints of the Church are surely Louis-Marie Grignion de Montfort and Maximilian-Maria Kolbe. Both of them insist in their writings and formulae of consecration on this principle of Mary's maternal mediation as justifying the "total gift of oneself" to Mary.[56] So does the eminent Thomistic scholar, Père Reginald Garrigou-Lagrange, O.P.[57] The matter was summarized succinctly by Pius XII in an address to a Marian Congress in India at the conclusion of the Marian Year of 1954:

> But let not those without the Household of the Faith mistake for a moment the meaning, the source and the scope of your age-old devotion to Mary. Every flower your children lay at her feet, every song you sing to her matchless beauty, every appeal to her power and compassion must be known for what it is, first and finally: the expression and reflexion of your personal dedication, after her example, to the living Christ; to the Divine Child Whom she

[53] Cf. above, 46–47. Interestingly Pius XII cites both of these early witnesses of Marian consecration as attesting to Mary's Queenship in his encyclical *Ad Caeli Reginam, AAS* 46 (1954): 629–30; *OL,* no. 690.

[54] Cf. above, 55–56, especially the prayer of Bartolomé de los Ríos on 56.

[55] Cf. above, 102–5.

[56] Cf. Arthur B. Calkins, "Mary's Maternal Mediation and the Practice of Marian Consecration", to be published in the *Proceedings of the National Marian Year Congress,* held in Chicago, August 11–15, 1988.

[57] Garrigou-Lagrange, *Mother of the Saviour,* 270–76; idem, *The Three Ages of the Interior Life,* vol. 2, trans. Sr. Timothea Doyle, O.P. (St. Louis: B. Herder Book Co., 1948), 265–71.

deserved, albeit through no merit of her own, to bear at Bethlehem; to the Divine Teacher, Who deigned to be taught human wisdom at her holy home in Nazareth; to the Divine Victim and Victor over sin and death, Whose redemptive Sacrifice she saw completed on Calvary. To Jesus, then, through Mary, leads the spiritual path of that authentic Marian devotion you proudly and publicly profess once more today, at the close of her historic Centenary. If you have entrusted to her maternal care and vigilance the most delicate and urgent of your family and social problems—witness the ardent resolution of your successive Marian Congresses—the light and strength you seek is not hers to give, but only to procure from the Sacred Heart of her Son and Saviour. She is the crystal-pure Channel, not the Fountain, of that superabundant divine grace you beg through her Immaculate Heart for home and Church and country.[58]

The theme of Mary's mediatory role in our salvation is not entirely absent in Father De Fiores' discussion of the problematic consecration/entrustment to Mary as he cites contemporary authors,[59] although he gives it scant attention elsewhere in his study of contemporary Mariology where he considers it in an ecumenical context and seems to opt for the concept of "presence" as a more auspicious route to be pursued in dialogue.[60]

Happily, Father Alfredo Marranzini, S.J., in his analysis of the theological significance of the Pope's Act of Consecration and Entrustment of 1984 touches upon both of these themes as he attempts to sum up the nature of this act. His definition would seem to provide an appropriate conclusion to our consideration of contemporary theological reflection

[58] *AAS* 46 (1954): 726–27.

[59] Cf. De Fiores, *Maria nella Teologia Contemporanea*, quoting K. Rahner, 320, and J. Alfaro, 322.

[60] Ibid., 248–50. Cf. also his "Linee di Sviluppo della Riflessione Teologica sul Ruolo Storico di Maria", in *Il Ruolo di Maria nell'oggi della Chiesa e del Mondo* (Rome: Edizioni Marianum, 1979), 205–18, especially 208, where he considers the same proposal. In his treatment of the history of Marian consecration, naturally, he averts to the principle, of necessity, "Cons.", 404–5, 408.

on the phenomenon of Marian consecration in the spiritual journey of the Church.

> This [consecration] is an act of love directed to a creature who was chosen by God in a unique manner for a mission which no one can leave out of consideration, and who has reciprocated such predilection by carrying out her duties in the most unconditional manner. Such an act of love, proximately oriented to a being who, notwithstanding her sublime holiness and her rank as Queen beside her Son, remains entirely in the human sphere, has as its only end the thrice "holy" Lord of whose glory the earth is full (cf. Is. 6:3). The acceptance of the mediation of a creature does not constitute an obstacle to an immediate offering to God and his exclusive adoration, but facilitates it and makes it concrete and in the final analysis is willed by God Himself and corresponds to our human makeup.[61]

[61] Alfredo Marranzini, S.J., "L' 'Atto di Affidamento e Consacrazione' a Maria", *Civiltà Cattolica* 135:2 (1984): 28 (my trans.). Also in "Consacrazione a Maria in Prospettiva Teologico-Antropologica", *Madonna: Rivista di Cultura Mariana* 27 (August 1979): 72–73.

PART TWO

THE THOUGHT OF POPE JOHN PAUL II

5

THE THEOLOGICAL PROBLEM OF MARIAN CONSECRATION AND THE PRINCIPLES OF ITS RESOLUTION

When one speaks of "consecration to Mary" or "to her Immaculate Heart", one immediately raises a theological question: How is it possible legitimately to apply to Mary a term which, in its elementary sense, applies only to God? Let us begin with a standard Catholic definition of the term *consecration*:

> In the strict sense, consecration signifies the total dedication of a person or thing to God and His service, and its consequent separation from ordinary human use. By the act of consecration a state or stable condition is inaugurated: what is consecrated thereafter belongs exclusively to God. In common Christian usage the term is applied to the conversion of bread and wine into the Body and Blood of Christ, to elevation to the episcopate, to the solemn blessing of churches, altars, sacred vessels, and cemeteries. But the idea of consecration is realized also in Baptism, which may indeed be called the fundamental consecration of the Christian life. Through it the baptized person, by a title distinct from that of creation, belongs and is consecrated to God. Confirmation also, and the Sacrament of Orders, involving the Christian more fully in the service of God, can be considered consecrations, or at least as enlargements of the consecration of Baptism.
>
> In addition to this type of consecration, there is another that exists when an individual not only belongs to God, but also sees the relationship and is freely determined by his own choice to

accept it, to live in accord with the responsibilities it imposes, and perhaps also to undertake good works or practices that are not obligatory by reason of his baptismal commitment. Thus, from the 4th century, the vow of virginity, accompanied by the liturgical blessing, was called a consecration. Later, the vows of religion were recognized as having a similar character. Similarly, any engagement undertaken by an individual to accept his already existing baptismal obligations, or to enlarge the scope of his service to God, can be considered a kind of consecration, although the idea is less perfectly realized in a determination not stabilized by vow and unratified by the authority of the Church.[1]

Given this definition which represents classical Catholic theology reaffirmed by the usage of the Second Vatican Council,[2] how can "consecration to Mary" escape the charge of idolatry or, at the very least, of being a misnomer? This is precisely the *status quaestionis* which must inevitably

[1] N. Lohkamp, "Consecration, Personal", in *NCE*, vol. 4 (New York: McGraw-Hill Book Co., 1967), 209; cf. also Joseph de Finance, S.J., "Consécration", in *DSp*, 2:1576–79.

[2] *LG*, no. 28, speaks of bishops as sharers in the consecration and mission of Jesus. *Christus Dominus* (Vatican II Decree on the Pastoral Office of Bishops in the Church), no. 15 (hereafter cited as *CD*), says that bishops have been consecrated as true priests of the New Testament. *Perfectae Caritatis* (Vatican II Decree on the Up-to-Date Renewal of Religious Life), no. 5 (hereafter cited as *PC*), speaks of the special consecration of religious as a fuller expression of their baptismal consecration. *AA*, no. 3, refers to the fact that all the laity by virtue of baptism and confirmation are consecrated in order to offer spiritual sacrifices and bear witness to Christ throughout the world. *Ad Gentes* (Vatican II Decree on Church's Missionary Activity), no. 18 (hereafter cited as *AG*), speaks of the deeper consecration made to God by religious as signifying the intimate nature of the Christian vocation. *AG*, no. 39, states that priests should be aware that their very lives are consecrated to the service of the missions. *Presbyterorum Ordinis* (Vatican II Decree on the Ministry and Life of Priests), no. 2 (hereafter cited as *PO*), describes bishops as sharers of the consecration and mission of Christ. *PO*, no. 7, speaks of the unity of the consecration and mission of priests and bishops. *PO*, no. 12, says that priests who have already received the consecration of baptism are consecrated to God in a new way through ordination so that they may become living instruments of Christ the Eternal Priest.

be addressed at the beginning of any such study.[3] Because this question has been posed explicitly since the dawning of the golden age of French spirituality inaugurated by Cardinal de Bérulle, which brought it into prominence, the same author cited above provides us further data that lead in the direction of a solution.

> Strictly speaking, one can consecrate himself only to God, for only God has the right to man's total dedication and service. Consecration to Christ, to the Sacred Heart, is legitimate because of the Hypostatic Union. But "consecration" to the Blessed Virgin, or even to St. Joseph or to other saints, is not unknown to Christian piety. In the case of St. Joseph or the other saints, this is to be understood as consecration in a broad sense of the term, and it signifies no more than an act of special homage to one's heavenly protector. The case of the Blessed Virgin, however, is not the same. The importance of her role in Christian spirituality is such that formulas of dedication to her appear to have more profound meaning. Her position in the economy of salvation is inseparable from that of her Son. Her desires and wants are His, and she is in a unique position to unite Christians fully, quickly, and effectively to Christ, so that dedication to her is in fact dedication to Christ. French spirituality has made much of consecration to Mary. Cardinal Bérulle encouraged the vow of servitude to Jesus and Mary. St. John Eudes propagated the devotion of consecration not only to the Sacred Heart, but to the heart of Mary as well. But the practice achieved its strongest expression in the *Traité de la vraie dévotion à la Sainte Vierge* of St. Louis Marie Grignion de Montfort. The act of personal consecration according to De Montfort, is an act of complete and total consecration. It consists in giving oneself entirely to Mary in order to belong wholly to Jesus through her.[4]

In effect the author of this article points to a resolution of this problem along two complementary lines. First and, admittedly, only very implicitly he evokes the principle of

[3] Cf. Bossard, "Se Consacrer à Marie", 97–98; Stefano De Fiores, S.M.M., *Maria: presenza viva nel popolo di Dio* (Rome: Edizioni Monfortane, 1980), 365–67; "Cons.", 395; Marranzini," L' 'Atto di Affidamento' ", 17, 19.

[4] Lohkamp, 209; cf. also de Finance, 1579–82.

analogy. Second and quite explicitly he points to the unique role of Mary in the mystery of Christ and the economy of our salvation, particularly her mediation.

The principle of analogy

I say that he evokes the principle of analogy implicitly because he says, "Strictly speaking, one can consecrate himself only to God." Father Stefano De Fiores frequently adverts to the principle of analogy in dealing with the subject of Marian consecration. Here are two excerpts from his article on consecration in the *Nuovo Dizionario di Mariologia*:

> The only way to be able to apply a term to God and to a creature is to have recourse to analogy which is based precisely on the likeness in the difference. The analogical use of consecration referred to Mary maintains a sense of "total and perpetual gift" which is required in order to bring this usage in line with the light of revelation and theology. . . .
>
> The gift to her is analogous to that which is made to God since it maintains the significance of the total and perpetual gift, but on the different level proper to a creature.[5]

Analogy, in the classical sense in which this term is used by Saint Thomas Aquinas and his followers, denotes "a kind of predication midway between univocation and equivocation".[6] Here is the Angelic Doctor's own description of what he meant by analogous predication:

> It is evident that terms which are used in this way [i.e., analogically] are intermediate between univocal and equivocal terms. In the case of univocity one term is predicated of different things according to a meaning [*ratio*] that is absolutely one and the same; for example, the term *animal*, predicated of a horse or of an ox,

[5] "Cons.", 409, 412 (my trans.); cf. also the section on the analogical use of "consecration" with regard to Mary in his *Maria nella Teologia Contemporanea,* 323–25.

[6] G. P. Klubertanz, "Analogy", in *NCE,* 1:463.

> signifies a living sensory substance. In the case of equivocity the same term is predicated of various things according to totally different meanings, as is evident from the term *dog*, predicated both of a constellation and of a certain species of animal. But in those things which are spoken of in the way mentioned previously [i.e., analogically], the same term is predicated of various things according to a meaning that is partly the same and partly different: different as regards the different modes of relation, but the same as regards that to which there is a relation. [*In his vero quae praedicto modo dicuntur, idem nomen de diversis praedicatur secundum rationem partim eamdem, partim diversam. Diversam quidem quantum ad diversos modos relationis. Eamdem vero quantum ad id ad quod fit relatio.*] [7]

Even more precisely, when one speaks of "consecration to God" and "consecration to Mary" one is effectively speaking in the first place of what the disciples of Saint Thomas call the "analogy of attribution". Gardeil says that

> in the analogy of attribution there is always a primary (or principal) analogate (or analogue), in which alone the idea, the formality, signified by the analogous term is intrinsically realized. The other (secondary) analogates have this formality predicated of them by mere extrinsic denomination.[8]

Following this paradigm, then, "consecration to God" is the primary analogate whereas "consecration to Mary" is a secondary analogate. In other words, the term "consecration" signifies something which is common to both analogates, the recognition of our dependence on them, but since God is our Creator and Mary is a creature that dependence cannot be exactly the same.[9]

[7] *In XI Metaph.* lect. 3, no. 2197, quoted in H. D. Gardeil, O.P., *Introduction to the Philosophy of St. Thomas Aquinas IV: Metaphysics,* trans. John A. Otto (St. Louis: B. Herder Book Co., 1967), 50–51.

[8] Gardeil, 53.

[9] Cf. J. Bittrémieux, "Consecratio Mundi Immaculato Cordi B. Mariae Virginis", *Ephemerides Theologicae Lovanienses* 20 (1943): 102; Roschini, "Consacrazione del Mondo", 60.

But it can be held as well that such usage of the term "consecration to Mary" is also an instance of the "analogy of proportionality" which Gardeil explains in this way:

> It will be remembered that in the analogy of attribution the (secondary) analogates are unified by being referred to a single term, the primary analogue. This marks a basic contrast with the analogy now under consideration, that of proportionality; for here the analogates are unified on a different basis, namely by reason of the proportion they have to each other. Example: in the order of knowledge we say there is an analogy between seeing (bodily vision) and understanding (intellectual vision) because seeing is to the eye as understanding is to the soul.[10]

Theologians have long recognized that there exists an analogy, a certain "likeness in difference" between Jesus and Mary, a certain symmetry and complementarity, though not identity, between them.[11]

We can say, then, that the consecration to the Immaculate Heart of Mary bears a proportionate relationship to the consecration to the Sacred Heart of Jesus because it is rooted in the latter.[12] It is interesting to note that Père Bossard, basing himself on the teaching of de Montfort, says that the consecration to Christ through Mary also implies a consecration to Mary. In that sense Mary is the means or proximate end which leads to Christ who is the final end of

[10] Gardeil, 54.

[11] On the principle of analogy as it pertains to Mariology, cf. José M. Bover, S.J., "El Principio Mariológico de Analogía", in *De Mariologia in Genere Nonnullisque Privilegiis ac Muneribus*, vol. 11 of *Alma Socia Christi: Acta Congressus Mariologici-Mariani Romae Anno Sancto MCML Celebrati* (Rome: Pontificia Academia Mariana Internationalis, 1953), 1–13 (latter hereafter cited as *ASC*); Gabriele M. Roschini, O.S.M., *Dizionario di Mariologia* (Rome: Editrice Studium, 1961), 30–31; Roschini, *Maria Santissima,* vol. 1, *Introduzione Generale,* 171–77; Brunero Gherardini, *La Madre: Maria in una sintesi storico-teologica* (Frigento: Casa Mariana Editrice, 1989), 309–10; Emile Neubert, S.M., *Mary in Doctrine* (Milwaukee: Bruce Publishing Co., 1954), 5–8.

[12] Cf. Bittrémieux, 102; Roschini, "Consacrazione del Mondo", 60.

the consecration.[13] This, in effect, is what Pius XII understood and taught regarding his consecration of the world to the Immaculate Heart of Mary.[14] In the words of Father Firmin Schmidt, O.F.M. Cap.:

> It is especially worthy of note that an obvious parallel is established between the consecration to the Sacred Heart by Leo XIII and this consecration by Pius XII to the Immaculate Heart. Consecration, by its very nature, is an expression of reverent submission and an acknowledgment of the dominion of him to whom the consecration is made. In the consecration to the Sacred Heart there is the recognition of Our Lord's supreme dominion. In the consecration to the Immaculate Heart there is also a true dominion recognized in Our Blessed Mother. However, Mary's dominion is subordinate to that of Christ and dependent upon Him. Pope Pius XII himself in subsequent documents confirmed the significant parallel between the two consecrations.[15]

In his great encyclical on the Queenship of Mary, *Ad Caeli Reginam*, the Servant of God Pius XII specifically taught that Mary's Queenship, one of the fundamental dogmatic bases of consecration to her, is analogous to the Kingship of Christ. "Mary," he said, "although in a restricted way and only by analogy [*quamvis temperato modo et analogiae ratione*], shares in the royal dignity as the Mother of Christ who is God."[16] Hence it might be said, in effect, that the magisterium of the Church recognizes an "analogy of attribution" between the consecration to the Sacred Heart of Jesus and that to the Immaculate Heart of Mary and, even more explicitly, an "analogy of proportionality". Monsignor John F. Murphy sums up the issue fairly succinctly, even while writing before the publication of *Ad Caeli Reginam*:

[13] Cf. above, 148.

[14] Cf. above, 101; 104.

[15] Firmin M. Schmidt, O.F.M.Cap., "The Universal Queenship of Mary", in *Mariology*, 2:510.

[16] *AAS* 46 (1954): 635; Mathews, 245.

In the devotion to the Sacred Heart, we consecrate ourselves to our Lord inasmuch as the redemption of Christ and the shedding of His blood gave Him a claim to all men. Analogously, a consecration can also be made to Mary because of her share in this Redemption and the all-embracing claims of her Motherhood. We say "analogously," for though the term "consecration" is used in reference to both Christ and to Mary, when used in reference to Mary and her Immaculate Heart, it has a partly identical and a partly different meaning. The difference arises because of the divergence in the sovereignty or dominion of Jesus and Mary upon which the consecration is based. The analogy, however, is not simply made metaphorically, but is an analogy of proper proportionality and, further, an analogy of attribution, for our dependence on Mary, the reason for our act, is essentially a dependence on God.[17]

On this issue we shall let Father De Fiores be a spokesman for contemporary theologians as well:

It has become an acquired datum for all that "consecration" in the strict sense and according to biblical usage implies an act of *latria* (adoration) and is reserved to God. Nevertheless it is possible to speak of consecration to Mary not merely in a metaphorical sense, but in a proper sense, even if analogical, secondary, derivative, and instrumental.[18]

Closely related to the principle of analogy in terms of seeing our relationship to Mary in proportion to our relationship to God is the traditional distinction made in Catholic theology about cult.[19] Here is a classical presentation of that doctrine:

Ordinarily understood, cult implies three acts: intellectual recognition of another's excellence, voluntary submission, and an act expressing this recognition and submission. If this cult is offered to

[17] Murphy, *Mary's Immaculate Heart,* 98.

[18] *Maria nella Teologia Contemporanea,* 323 (my trans.). Cf. also de Finance, 1579, whom he seems to follow closely on this point.

[19] Ordinarily I prefer to use this word in its Latin form [*cultus*] in order to avoid the connotations of the word "cult" in present English usage.

a person whose excellence is uncreated, it is called *latria*; if to a person whose excellence is created, it is called *dulia*. If, however, this created excellence is altogether and entirely singular, as in the case of the Blessed Mother, the cult offered is called *hyperdulia*. . . .

Participating in the virtue of religion, moreover, is the virtue of supernatural dulia and consequently that of hyperdulia. Accordingly, the devotion we manifest towards Our Lady, though immediately elicited by hyperdulia, does not for that reason fail to participate in the nature of that devotion which is the act of the virtue of religion. The devotion one has to God's saints does not terminate in them, but reaches even to God in the servants of God. . . .

Now the privileges of the Blessed Mother upon which hyperdulia is founded differ in degree and *nature* from those of the saints which cause us to venerate them. Mary shares more than the ordinary grace of adoptive filiation. To her is attributed the plenitude of grace, and over and above this great gift is added the specifically distinct privilege of special affinity to God, the grace of Divine Motherhood. Mary, as the Mother of God, enjoys therefore a special relationship not only with the Second Person of the Blessed Trinity, but mediately, through Him, with the other Persons of the Godhead. All other creatures, even St. Joseph, no matter how closely associated with Christ, pertain to the Hypostatic Union only extrinsically; the Blessed Mother, however, intrinsically.[20]

It ought to be noted that these distinctions are deeply rooted in the practice of the Church and the theology of the medieval schoolmen, especially Saint Thomas Aquinas, who discusses *hyperdulia* in his *Summa Theologiae*.[21] For him the homage and worship which we owe God comes under the cardinal or moral virtue of justice of which the virtue of religion is a specific part.[22] This is to be distinguished from the infused theological virtues, such as faith, hope, and

[20] John F. Murphy, "Origin and Nature of Marian Cult", in *Mariology*, 3:10–11; cf. also A. Buono, "Hyperdulia", in *Dictionary of Mary* (New York: Catholic Book Publishing Co., 1985), 129–30.

[21] Cf. *ST*, II–II, q. 103, a. 4; III, q. 25, a. 5.

[22] Ibid., II–II, q. 81, a. 4.

charity, which have God as their object whereas the virtue of religion has as its object the honor, reverence, and worship which are owed to God as a matter of justice. Saint Thomas further distinguishes between the proper and immediate acts which this virtue elicits—acts of *cultus* in the strict sense—and those acts directed to our neighbor but ultimately motivated by the desire to honor God.[23] Hence when Monsignor Murphy speaks of *dulia* and *hyperdulia* as participating in the virtue of religion, he is following this well-established terminology.

While by no means repudiating the traditional teaching on *hyperdulia*, the Second Vatican Council, evidently because of its pastoral orientation, did not use the term in its treatment of Our Lady. However, the reality was surely confirmed.

> This cult of Mary, as it has always existed in the Church, though it is altogether singular, differs essentially from the cult of adoration, which is shown to the Incarnate Word equally with the Father and the Holy Spirit, and which the Marian cult promotes in a special way.[24]

Again, in his great *magna charta* of Marian devotion, *Marialis Cultus*, Paul VI underscores the reality of *hyperdulia* without using the term.

> The development, desired by us, of devotion to the Blessed Virgin Mary is an indication of the Church's genuine piety. This devotion fits—as we have indicated above—into the only worship that is rightly called "Christian," because it takes its origin and effectiveness from Christ, finds its complete expression in Christ, and leads through Christ in the Spirit to the Father. In the sphere of worship this devotion necessarily reflects God's redemptive plan, in which a special form of veneration is appropriate to the singular place

[23] Ibid., a. 1, ad 1.

[24] *LG*, no. 66; Unger, 16. In *Redemptoris Mater,* no. 42, John Paul II adds a further gloss to this assertion of the Council: "This cult is altogether special; it bears in itself and *expresses* the profound *link* which exists *between the Mother of Christ and the Church*" (*Inseg* X:1 [1987], 731; St. Paul ed., 60).

which Mary occupies in that plan. Indeed every authentic development of Christian worship is necessarily followed by a fitting increase of veneration for the Mother of the Lord. Moreover, the history of piety shows how "the various forms of devotion towards the Mother of God that the Church has approved within the limits of wholesome and orthodox doctrine" have developed in harmonious subordination to the worship of Christ, and have gravitated towards this worship as to their natural and necessary point of reference.[25]

Before continuing the thread of our exposition of the *status quaestionis* following the lines suggested in Father Lohkamp's article cited above, I would like to discuss briefly the question of the nature of Marian consecration as an act of the virtue of religion in order to establish a further point of reference in our inquiry into the "program of consecration and entrustment" to Mary of Pope John Paul II. I present first the conclusion of a rigorous study of Marian consecration according to the canons of classic Thomistic theology. This study was done by Father Juan Ramón Urquía Barroso, S.M., and presented to the Faculty of Theology of the University of Fribourg in 1958. Father Urquía draws a conclusion which we are now in a position to comprehend more readily, given the exposition of terms already presented.

Marian consecration, we say, is an elicit act of Religion. It is what is deduced in projecting over the previous positive results the light of Moral Theology, such as St. Thomas and his best commentators expound it. Thus we emphasize the essential religious value of certain acts of cult which are performed in honor of Mary. Not all of them are elicit acts of hyperdulia. There are some, such as prayer and sacrifice, whose intrinsic religious nature can not be justified either by the implicit religious character of hyperdulia, or by the governance of religion, or even less by attributing a strictly religious but relative value to them. The same thing occurs with Marian consecration. It is not an act of hyperdulia, but of religion.

[25] *AAS* 66 (1974): 134; Paul VI, *Mary—God's Mother and Ours,* 97.

> From religion it receives its essential content. Only God can require of man an act such as implies an absolute submission. Strictly speaking, we do not consecrate ourselves to Mary as the object *cui*, but to God through Her mediation. Such a consecration renders religious cult to God as Supreme Being, and a cult of hyperdulia to Mary as Mediatrix at the same time. By this we do not impoverish Marian consecration. On the contrary, it is precisely as an act of religion that it acquires its full value, that which has been given to it throughout history, and which with greater or less clarity we really express in saying that we consecrate ourselves to Mary, and through her to God, or that we consecrate ourselves to God through Mary.[26]

Quite deliberately, Father Urquía rejects the principle of analogy as a solution to the theological question of Marian consecration. He is not willing to recognize that Marian consecration could be addressed immediately to God (as an act of *latria*) as well as being addressed mediately to Mary (as an act of *hyperdulia*). He will not allow that Mary could be the object *cui*, the person to whom the consecration is made, even if not the final object of the consecration. His argument seems somewhat confusing since in the final analysis, he does admit that Marian consecration renders "a cult of hyperdulia to Mary as Mediatrix at the same time".

It would seem that the crux of Urquía's problem is that he refuses to recognize what Monsignor Murphy points out, i.e., that *hyperdulia* participates in the virtue of religion. A more balanced solution of the question, which makes implicit use of the principle of analogy, still seems to be that offered by Saint Louis-Marie Grignion de Montfort: "It follows that we consecrate ourselves at one and the same time to Mary and to Jesus. We give ourselves to Mary because Jesus chose her as the perfect means to unite himself to us

[26] Juan Ramón Urquía Barroso, S.M., *The Theological Content of Consecration to Mary*, trans. Robert Wood, S.M. (Dayton: Marianist Resources Commission, n.d.), 102–3.

and unite us to him. We give ourselves to Jesus because he is our last end." [27]

I submit that this is also the sense which is assumed by the magisterium. The consecration made by Pius XII on October 31, 1942, really was addressed to Mary, as have been the subsequent pontifical acts, and he readily adverted to the fact that this consecration was complementary (analogical) to that made to the Sacred Heart of Jesus and that it was addressed to Mary as the object *cui*:

> Finally, just as the Church and the entire human race were consecrated to the Heart of your Jesus, because by placing in Him every hope, it may be for them a token and pledge of victory and salvation; so, henceforth, may they be perpetually consecrated to you, to your Immaculate Heart [*così parimenti da oggi siano essi in perpetuo consacrati anche a Voi, al vostro Cuore Immacolato*], O Our Mother and Queen of the world, in order that your love and protection may hasten the triumph of the Kingdom of God.[28]

To what extent do the Marian consecrations of Pope John Paul II verify the conclusions we have reached? Surely he uses the language of analogy while favoring the term *entrust* by using it much more frequently than *consecrate.* Granted that he does not explicitly call our attention to the fact that he is making use of the principle of analogy in the examples which we are about to cite, in a number of his more theological addresses and documents he does advert to that principle.[29] His most illuminating statements on this

[27] *True Devotion,* no. 125; cf. also Franzi, "Per un orientamento", 8.

[28] *AAS* 34 (1942): 318–19, 325; *OL,* no. 380 (alt.). Pius was quite explicit about the analogy between the Kingship of Christ and the Queenship of Mary, which both provide solid doctrinal bases for the respective consecrations, as we have noted above on pages 91–92 and 154.

[29] Cf. his encyclical *Dominum et Vivificantem,* no. 64 (*Inseg* IX:1 [1986], 1543; *ORE* 940:14); his address to entrepreneurs in Buenos Aires of April 11, 1987 (*Inseg* X:1 [1987], 1250; *ORE* 988:13); his homily for the First Sunday of Lent, February 21, 1988 (*Inseg* XI:1 [1988], 492–93; *ORE* 1030:10); his address to the first group of the bishops of India on the "ad limina" visit, April 6, 1989 (*Inseg* XII:1 [1989], 749; *ORE* 1085:3).

subject for our purposes would seem to be in his apostolic letter *Mulieris Dignitatem* issued on the occasion of the closing of the Marian Year:

> *God speaks in human language*, using human concepts and images. If this manner of expressing himself is characterized by a certain anthropomorphism, the reason is that man is "like" God: created in his image and likeness. But then, *God too* is in some measure "like man", and precisely because of this likeness, he can be humanly known. At the same time, the language of the Bible is sufficiently precise to indicate the limits of the "likeness", the limits of the "analogy". For biblical Revelation says that, while man's "likeness" to God is true, the "*non-likeness*" which separates the whole of creation from the Creator is *still more essentially true.* Although man is created in God's likeness, God does not cease to be for him the one "who dwells in unapproachable light" (1 Tim. 6:16): he is the "Different One", by essence the "totally Other".[30]
>
> If God's love for the human person, for the Chosen People of Israel, is presented by the Prophets as the love of the bridegroom for the bride, such an analogy expresses the "spousal" quality and the divine and non-human character of God's love: "For your Maker is your husband . . . the God of the whole earth he is called" (Is. 54:5). The same can also be said of the spousal love of Christ the Redeemer: "For God so loved the world that he gave his only Son" (Jn. 3:16). It is a matter, therefore, of God's love expressed by means of the Redemption accomplished by Christ. According to Saint Paul's Letter, this love is "like" the spousal love of human spouses, but naturally it is not "the same". For the analogy implies a likeness, while at the same time leaving ample room for non-likeness.[31]

Here, then, follow some examples of his analogous use of the term *entrustment* (and other cognate forms) on the levels of both *latria* and *hyperdulia*:

[30] *Inseg* XI:3 (1988), 258–59, 330; *ORE* 1058:4.

[31] *Inseg* XI:3 (1988), 301, 366; *ORE* 1058:11. In this case the Latin word rendered into English as "analogy" is *comparatio*, but the text still serves admirably as a depiction of the classic scholastic concept of analogy, likeness in difference.

I am going to the Basilica of Notre-Dame, the Mother of the Churches of this diocese and one of the most venerable religious buildings of this nation. There I wish to entrust to the Lord and to the Blessed Virgin my wishes for the whole of the French people.[32]

God bless Brazil! I entrust it to Christ and to his Mother: Mary "Aparecida."[33]

Praying, I entrust to Christ and his Mother all that has been accomplished in the last few months and is being accomplished.[34]

Entrust yourselves to him [Christ] in your daily prayer, entrust yourselves to Mary, the Mother of Sorrows.[35]

And now, Lord, I beseech You for my brothers and sisters, the Catholics of the Congo. I entrust them to You, since You have permitted me to visit them in their country. . . . I entrust them also to Your holy Mother, the Blessed Virgin Mary, Mother of the Church and our Mother. May she take them under her motherly protection and watch over them in their difficulties! May she teach them to stand at the foot of Your cross and to gather around her while waiting for Your coming at the end of time![36]

Here are representative instances of the linking of *hyperdulia* and *dulia*:

May God preserve you, Turin! And you, always keep his Law! May God reward you, Turin, for this hospitality that you have given today to this Pope John Paul II who came to you as a pilgrim! This is my wish, which I entrust to the Great Mother of God, to the intercession of your Saints, to your goodwill![37]

I entrust these sentiments to the prayer that we now raise to Our Lady and to the intercession of the Martyr Paul Miki and his

[32] *Inseg* III:1 (1980), 1522; *France: Message of Peace, Trust, Love and Faith* (Boston: St. Paul Editions, 1980), 26 (hereafter cited as *France*).

[33] *Inseg* III:2 (1980), 270; *Brazil,* 390.

[34] *Inseg* III:2 (1980), 1792, 1794; *ORE* 668:18.

[35] *Inseg* IV:1 (1981), 910; *ORE* 679:7.

[36] *Inseg* III:1 (1980), 1147; *Africa Ap,* 148.

[37] *Inseg* III:1 (1980), 918; *ORE* 630:11.

heroic companions who met death proclaiming the blessed names of Jesus and Mary.[38]

I am happy to entrust this prayer to the intercession of the Blessed Virgin, "Salus Populi Romani," who has so often, in the course of the centuries, borne witness to her motherly care for this city. And I entrust it also to the intercession of the Holy Apostles Peter and Paul, whose blood bathed this Rome of ours, drawing from it that germination of Christian faith, which no event, however adverse, was ever subsequently able to suffocate.[39]

Finally, I entrust you to the intercession of all the holy martyrs of Nagasaki, and especially to the protection of Mary, Queen of Martyrs and Mother of the Church.[40]

I entrust these wishes to Saints Benedict, Cyril and Methodius, the Patron Saints of Europe; I entrust these wishes to the Blessed Virgin, the Queen of Peace; finally I entrust these wishes of mine to the Blessed Virgin of Jasna Góra, the Mother of Poland.[41]

In all your efforts I commend you to the Blessed Virgin Mary and to Saint Joseph, to whom the Cathedrals of Trivandrum are dedicated.[42]

To him [Saint Joseph], and to the Virgin Mary, I wish to entrust all of you today, along with your fellow workers—your brothers and sisters—throughout Italy and the world.[43]

Lastly, here are illustrations of the analogous application of entrustment on the level of *latria*, *hyperdulia*, and *dulia* simultaneously:

[38] *Inseg* III:2 (1980), 1103; *ORE* 658:2.

[39] *Inseg* IV:1 (1981), 120; *ORE* 671:7.

[40] *Inseg* IV:1 (1981), 559; *The Far East: Journey of Peace and Brotherhood* (Boston: St. Paul Editions, 1981), 308 (hereafter cited as *Far East*).

[41] *Inseg* IV:1 (1981), 806; *ORE* 678:2.

[42] *Inseg* IX:1 (1986), 393.

[43] *Inseg* XI:2 (1988), 1095; *ORE* 1040:8.

> To the Holy Family of Nazareth I entrust every family, and I cordially impart to you, Venerable Brothers and beloved sons and daughters, especially to every home, my Apostolic Blessing.[44]

> To this Holy Family of Nazareth, unparalleled model of every familial community, human and Christian, I entrust the sacred pledge which you have assumed before God, the Church, and society, as well as your intentions, your ideals, and your plans.[45]

> I entrust each family to Him [Christ the Lord], to Mary, and to Joseph. To their hands and their hearts I offer this Exhortation: May it be they who present it to you, venerable Brothers and beloved sons and daughters, and may it be they who open your hearts to the light that the Gospel sheds on every family.[46]

While, then, it may be readily admitted that the Holy Father speaks of entrustment (and its cognate forms) to God, to Mary, and to the saints analogously, even though in each of these cases the meaning is proportionately different, would he hold that Marian consecration (or entrustment) is in the first instance an act of religion (hence *latria*) and secondarily an act of *hyperdulia*? The following illustrations should point in the direction of a reply:

> Once more I entrust you to Christ through the hands and the heart of *the Mother of God*.[47]

> Therefore in particularly difficult days my thought turns to Divine Providence and, *through the intercession of the Queen of Poland, the Mother of Christ,* entrusts to it this beloved nation of mine, my homeland.[48]

> I entrust your concerns and your hopes—through the hands of the *Blessed Virgin*, venerated with such love and confidence by the Rumanian ecclesiastical community—to the Almighty and Merciful Lord.[49]

[44] *Inseg* III:2 (1980), 391, 394; *ORE* 646:19.

[45] *Inseg* IV:1 (1981), 35 (my trans.).

[46] *Inseg* IV:2 (1981), 1045, 1130; *ORE* 715:18.

[47] *Inseg* I (1978), 57; *Talks*, 118 (my emphasis).

[48] *Inseg* IV:2 (1981), 1279, 1280–81; *ORE* 717:14 (my emphasis).

[49] *Inseg* V:1 (1982), 52; *ORE* 724:12 (my emphasis).

> And through *the motherly intercession of the Virgin of the Angels*, I entrust all of you to the goodness of God.[50]

> I entrust you to Jesus, the Good Shepherd, through the mediation of his Mother, who is also our Mother.[51]

> Our Lady of Peace, once again we entrust to you the Church of this diocese, of all the dioceses of this country. Through your mediation we consecrate them to your Son.[52]

> Let us commend the souls of our loved ones to the Blessed Virgin, whom we invoke as "Queen of Saints". Through her, whose image is often found on Christian tombs, let us entrust to God's mercy all the souls who are waiting to be received into the eternal dwellings.[53]

These examples clearly demonstrate a Christocentric, and ultimately theocentric, perspective on the Pope's part. But is this always the case, especially in the explicitly Marian consecrations? First, let us listen to the Pope's description of what he was about to do at Fatima on May 13, 1982, in the homily which preceded the act of consecration.

> Consecrating the world to the Immaculate Heart of Mary means drawing near, *through the Mother's intercession*, to the very Fountain of life that sprang from Golgotha. . . . It means consecrating this world to the pierced heart of the Savior, bringing it back to the very source of its redemption. . . .
>
> *Consecrating ourselves to Mary means accepting her help to offer ourselves and the whole of mankind to Him* who is holy, infinitely holy; it means accepting her help—by having recourse to her motherly heart, which beneath the cross was opened to love for every human being, for the whole world—in order to offer the world, the individual human being, mankind as a whole, and all the nations to Him who is infinitely holy. . . .

[50] *Inseg* V:1 (1982), 854; *ORE* 728:10 (my emphasis).

[51] *Inseg* IX:2 (1988), 1224; *ORE* 1041:5.

[52] *ORE* 1157:13.

[53] *ORE* 1215:1.

My heart is oppressed when I see the sin of the world and the whole range of menaces gathering like a dark cloud over mankind, but it also rejoices with hope as I once more do what has been done by my Predecessors, when they consecrated the world to the heart of the Mother, when they consecrated especially to that heart those peoples which particularly need to be consecrated. Doing this means consecrating the world to Him who is infinite holiness.[54]

Next let us listen to his greeting to English-speaking pilgrims at his first general audience in Rome after his return from Fatima.

Last week I myself went on pilgrimage to Portugal, especially to Fatima, in order to give thanks that the mercy of God and the protection of the Mother of Christ had saved my life last year. The message of Fatima is a call to conversion and penance, the first and most basic call of the Gospel. Today it is more urgent than ever, when evil is threatening us through errors based on denial of God. The message of Fatima puts us on our guard. It also invites us to approach anew the Fountain of Mercy by an act of consecration. Mary wishes us to draw near to it: each one of us, each nation, and the whole world.[55]

In this context it would be difficult not to see the above reference to "approaching anew the Fountain of Mercy by an act of consecration" as a specific reference in fact to what he did at Fatima, particularly since he used the same terminology in the homily he delivered there. Moreover in his annual visit to the Gesù on New Year's Eve of 1984, he referred to the consecration of March 25 of that year in this way:

This Act of Consecration was a drawing nearer of the world, *through the Mother of Christ and Our Mother,* to the source of life, poured out on Golgotha: it was a bringing back of the world to the same fount of Redemption, and at the same time, a recourse to

[54] *Inseg* V:2 (1982), 1573–76, 1582–84; *Portugal,* 79–83 (my emphases).
[55] *Inseg* V:2 (1982), 1763.

> the Madonna's help in order to offer men and peoples to him who is infinitely holy.[56]

Consistently, then, and hardly surprisingly, we see that the Holy Father's own testimony corroborates the great theological tradition which we have already delineated in broad strokes, i.e., that Marian consecration is in the first instance an act of religion directed to God (*latria*) without ceasing at the same time to be also an act of *hyperdulia*. The last cited quotation says this quite succinctly.

The principle of Mary's maternal mediation

We are now ready to consider the other theological principle underlying Marian consecration already alluded to in Father Lohkamp's treatment of "personal consecration". He says:

> [Mary's] position in the economy of salvation is inseparable from that of her Son. *Her desires and wants are His, and she is in a unique position to unite Christians fully, quickly, and effectively to Christ, so that dedication to her is in fact dedication to Christ.* . . . The act of personal consecration according to De Montfort, is an act of complete and total consecration. *It consists in giving oneself entirely to Mary in order to belong wholly to Jesus through her.*[57]

In effect he is simply recapitulating the fundamental thrust of Marian consecration throughout the ages and at the same time reaffirming the teaching on Mary which is detailed in the eighth chapter of *Lumen Gentium*, the Second Vatican Council's Dogmatic Constitution on the Church. While the entire eighth chapter (nos. 52–69) touches upon Mary's role in our Redemption, the following passages seem particularly pertinent to our consideration of Marian consecration:

[56] *Inseg* VII:2 (1984), 1684; *ORE* 869:4 (alt.; my emphasis).

[57] Lohkamp, 209 (my emphasis).

> This Sacred Synod, which is engaged in expounding the doctrine about the Church, in which the divine Redeemer works out our salvation, intends diligently to explain both the role of the Blessed Virgin in the mystery of the Incarnate Word and of the Mystical Body [*munus Beatae Virginis in mysterio Incarnati Verbi et Corporis Mystici*], and the duties of the redeemed people toward God's mother, that is, the Mother of Christ and the Mother of all people, especially of the believers.[58]

> To that heavenly messenger she gave the reply: "Behold the handmaid of the Lord, be it done to me according to thy word" (Lk. 1:38). In that way Mary, a daughter of Adam, by giving consent to the Divine Word, became the Mother of Jesus. And as she embraced God's salvific will with all her heart and unhampered by any sin, she devoted herself totally as the Lord's handmaid to the person and work of her Son. Thus, in virtue of the grace of God Almighty, *she put herself, under him and together with him, in the service of the mystery of redemption.* [*Semetipsam ut Domini ancillam personae et operi Filii sui totaliter devovit, sub Ipso et cum Ipso, omnipotentis Dei gratia, mysterio redemptionis inserviens.*] Rightly therefore the Holy Fathers believe that Mary was used by God not merely passively, but that she cooperated by a free faith and obedience in human salvation. Really, as St. Irenaeus said, she, being "obedient became the cause of salvation both for herself and for the whole human race."[59]

If the above texts underscore the unique, unparalleled role of Mary in our salvation (in the language of *Lumen Gentium*, "in the mystery of Christ and of the Church"), then the ensuing passage does so in a way that bears very directly on the issue of Marian consecration:

> This motherhood of Mary in the economy of grace, moreover, perdures unceasingly, beginning with the consent she trustingly gave at the annunciation, which she upheld unwaveringly under the cross, even to the perpetual fulfillment of all the elect. To wit, when she had been taken into heaven, she did not lay aside this

[58] *LG*, no. 54; Unger, 7.

[59] *LG*, no. 56; Unger, 9 (my emphasis).

> saving role; rather, she continues by her manifold intercession to win for us the gifts of eternal salvation. . . . No creature, really, can ever be put in a class with the Incarnate Word and Redeemer. Nevertheless, just as Christ's priesthood is shared in, by various ways, both by the ministers and by the believing people, and just as the one goodness of God is in reality poured out upon creatures in diverse ways, in the same manner, the unique mediation of the Redeemer does not exclude, in fact it calls forth, from the one fountainhead, a varied cooperation shared among the creatures. The Church does not hesitate to profess such a subordinate role of Mary. She has experience of it constantly and commends it to the hearts of the faithful, with a view that, supported by her motherly protection, they may cling more intimately to the Mediator and Savior. [*Tale autem munus subordinatum Mariae Ecclesia profiteri non dubitat, iugiter experitur et fidelium cordi commendat, ut hoc materno fulti praesidio Mediatori ac Salvatori intimius adhaereant.*] [60]

The conciliar teaching on the presence of Mary in the mystery of Christ and the Church was readily assimilated by the archbishop of Krakow and given expression in his *vademecum* on the documents of the Second Vatican Council. Here is how he presented it to the clergy, religious, and faithful of his archdiocese:

> In our present study, which is concerned with the enrichment of faith in the ways pointed out by Vatican II, we must first underline the solution chosen by the Council with its decision not to promulgate a separate document concerning Our Lady but to include what would have been the content of such a document in the Dogmatic Constitution on the Church. This in a sense confirms that *the mind of the Church is permeated in a special way by the mystery of the Mother of God, which is fully present in the mystery of Christ the Incarnate Word and hence in that of the Mystical Body of Christ.* [61]
>
> As will be seen, the whole attitude of the ancient and modern Church to the Mother of God is based not only on the exceptional honour due to her divine maternity but also on her awareness of

[60] *LG,* no. 62; Unger, 13.

[61] Wojtyła, *Sources of Renewal,* 100–101 (my emphasis).

the redemption and her own participation in the work of Christ: she "cooperated in the work of man's salvation," as the Constitution says. This active cooperation on Mary's part is expressed above all in her obedience. By being thus obedient she did not merely submit passively to the salvific action of the Most Holy Trinity, but with all her life and behaviour embraced it and shared in it: so that *our consciousness of redemption must always see the "maternal act" as united to not only the "act of Christ" but also "under and with him,"* as the Council declares.[62]

Very significantly, in the immediate postconciliar period Cardinal Wojtyła was already giving positive attention to the mediatorial role of Mary. Others at that time were preoccupied with explaining that Mary's mediation does not compete with that of Christ and with debunking the caricature of Mary's mediation as a shield of mercy against the wrath of her Son.[63] It is also interesting to note the consistency of Wojtyła's thought. He already uses the term "maternal mediation", which will be one of the great highlights of his Marian Year encyclical *Redemptoris Mater*:

Mary's divine maternity is a unique fact in the history of our salvation, closely linked with the incarnation of the Word to which it belongs. But her spiritual maternity in the order of grace goes far beyond that fact, extending as widely as her Son's work of redemption "until the eternal fulfillment of all the elect" (*LG* 62). *The Mother of God fulfills her universal maternity as a mediatrix in the economy of grace.* The Church professes its faith in that maternal

[62] Ibid., 105 (my emphasis).

[63] Cf. Eamon R. Carroll, O. Carm., *Understanding the Mother of Jesus* (Wilmington, Del.: Michael Glazier, 1979), 81–82, 92–96; Frederick M. Jelly, O.P., "The Mystery of Mary's Mediation", *Homiletic and Pastoral Review* 80, no. 8 (1980): 11–20; Anthony J. Tambasco, *What are they saying about Mary?* (New York: Paulist Press, 1984), 46–48. The brief treatment of this matter by Dr. Tambasco seems notably flawed by his unwillingness to take a clear position with regard to the reparative value of the Redemption and, consequently, with regard to Mary's unique collaborative role in it. For a résumé of the whole question, cf. Roschini, *Maria Santissima,* vol. 2, *Il Dogma Mariano, Parte I,* 111–252; Gherardini, 287–324.

mediation of divine grace, while clearly distinguishing it from the mediation of the Redeemer himself. . . .

Thus the mediation of the Mother of God is subordinate to the unique mediation of Christ, which alone constitutes the foundation and source of the supernatural economy of grace and salvation. *Nevertheless Mary's mediation, as an expression of her spiritual maternity in the order of grace, is universal in its range and is specially efficacious.*[64]

Not only was the conciliar teaching on Mary's insertion into the mystery of Christ and her maternal mediation deeply appreciated and consistently preached by our Holy Father as archbishop of Krakow,[65] but it also has become a keystone of his papal service as Bishop of Rome. Here is a portion of his treatment of this theme in his first encyclical letter.

The aim of any service in the Church, whether the service is apostolic, pastoral, priestly or episcopal, is to keep up this dynamic link between the mystery of the Redemption and every man.

If we are aware of this task, then we seem to understand better what it means to say that the Church is a mother and also what it means to say that the Church always, and particularly at our time, has need of a Mother. We owe a debt of special gratitude to the Fathers of the Second Vatican Council, who expressed this truth in the Constitution *Lumen Gentium* with the rich Mariological doctrine contained in it. . . .

We who form today's generation of disciples of Christ all wish to unite ourselves with her [Mary] in a special way. We do so with all our attachment to our ancient tradition and also with full respect and love for the members of all the Christian Communities.

We do so at the urging of the deep need of faith, hope and charity. For if we feel a special need, in this difficult and responsible phase of the history of the Church and of mankind, to turn to Christ, who is Lord of the Church and Lord of man's history on

[64] *Sources of Renewal,* 107–8 (my emphases).

[65] E.g., *Omelie,* passim.

account of the mystery of the Redemption, we believe that *nobody else can bring us as Mary can into the divine and human dimension of this mystery.*[66] Nobody has been brought into it by God himself as Mary has. [*Probe arbitramur neminem ut Mariam nos inducere posse in rationem divinam et humanum eiusmodi mysterii. Nemo ut Maria eo introductus est ab ipso Deo.*] It is in this that the exceptional character of the grace of the divine Motherhood consists. Not only is the dignity of this Motherhood unique and unrepeatable in the history of the human race, but Mary's participation, due to this Maternity, in God's plan for man's salvation through the mystery of the Redemption is also unique in profundity and range of action. . . .

The Father's eternal love, which has been manifested in the history of mankind through the Son whom the Father gave, "that whoever believes in him should not perish but have eternal life," comes close to each of us through this Mother and thus takes on tokens that are of more easy understanding and access by each person. Consequently, *Mary must be on all the ways for the Church's daily life.* [*Ita fit, ut Maria in omnibus viis cotidianae vitae Ecclesiae versetur oporteat.*] *Through her maternal presence the Church acquires certainty that she is truly living the life of her Master and Lord and that she is living the mystery of the Redemption in all its life-giving profundity and fullness.*[67]

In this highly significant excerpt of *Redemptor Hominis*, one sees how fully John Paul II has appropriated the eighth chapter of *Lumen Gentium* on the presence of Mary in the mystery of Christ and the Church and at the same time made it uniquely his own. Already in this text one can clearly see the foundation of the teaching he will develop on Mary's maternal mediation in *Redemptoris Mater*: no one

[66] Interestingly, in this passage the Pope is reiterating a theme which he had sounded already in his article entitled, "Oddanie Bogurodzicy w świetle nauki Soboru" [Self-giving to the Mother of God in the light of the Council's teaching]: "No one knows how to introduce us to the work of Christ, into His work, into Redemption, as His Mother—because no one else is so present to 'the mystery of Christ and His Church' as she is" (trans. Dr. John Grondelski/Fr. Bernard Przewozny, O.F.M. Conv.).

[67] *Redemptor Hominis,* no. 22, *Inseg* II:1 (1979), 606–8, 658–59; *Messages,* 558–61 (my emphases).

else can conduct us as Mary can into the mystery of the Redemption.

By his vigorous insistence on the conciliar teaching on Mary's role in the mystery of Christ and the Church, which is "a mystery best described dynamically as her maternal mediation",[68] he is effectively providing a necessary theological foundation for his "program of consecration and entrustment". The most developed presentation of his teaching on Mary's mediation is to be found in *Redemptoris Mater*, numbers 38–41. Although a very significant body of papal doctrine had already evolved on this issue,[69] the cli-

[68] Peter D. Fehlner, O.F.M. Conv., "Mulieris Dignitatem", *Miles Immaculatae* 25 (1989): 9.

[69] Benedict XIV, apostolic constitution *Gloriosae Dominae* of September 27, 1748 (*OL*, no. 4); Pius VII, apostolic constitution *Quod Divino Afflata Spiritu* of January 24, 1806 (*OL*, no. 14); Venerable Pius IX, encyclical letter *Ubi Primum* of February 2, 1849 (*OL*, no. 23); apostolic constitution *Ineffabilis Deus* of December 8, 1854 (*OL*, no. 64); Leo XIII, encyclical letter *Supremi Apostolatus* of September 1, 1883 (*ASS* 16 [1889]: 113; *OL*, no. 81); encyclical letter *Octobri Mense* of September 22, 1891 (*ASS* 24 [1891–1892]: 195–96; *OL*, nos. 113–14); encyclical letter *Jucunda Semper* of September 8, 1894 (*ASS* 27 [1894–1895]: 178–80, 182–84; *OL*, nos. 149–52, 155–56, 161, 163); encyclical letter *Adiutricem Populi* of September 5, 1895 (*ASS* 28 [1895–1896]: 130–31; *OL*, nos. 169–72); encyclical letter *Fidentem Piumque* of September 20, 1896 (*ASS* 29 [1896–1897]: 206; *OL*, no. 194); letter to the archbishop of Turin *Mariani Coetus* of August 2, 1898 (*OL*, no. 209); St. Pius X, encyclical letter *Ad Diem Illum* of February 2, 1904 (*ASS* 36 [1903–1904]: 450–51; *OL*, nos. 222, 224, 226–28, 233–35); letter *Summa Deus Hominum* of November 27, 1907 (*OL*, no. 253); Benedict XV, Allocution to the Consistory of December 24, 1915 (*OL*, no. 261); letter *Il 27 Aprile 1915* to Cardinal Pietro Gaspari of May 5, 1917 (*AAS* 9 [1917]: 266; *OL*, no. 263); letter *Inter Sodalicia* of May 22, 1918 (*AAS* 10 [1918]:182; *OL*, nos. 267–68); allocution *Il Nous serait difficile* of April 6, 1919 (*OL*, nos. 271–72); Pius XI, encyclical letter *Miserentissimus Redemptor* of May 8, 1928 (*AAS* 20 [1928]: 178; *OL*, no. 287); encyclical letter *Caritate Christi Compulsi* of May 3, 1932 (*AAS* 24 [1932]: 192; Carlen 3:482); Homily given at reading of Decree "de tuto" for the Canonization of St. Jeanne Antide Thouret of August 15, 1933 (*OL*, nos. 323, 325); encyclical letter *Ingravescentibus Malis* of September 29, 1937 (*AAS* 29 [1937]: 375, 380; *OL*, nos. 338, 343); Servant of God Pius XII, letter to Cardinal Luigi Maglione *Superiore Anno* of April 15, 1940 (*AAS* 32 [1940]: 145; *OL*, nos. 356–57); Decree "de tuto" of January 11, 1942, for the

mate at the Second Vatican Council was not auspicious for its full assimilation.[70] What John Paul has managed to do is to re-present the teaching on Marian mediation, completely in the context of the Council's presentation of Mary in the mystery of Christ and the Church and in terms of his own unique mode of thought and style of exposition.

Canonization of St. Louis-Marie Grignion de Montfort (*AAS* 34 [1942]: 44; Michael O'Carroll, C.S.Sp., *Mediatress of All Graces* [Westminster, Md.: Newman Press, 1958], 161); encyclical letter *Mystici Corporis* of June 29, 1943 (*AAS* 35 [1943]: 247–48; *OL,* no. 384); radio message *Bendito Seja O Senhor* of May 13, 1946 (*AAS* 38 [1946]: 264; *OL,* no. 407); apostolic letter *Per Christi Matrem* of May 15, 1947 (*AAS* 40 [1948]: 536; *OL,* no. 428); Allocution on the Canonization of St. Louis-Marie Grignion de Montfort of July 21, 1947 (*AAS* 39 [1947]: 410–13; *OL,* nos. 431–32); encyclical letter *Mediator Dei* of November 20, 1947 (*AAS* 39 [1947]: 582–83; *OL,* no. 440); letter *Ex Officiosis Litteris* of February 15, 1948 (*AAS* 40 [1948]: 107–8; *OL,* no. 444); exhortation to priests *Menti Nostrae* of November 23, 1950 (*AAS* 42 [1950]: 701; *OL,* nos. 465, 466); encyclical letter *Doctor Mellifluus* of May 25, 1953 (*AAS* 45 [1953]: 382; *OL,* no. 578); Radio Message to Italian Catholic Action of December 8, 1953 (*AAS* 45 [1953]: 850–51; *OL,* nos. 624–25); encyclical letter *Sacra Virginitas* of March 25, 1954 (*AAS* 46 [1954]; 189; *OL,* no. 641); encyclical letter *Ad Caeli Reginam* of October 11, 1954 (*AAS* 46 [1954]: 636–37; *OL,* no. 709); Radio Message to National Marian Congress of India of December 8, 1954 (*AAS* 46 [1954]: 727; *OL,* no. 760); letter *Gloriosam Reginam* of December 8, 1955 (*AAS* 48 [1956]: 75; *OL,* no. 770); encyclical letter *Haurietis Aquas* of May 15, 1956 (*AAS* 48 [1956]: 352; *OL,* no. 778); apostolic constitution *Sedes Sapientiae* of May 31, 1956 (*AAS* 48 [1956]: 354; *OL,* no. 779); Servant of God John XXIII, Allocution at St. Mary Major of February 15, 1959 (*AAS* 51 [1959]: 136; *OL,* no. 851); Paul VI, Address at Lombard Seminary of December 8, 1966 (Domenico Bertetto, S.D.B., *La Madonna nella Parola di Paolo VI,* 2nd ed. [Rome: Libreria Ateneo Salesiano, 1980], 408); letter *Gloriosa Dicta* of April 15, 1967 (*AAS* 59 [1967]: 484); apostolic exhortation *Signum Magnum* of May 13, 1967 (*AAS* 59 [1967]: 465–75; St. Paul Editions, National Catholic Welfare Conference [NCWC] trans. 4, 7, 8); Homily at Beatification of St. Maximilian Kolbe of October 17, 1971 (*Insegnamenti di Paolo VI* IX [1971], 907–9; *TPS* 16 [1971]: 240–41); letter *E' con sentimenti* of May 13, 1975, to Cardinal Suenens (*AAS* 67 [1975]: 358; *Mary—God's Mother and Ours,* 194–95).

[70] Cf. *Theotokos,* 242–45; Michael O'Carroll, C.S.Sp., "Still Mediatress of All Graces?" *Miles Immaculatae* 24 (1988): 122–25; Thomas Mary Sennott, "Mary, Mediatrix of All Graces, Vatican II and Ecumenism", *Miles Immaculatae* 24 (1988): 151–54; Most, "Marian Consecration as Service", 453, n. 52.

At the press conference on the day of the release of *Redemptoris Mater*, March 25, 1987, Cardinal Joseph Ratzinger, prefect of the Congregation for the Doctrine of the Faith, said of the Pope's treatment of the issue of Our Lady's mediation:

> Without doubt this is the point on which theological and ecumenical discussion will be concentrated. The Second Vatican Council also had already made use of the title "Mediatrix" (*LG* 62) and spoke of the extent of Mary's mediation (*LG* 60 and 62). However, until the present time this subject had never been dealt with so extensively in a document of the Magisterium. As regards its content, the encyclical does not go beyond what was already said by the Council, whose terminology it follows. However, it examines more deeply the Council's statements and gives them a new weight for theology and religious piety.[71]

Here I simply wish to allow the Pope to present his own teaching on Mary's "maternal mediation":

> In effect, Mary's mediation *is intimately linked with her motherhood.* It possesses a specifically maternal character, which distinguishes it from the mediation of the other creatures who in various and always subordinate ways share in the one mediation of Christ, although her own mediation is also a shared mediation. In fact, while it is true that "no creature could ever be classed with the Incarnate Word and Redeemer," at the same time "the unique mediation of the Redeemer does not exclude but rather gives rise among creatures to *a manifold cooperation* which is but a sharing in this unique source."[72]
>
> Mary *entered, in a way all her own, into the one mediation "between God and men" which is the mediation of the man Christ Jesus.* If she was the first to experience within herself the supernatural consequences of this one mediation—in the Annunciation she had been greeted as "full of grace"—then we must say that through

[71] *ORE* 981:21.

[72] *Inseg* X:1 (1987), 724–25; St. Paul ed., 54.

this fullness of grace and supernatural life she was especially predisposed to cooperation with Christ, the one Mediator of human salvation. *And such cooperation is precisely this mediation subordinated* to the mediation of Christ.[73]

Mary, who from the beginning had given herself without reserve to the person and work of her Son, could not but pour out upon the Church, from the very beginning, her maternal self-giving. After her Son's departure, her motherhood remains in the Church as maternal mediation: interceding for all her children, the Mother cooperates in the saving work of her Son, the Redeemer of the world. In fact the Council teaches that the "motherhood of Mary in the order of grace . . . *will last without interruption* until the eternal fulfillment of all the elect" (*Lumen Gentium* no. 62). With the redeeming death of her Son, the maternal mediation of the handmaid of the Lord took on a universal dimension, for the work of redemption embraces the whole of humanity.[74]

The excerpts which we have presented, especially the above selections of *Redemptoris Mater*, provide strong evidence of the Pope's thorough grasp of Mary's mediation, subordinate and secondary to that of Christ, completely derivative from it and totally dependent upon it and at the same time "special and extraordinary" [*Quod munus est et peculiare et extraordinarium*].[75] Since her capacity for being a mediatrix is proportionally analogous to her being [*agere sequitur esse*], Mary's is the highest form of all modes of creaturely mediation. This in turn is proportionally analogous to the honor which we owe her [*hyperdulia*] which surpasses that owed to all the saints and angels. All of this, then, provides the context of the proposal which John Paul II makes toward the end of his Marian Year encyclical:

I would like to recall, among the many witnesses and teachers of this [Marian] spirituality, the figure of Saint Louis-Marie Grignion

[73] *Inseg* X:1 (1987), 727; St. Paul ed., 56.

[74] *Inseg* X:1 (1987), 727–28; St. Paul ed., 57.

[75] *Inseg* X:1 (1987), 725, 727; St. Paul ed., 54, 56.

de Montfort, who proposes *consecration to Christ through the hands of Mary*, as an effective means for Christians to live faithfully their baptismal commitments. I am pleased to note that in our own time too new manifestations of this spirituality and devotion are not lacking.[76]

Without a clear grasp of the authentic doctrine of Marian mediation, it is impossible to build a solid foundation for the practice of Marian consecration. This John Paul has no doubt perceived since his reading of de Montfort as a young man. An excellent illustration of his thorough grasp and application of this principle may be found in his prayer of entrusting Zaire to Our Lady on the hundredth anniversary of its initial consecration and evangelization:

Permit me, O Mother of Christ and Mother of the Church, permit me, Pope John Paul II, who has the privilege of taking part in this jubilee, to recall and at the same time renew this missionary consecration which took place in this land at the beginning of its evangelization.

To consecrate itself to Christ through you! To consecrate itself to you for Christ![77]

[76] *Inseg* X:1 (1987), 739; St. Paul ed., 68 (my emphasis).

[77] *Inseg* III:1 (1980), 1069; *Africa Ap*, 41 (my emphasis).

6

THE CHRIST-CENTERED CHARACTER OF THE ACT OF CONSECRATION

In his annual "Survey of Recent Mariology" for 1984, Father Eamon R. Carroll, O. Carm., noted that "the deeply Christological character of the 'act of entrusting' " of March 25, 1984, had gone largely unnoticed.[1] He took up this theme again in a talk presented on September 7, 1985, to a conference of the Western Region of the Mariological Society of America at Saint Mary's Cathedral in San Francisco. Speaking about that "act of entrusting of the world to the Blessed Virgin" near the end of the Extraordinary Holy Year of the Redemption he said:

> What was missed was the intensely Christ-centered character of the "act of entrusting," that it was basically an association with the consecration that Jesus made of himself to the Father's will and to his redemptive mission, that, after the example of our Lady and with her assistance, we too are to enter into the consecration Jesus made of himself, just as in the Eucharist (Prayer Three) we beg the Father to send upon us the Spirit of his Son to make us an "everlasting gift," that is a permanent victim together with Christ. . . .
>
> Any genuine Christian consecration can only be a sharing in the consecration of Christ, a participation in his self-consecration: "For these I consecrate myself, so that they may be consecrated in truth" (Jn. 17:19). Any consecration we make can only be a

[1] *Marian Studies* 35 (1984): 167–68.

> response to the consecratory action of God, to his gift in Christ Jesus. The Savior shares his own self-consecration in various ways: he communicates his holiness to us by many gifts, for example, the sacraments of baptism and the Eucharist, his holy word, his Spirit and his Mother.[2]

Rightly Father Carroll emphasizes the Christocentrism of the 1984 act of entrusting. Of course, the same may be said for the 1982 act at Fatima which was substantially the same text, as the Holy Father himself told the bishops of the world in his letter to them dated December 8, 1983.[3]

What he underscores in both of these references is the Holy Father's quotation of John 17:19. This occurs in both the 1982[4] and 1984[5] acts of consecration/entrustment and in the homily given at the Mass in Fatima which preceded the act of consecration.[6] This is surely one of John Paul II's major contributions to the theology of Marian consecration, as well as an irrefutable proof that he envisions consecration/entrustment to Mary as first and foremost an act of *latria* with a solid Christological foundation. Let us examine his use of the Johannine text in its immediate context in each instance. First let us listen to his homily of May 13, 1982, in Fatima:

> *Consecrating ourselves to Mary means accepting her help to offer ourselves and the whole of mankind to Him who is holy, infinitely holy*; it means accepting her help—by having recourse to her motherly heart, which beneath the cross was opened to love for every human being, for the whole world—*in order to offer the world, the individual human being, mankind as a whole, and all the nations to Him who is infinitely holy.* God's holiness showed itself in the redemption of

[2] "Mary: the Woman Come of Age", *Marian Studies* 36 (1985): 151, 153–54. Several other authors also readily recognized the Christological emphasis in the text of the Pope's consecration. Cf. Marranzini, "L' 'Atto di Affidamento' ", 12–29.

[3] Cf. *Inseg* VII:1 (1984), 417; *ORE* 823:2; cf. also above, 34–35.

[4] *Inseg* V:2 (1982), 1587, 1591; *ORE* 735:12.

[5] *Inseg* VII:1 (1984), 775–76; *ORE* 828:9.

[6] *Inseg* V:2 (1982), 1574, 1583; *Portugal*, 80.

man, of the world, of the whole of mankind, and of the nations: a redemption brought about through the sacrifice of the cross. *"For their sake I consecrate myself," Jesus had said* (Jn. 17:19).

By the power of the redemption the world and man have been consecrated to Him who is infinitely holy. They have been offered and entrusted to Love itself, merciful Love.

The Mother of Christ calls us, invites us to join with the Church of the living God in the consecration of the world, in this act of confiding by which the world, mankind as a whole, the nations, and each individual person are presented to the Eternal Father with the power of the redemption won by Christ. They are offered in the Heart of the Redeemer which was pierced on the cross.[7]

Next we listen to the words of that act of consecration which he made that same day:

"For God so loved the world that he gave his only Son, that whoever believes in him should not perish but have eternal life" (Jn. 3:16).

It was precisely by reason of this love that the Son of God consecrated himself for all mankind: "And for their sake I consecrate myself, that they also may be consecrated in truth" (Jn. 17:19).

By reason of that consecration the disciples of all ages are called to spend themselves for the salvation of the world, and to supplement Christ's afflictions for the sake of his body, that is the Church (cf. 2 Cor. 12:15; Col. 1:24).

Before you, Mother of Christ, before your Immaculate Heart, *I today, together with the whole Church unite myself with our Redeemer in this his consecration for the world and for people,* which only in his divine Heart has the power to obtain pardon and to secure reparation.

The power of this consecration lasts for all time and embraces all individuals, peoples and nations. It overcomes every evil that the spirit of darkness is able to awaken, and has in fact awakened in our times, in the heart of man and in his history.

The Church, the Mystical Body of Christ, unites herself, through the service of Peter's successor, to this consecration by our Redeemer. . . .

[7] *Inseg* V:2 (1982), 1574, 1583; *Portugal,* 80–81 (my emphases).

Hail to you, who are wholly united to the redeeming consecration of your Son!

Mother of the Church! Enlighten the People of God along the paths of faith, of hope and love! *Help us to live with the whole truth of the consecration of Christ for the entire human family of the modern world.*

In entrusting to you, O Mother, the world, all individuals and peoples, *we also entrust to you the consecration itself, for the world's sake, placing it in your motherly Heart.*[8]

Finally, here is his Act of Consecration of March 25, 1984:

> Behold, as we stand before you, Mother of Christ, before your Immaculate Heart, *we desire, together with the whole Church, to unite ourselves with the consecration which, for love of us, your Son made of himself to the Father: "For their sake," he said, "I consecrate myself that they also may be consecrated in the truth"* (Jn. 17:19). *We wish to unite ourselves with our Redeemer in this his consecration for the world and for the human race,* which, in his divine Heart, has the power to obtain pardon and to secure reparation.
>
> *The power of this consecration lasts for all time and embraces all individuals, peoples and nations. It overcomes every evil that the spirit of darkness is able to awaken,* and has in fact awakened in our times, in the heart of man and in his history. . . .
>
> *Hail to you, who are wholly united to the redeeming consecration of your Son!*
>
> Mother of the Church! Enlighten the People of God along the paths of faith, hope and love! Enlighten especially the peoples whose consecration and entrustment by us you are awaiting. *Help us to live in the truth of the consecration of Christ for the entire human family of the modern world.*
>
> *In entrusting to you, O Mother, the world, all individuals and peoples, we also entrust to you this very consecration of the world, placing it in your motherly Heart.*[9]

It will be readily noted that what the Pope stresses in each of these passages is the self-consecration of Christ as stated in John 17:19 and the Church's desire to be united with that

[8] *Inseg* V:2 (1982), 1587–89, 1591–92; *ORE* 735:12 (my emphases).

[9] *Inseg* VII:1 (1984), 775–76; *ORE* 828:9–10 (my emphases).

consecration. The specifically Marian dimension is introduced by invoking the help of Mary who is "wholly united to the redeeming consecration of her Son" for the Church to live this consecration and by entrusting the consecration itself to her.

The consecration of Christ

Let us consider a few of the implications of this so-called self-consecration of Christ as expressed in John 17:19. Perhaps the first point to be noted is that it presupposes Jesus' prior consecration by the Father as a priest upon his entry into the world (Jn 10:36).[10] This is a datum of the tradition that is found deeply embedded in the New Testament, particularly in the Letter to the Hebrews (2:17; 5:5–6; 6:20), and is attested to by the representatives of the sub-apostolic and patristic tradition[11] and by one of the canons of Saint Cyril of Alexandria against Nestorius.[12] By taking on a human nature, the Son of God became the perfect mediator, the perfect priest because in his two natures he could represent God to man and man to God.[13]

This is a theme frequently alluded to by John Paul II. Speaking in Bolivia to priests, brothers, and seminarians he

[10] Cf. André Feuillet, P.S.S., *The Priesthood of Christ and His Ministers,* trans. Matthew J. O'Connell (Garden City, N.Y.: Doubleday & Co., 1975), 37, 39, 96–97, 121, especially 125, 213. On the question of Jesus' consecration by the Father (Jn 10:36) and His self-consecration (Jn 17:19) in terms of the biblical evidence this study is *facile princeps.*

[11] Cf. M. E. McIver, "Priesthood of Christ", in *NCE,* 11:774–75.

[12] Henricus Denzinger and Adolfus Schonmetzer, S.J., eds., *Enchiridion Symbolorum Definitionum et Declarationum de Rebus Fidei et Morum,* 32nd ed. (Freiburg-im-Breisgau: Herder, 1963), no. 261 (hereafter cited as Denz-Schon.); J. Neuner, S.J., and J. Dupuis, S.J., eds., *The Christian Faith in the Doctrinal Documents of the Catholic Church* (New York: Alba House, 1982), no. 606, canon 10. St. Cyril also touched on this theme in his preaching, cf. *PG,* 74, 505–8, 544–45.

[13] The priesthood of Christ is discussed in six articles by St. Thomas Aquinas in *ST,* III, q. 22.

said: "In this Marian Year, I invite all, priests, religious and seminarians, to meditate on the priesthood of Christ, whose anointing by the Holy Spirit took place in Mary's womb, when the Word became flesh." [14] In his 1989 Holy Thursday Letter to Priests he said simply, "As man, Christ is priest".[15] And a few weeks later he declared to the Plenary Assembly of the Congregation for the Evangelization of Peoples: "By the Sacrament of Orders, priests participate in the 'consecration' of Christ the Priest, which took place at the moment of the Incarnation of the Word in Mary's womb, and they become living instruments to continue his wonderful work." [16]

This prior consecration of Christ by virtue of his Incarnation is carefully discussed from a scriptural perspective by the French Sulpician exegete, Father André Feuillet.

> The consecration that Christ received from his Father (Jn. 10:36) has been explained in two ways. Some have connected it with the consecration of Jeremiah before his birth (Jer. 1:5; Sir. 49:7). In both instances God sets someone apart, even before his coming into this world, because God intends to speak to men through this individual; thus, after speaking to us through the prophets, God now speaks to us through his Son (Heb. 1:1–2). But, as we noted in Chapter 1, other commentators prefer to think of priests and to say that Jesus was consecrated a priest. As in Hebrews 5:5, so in John, Jesus receives the high priestly dignity from his Father. And, in point of fact, in New Testament times people thought of priests when they spoke of consecrated individuals.
>
> These two interpretations are by no means exclusive of each other since Jesus was conscious of being the Servant of God who resembled both prophets and priests. Nonetheless, the priestly perspective is certainly to the fore in John 10:36, for there is an evident connection between the consecration meant here and the consecration in 17:19. In short, if the Father consecrates Christ, it

[14] *Inseg* XI:2 (1988), 1312; *ORE* 1043:11.

[15] *Inseg* XII:1 (1989), 543; *ORE* 1081:6.

[16] *Inseg* XII:1 (1989), 812; *ORE* 1087:4.

> is that Christ may then consecrate himself and offer himself as a victim. . . .
>
> To say that the Son of God was consecrated a priest at the moment of his being sent into the world amounts to saying that he is a *priest in his very being as the incarnate Son of God.* The two concepts of priest and mediator are closely connected. A mediator acts as intermediary between two or more parties with which he has something in common. A priest is "consecrated" for the purpose of acting as intermediary between the holy God and men. By the very fact that divinity and manhood are united in him, the incarnate Son of God is already the perfect priestly mediator and infinitely superior to all other priests.[17]

This interpretation is verified by a number of authors, although not always put in such sharp relief as by Feuillet here.[18]

If John 10:36 may be understood as a reference to Jesus' priestly consecration by virtue of the Incarnation, then

> the second consecration of Jesus of which the fourth gospel speaks—"For their sake I consecrate myself" (17:19)—corresponds to this atoning death. . . . In consecrating himself as a victim, Jesus expresses his full acceptance of the Father's plan of salvation; he brings to fulfillment the intention behind the consecration effected by the Father in the incarnation. The sacrificial interpretation of John 17:19 is proposed by a large number of the Fathers, and we can make our own the comment of St. John Chrysostom which Bultmann quotes approvingly: "What does he mean, 'I consecrate myself'? He means, 'I offer sacrifice.' "[19]

[17] Feuillet, *Priesthood of Christ,* 97–98 (author's emphasis).

[18] Cf. Raymond Brown, S.S., *The Gospel According to John I–XII,* Anchor Bible, vol. 29 (Garden City, N.Y.: Doubleday & Co., 1966), 411; idem., *The Gospel According to John XIII–XXI,* Anchor Bible, vol. 29A (Garden City, N.Y.: Doubleday & Co., 1970), 765–67; Ignace de la Potterie, S.J., *La Vérité dans Saint Jean,* vol. 2, Analecta Biblica, no. 74 (Rome: Pontificium Institutum Biblicum, 1977), 763–67; Jean Galot, S.J., *Theology of the Priesthood,* trans. Roger Balducelli, O.S.F.S. (San Francisco: Ignatius Press, 1984), 203.

[19] Feuillet, *Priesthood of Christ,* 44; cf. also de la Potterie, *La Vérité,* 761–75, for further discussion of patristic interpretation.

This understanding of Jesus as consecrated by the Father as priest in order to consecrate himself as victim is implicit in the doctrine of the priesthood of Christ.[20] It is considered by Saint Thomas as a separate article in his treatment of this question in the *Summa Theologiae*[21] and was held as a fundamental principle of priestly spirituality by the members of *L'École Française*.[22] This datum of the tradition is faithfully passed on by Pope John Paul II. Here he does so in the context of an Advent homily:

> The mystery of the Incarnation represents the beginning of the new sacrifice: *of the perfect sacrifice*. He who is conceived in the womb of the Virgin through the work of the Holy Spirit, he who is born that night in Bethlehem, is the eternal priest. He already brings and fulfills the sacrifice in his Incarnation. And it is that *sacrifice which "is pleasing to God"*.
>
> God is pleased by that sacrifice in which the whole interior truth of man is expressed: the sacrifice *of the will and the heart*. The Son of God assumes human nature, a human body, precisely in order to initiate that sacrifice in human history.
>
> He will definitively fulfil it through his "obedience unto death" (cf. Phil. 2:8). Still, *the beginning of this obedience* is already to be found in the womb of the Virgin Mary. *Already on that night in Bethlehem:* "Lo, I have come . . . to do thy will, O God".[23]

He chose to underscore this reality of Christ's priest/victimhood again in his 1987 Holy Thursday Letter to Priests:

[20] Cf. Marranzini, "Consacrazione a Maria", 52; and Joseph de Sainte-Marie, *Teologia,* III:41 (the latter explicitly cites both Jn 10:36 and 17:19).

[21] *ST,* III, q. 22, a. 2.

[22] Cf. Cardinal Pierre de Bérulle, *La Vie de Jésus* (Paris, 1629), 188–94; Pierre Pourrat, P.S.S., *Christian Spirituality,* vol. 3, trans. W. A. Mitchell (Westminster, Md.: Newman Press, 1953), 372–73; Jean Gautier, P.S.S., *Some Schools of Catholic Spirituality,* trans. Kathryn Sullivan, R.S.C.J. (Tournai: Desclée Co., 1959), 338–39; Eugene A. Walsh, S.S., *The Priesthood in the Writings of the French School: Bérulle, De Condren, Olier* (Washington, D.C.: Catholic University of America Press, 1949).

[23] *Inseg* VIII:2 (1985), 1587; *ORE* 919:9, 11.

> On this extraordinary day, I wish—the same as every year—to be with you all, as also with your bishops, since we all feel a deep need to renew in ourselves the awareness of the grace of this sacrament which unites us closely to Christ, Priest and Victim. . . .
>
> In fact, if he was a priest from the beginning of his existence, nevertheless he "became" in a full way the unique priest of the new and eternal Covenant through the redemptive sacrifice which had its beginning in Gethsemane.[24]

A further conclusion drawn by Father Feuillet as to the meaning of this text in the larger context of the high-priestly prayer of Jesus (Jn 17) is that

> the connection which Christ makes between his own consecration as victim and the consecration of the apostles as priests ("I have consecrated myself so that they too may be consecrated in truth") shows clearly that, like all the other blessings of the new covenant, the priesthood of the apostles is the fruit of Christ's self-giving on the cross as an expiatory victim that men may have eternal life.[25]

Father Feuillet is not the first to offer this interpretation of the text, even if he does so with a highly developed exegetical argument. The famous "eagle of Meaux", Jacques-

[24] *Inseg* X:1 (1987), 1306, 1312; *ORE* 983:21, 22.

[25] Feuillet, *Priesthood of Christ,* 126. On this point Galot concurs, drawing the further application that the consecration of Jesus by the Father (Jn 10:36) is an analogue for the priesthood of the faithful, while his self-consecration (Jn 17:19) is an analogue for the hierarchical priesthood as well as specifically undertaken to effect that priestly consecration, cf. Galot, *Theology of the Priesthood,* 121–25. Ferdinand Prat, S.J., in his *Jesus Christ: His life, His Teaching, and His Work,* vol. 2, trans. John J. Heenan, S.J. (Milwaukee: Bruce Publishing Co., 1950), 302–3, and F. X. Durwell, C.SS.R., in his *The Resurrection: A Biblical Study,* trans. Rosemary Sheed (New York: Sheed and Ward, 1960), 236, 307, also link this text with either apostleship or the ministerial priesthood. This application of John 17:19 to the hierarchical priesthood by Feuillet has been contested by Jean Delorme, "Sacerdoce du Christ et Ministère (A propos de Jean 17): Sémantique et théologie biblique", *Recherches de Science Religieuse* 62 (1974): 199–219. This, in turn, elicited in response the article by Henri Cazelles, "Note sur le ministère apostolique de consécration", *Bulletin de Saint-Sulpice* 1 (1975): 302–7. Delorme again responded with "Sacrifice, sacerdoce, consécration", *Recherches de Science Religieuse* 63 (1975): 343–66.

Bénigne Bossuet, had already given classic expression to this concept when he said of Christ:

> He was holy, then, and consecrated to God, not only in his capacity as pontiff, but also as victim. . . . It is for this that he sanctifies himself, offers himself, consecrates himself as property dedicated and holy to the Lord. But he also adds in speaking to his apostles: "I sanctify myself for them", so that participating by their ministry in the grace of his priesthood, they might enter at the same time into the state of victimhood, and, not having at all on their own the holiness which was required to be messengers and ministers of Jesus Christ, they might find this in him.[26]

In point of fact John Paul II has several times made this specifically hierarchical priestly application in the citation of this text[27] and has also applied it to those who live the consecrated religious life,[28] but more frequently he applies it in a broader sense to all members of the Body of Christ, who share in the common priesthood of all believers, as described in *Lumen Gentium*, number 10, and *Presbyterorum Ordinis*, number 2.[29] Perhaps he said this most strongly in his Letter to All Consecrated Persons on the Occasion of the Marian Year:

> Every vocation of a baptized person reflects some aspect of that "consecration in the truth" which Christ accomplished by his Death and Resurrection and made part of his Paschal Mystery:

[26] Quoted in M. J. Lagrange, O.P., *L'Évangile selon Saint Jean* (Paris: Gabalda & Cie., 1936), 448 (my trans.).

[27] *Inseg* II:2 (1979), 642; *U.S.A.*, 192; *Inseg* III:1 (1980), 112; *ORE* 618:10; *Inseg* III:1 (1980), 1762; *ORE* 640:19; *Inseg* XII:1 (1989), 139; *ORE* 1076:10; *Inseg* XII:1 (1989), 536; *ORE* 1081:3; *Inseg* XII:1 (1989), 1373; *ORE* 1096:6; *ORE* 1136:11.

[28] *Inseg* IX:1 (1986), 780; *ORE* 931:11; *Inseg* IX:1 (1986), 1659; *ORE* 941:6; *Inseg* XI:3 (1988), 714–15; *ORE* 1056:10.

[29] *Inseg* II:2 (1979), 493; *Ireland,* 117; *Inseg* III:2 (1980), 738, 741; *ORE* 652:3; *Inseg* VIII:1 (1985), 390–97; *ORE* 880:6–7; *Inseg* VIII:1 (1985), 1515; *ORE* 892:10; *Inseg* IX:2 (1986), 106; *ORE* 924:4; *Inseg* XI:2 (1988), 1928; *ORE* 1046:4; *Inseg* XII:1 (1989), 1588; *ORE* 1094:14; *ORE* 1211:11.

> "*For their sake I consecrate myself,* that they also may be consecrated in truth" (Jn 17:19).[30]

Such is clearly his intention in his use of the text in the acts of consecration/entrustment in 1982 and 1984. In fact in the earlier act made at Fatima he immediately follows the quotation of John 17:19 with this clarification: "By reason of that consecration the disciples of all ages are called to spend themselves for the salvation of the world, and to supplement Christ's afflictions for the sake of his body, that is the Church (cf. 2 Cor. 12:15; Col. 1:24)." [31]

Clearly then, by this apposition he wishes to underscore Christ's self-consecration to victimhood as a paradigm for all believers, an invitation to become "co-victims" with Him in order to supplement His afflictions for the sake of His body, the Church (Col 1:24).[32]

Mary "wholly united to the redeeming consecration of her Son"

It is in this light that Mary reappears in the acts of both 1982 and 1984. "Hail to you, who are wholly united to the redeeming consecration of your Son!" [33] She, by God's inscrutable design, was the first to share in Christ's sufferings

[30] *Inseg* XI:2 (1988), 1594, 1606–7; *ORE* 1043:2.

[31] *Inseg* V:2 (1982), 1587, 1591; *ORE* 735:12.

[32] This very understanding of the text of John 17:19 was presented by Bernard Leeming, S.J., in his essay "Consecration to the Sacred Heart", in *Pars Theologica,* vol. 1 of *Cor Jesu: Commentationes in Litteras Encyclicas Pii PP. XII "Haurietis Aquas",* ed. Augustinus Bea, S.J., et al. (Rome: Casa Editrice Herder, 1959), 640–52.

It is also interesting to note the development of what René Laurentin calls "La Perspective Victimale" in the spiritual and Marian theology of the 19th and 20th centuries. This perspective provides further elaboration of this implied theme of "co-victimhood" with Christ as realized in Mary and in the Christian. Cf. René Laurentin, *Essai sur le Développement d'une Idée Religieuse,* vol. 1 of *Maria, Ecclesia, Sacerdotium* (Paris: P. Lethielleux "Nouvelles Editions Latines", 1952), 422–67.

[33] *Inseg* V:2 (1982), 1588, 1592; *ORE* 735:12; *Inseg* VII:1 (1984), 776.

as a co-victim and the one to be most fully united with that consecration consummated on the Cross. She is described in *Lumen Gentium*, no. 56, as the one who "devoted herself totally as the Lord's handmaid to the person and work of her Son" [*semetipsam ut Domini ancillam personae et operi Filii sui totaliter devovit*].[34] Further, the Council Fathers declare that

> that association of the Mother with her Son in the work of salvation is manifested from the time of Christ's virginal conception up to his death. . . . So too the Blessed Virgin advanced in the pilgrimage of faith and kept up her union with her Son faithfully till the cross, where she was standing, not without divine design (cf. Jn. 19:25). There she sorrowed grievously together with her Only Son and united herself with motherly heart to his sacrifice, giving loving consent to the Immolation of the Victim born of her. [*Ita etiam B. Virgo in peregrinatione fidei processit, suamque unionem cum Filio fideliter sustinuit usque ad crucem, ubi non sine divino consilio stetit (cf. Io. 19:25), vehementer cum Unigenito suo condoluit et sacrificio Eius se materno animo sociavit, victimae de se genitae immolationi amanter consentiens*].[35]

While it evidently remained in the providence of God for this recognition of Mary as "wholly united to the redeeming consecration of her Son" to be highlighted by John Paul II, it is clear that the groundwork had already been laid in the documents of the Second Vatican Council and not just in chapter eight of *Lumen Gentium*.[36] Perhaps these texts are the most explicit:

> Perfect model of this apostolic spiritual life is the Blessed Virgin Mary, Queen of Apostles.[37]

> They [priests] always find a wonderful example of such docility in the Blessed Virgin Mary who under the guidance of the Holy

[34] Unger, 9.

[35] *LG*, nos. 57, 58; Unger, 9, 10.

[36] Cf. *LG*, no. 46; *PC*, no. 25.

[37] *AA*, no. 4; Flan., 771.

Spirit made a total dedication of herself for the mystery of the redemption of men.[38]

Without doubt Jesus is the preeminent One consecrated by God (Jn 10:36) and consecrating Himself for our Redemption (Jn 17:19), but analogously and subordinately[39] Mary is consecrated "under him and together with him, in the service of the mystery of redemption".[40] She "was predestined as God's Mother from all eternity together with the Incarnation of the Divine Word." [41] As Jesus' consecration began in Mary's womb at the moment of the Incarnation, so Mary's began at the first moment of her existence.[42] As His consecration was consummated on the Cross, so was hers beneath it and in the most total cooperation with His.[43]

At the very beginning of this chapter, I cited the testimony of Father Lohkamp on consecration. There he stated that baptism "may be called the fundamental consecration of Christian life." [44] This assertion is absolutely basic in the Christian tradition because baptism identifies one with the consecration of Christ (cf. Rom 6:3) and hence it is simply confirmed by the Second Vatican Council.[45] Hence also the

[38] *PO,* no. 18; Flan., 896–97.

[39] Cf. *LG,* no. 62.

[40] *LG,* no. 56; Unger, 9.

[41] *LG,* no. 61. This doctrine that "God by one and the same decree [*uno eodemque decreto*], had established both the origin of Mary and the Incarnation of Divine Wisdom" was first declared by the Venerable Pius IX in *Ineffabilis Deus, Pii IX Acta* I:599; *OL,* no. 34. It was reiterated by the Servant of God Pius XII in *Munificentissimus Deus, AAS* 42 (1950): 768; *OL,* no. 520, and alluded to by Paul VI in *Marialis Cultus, AAS* 66 (1974): 136, and *Mary—God's Mother and Ours,* 23. In *Redemptoris Mater,* John Paul II says: "In the mystery of Christ she is *present* even 'before the creation of the world', as the one whom the Father 'has chosen' as *Mother* of his Son in the Incarnation" (*Inseg* X:1 [1987], 687; St. Paul ed., 14).

[42] Denz-Schon., nos. 2800, 2803; *OL,* nos. 31, 62; *LG,* nos. 53, 56.

[43] *LG,* no. 58.

[44] Lohkamp, 209.

[45] Cf. *LG,* no. 10; *PC,* no. 5; *PO,* no. 12.

Pope can simply state categorically: "Baptism is the first and fundamental consecration of the human person."[46] The Church further singles out two kinds of consecration which build on the fundamental consecration of baptism. The first is the religious life under the vows of poverty, chastity, and obedience.

> They [religious] have dedicated their whole lives to his servitude. *This constitutes a special consecration, which is deeply rooted in their baptismal consecration and is a fuller expression of it.*[47]

> Right from the planting of the Church the religious life should be carefully fostered, because not only does it provide valuable and absolutely necessary help for missionary activity, but *through the deeper consecration made to God in the Church* it clearly shows and signifies the intimate nature of the Christian vocation.[48]

The other kind of consecration is accomplished in the sacrament of holy orders and given for special ministerial services in the Church.

> *Like all Christians they* [priests] *have already received in the consecration of baptism the sign and gift of their great calling and grace.* So they are enabled and obliged even in the midst of human weakness to seek perfection, according to the Lord's word: "You, therefore, must be perfect, as your heavenly Father is perfect" (Mt. 5:48).
>
> But priests are bound by a special reason to acquire this perfection. *They are consecrated to God in a new way in their ordination* and are made the living instruments of Christ the eternal priest, and so are enabled to accomplish throughout all time that wonderful work of his which with supernatural efficacy restored the whole human race.[49]

With obviously no desire to derogate from the "fundamental consecration of Baptism" or the unique ministerial

[46] *Inseg* VII:2 (1984), 1576; *ORE* 865:18.
[47] *PC,* no. 5; Flan., 614 (my emphasis).
[48] *AG,* no. 18; Flan., 834 (my emphasis).
[49] *PO,* no. 12; Flan., 885 (my emphases).

consecration of holy orders, Pope John Paul II uses the term "consecrated life" most frequently of the vowed religious life. And to religious men and women, therefore, he very frequently proposes Mary as the model of consecrated life,[50] the one most "wholly united to the redeeming consecration of her Son". Perhaps in none of his very numerous addresses to religious has he drawn Mary as model of consecrated souls more compellingly than in his apostolic exhortation *Redemptionis Donum*, of which this section forms the conclusion.

> On the feast of the Annunciation in this Holy Year of the Redemption, I place the present exhortation *in the heart of the immaculate Virgin*. Among all persons consecrated unreservedly to God, she is the first. She—the Virgin of Nazareth—is also the one *most fully consecrated to God*, consecrated in the most perfect way. Her spousal love reached its height in the divine Motherhood through the power of the Holy Spirit. She, who as Mother carries Christ in her arms, at the same time *fulfills* in the most perfect way *His call*, "Follow me." And she follows Him—she, the Mother—as her Teacher of chastity, poverty and obedience.
>
> How *poor* she was on Bethlehem night and how poor on Calvary! How *obedient* she was at the moment of the Annunciation, and then—at the foot of the cross—*obedient* even to the point of assenting to the death of her Son, who became obedient "unto death!" How *dedicated* she was in all her earthly life to the cause of the kingdom of heaven *through most chaste love*.
>
> If the entire Church finds in Mary her *first model*, all the more reason do you find her so—you as consecrated individuals and communities within the Church! On the day that calls to mind the inauguration of the Jubilee of the Redemption, which took place last year, I address myself to you with this present message, to

[50] Cf. Domenico Bertetto, S.D.B., *Maria nel Magistero di Giovanni Paolo II: Primo Anno di Pontificato, 16 ottobre 1978–21 ottobre 1979* (Rome: Libreria Ateneo Salesiano, 1980), 56, 179; *Secondo Anno* (1981), 159–60; *Terzo Anno* (1983), 163–65; *Quarto Anno* (1984), 272–74; *Quinto Anno* (1986), 129, 198, 217; *Sesto Anno* (1986), 181, 239.

invite you to renew *your religious consecration according to the model of the consecration of the very Mother of God.*[51]

Likewise, in his Letter to All Consecrated Persons on the Occasion of the Marian Year, he exhorted those who live the vowed life:

Through an increased resolve on your part to live your consecration to the full, taking Mary the Mother of Jesus and of the Church as the sublime model of perfect consecration to God, your evangelical witness will grow in effectiveness and lead to a greater fruitfulness of *pastoral work for vocations.*[52]

On October 7, 1979, speaking to women religious at the National Shrine of the Immaculate Conception in Washington, he put it succinctly: "This is the woman of history and destiny who inspires us today, the woman who speaks to us of femininity, human dignity, and love, and *who is the greatest expression of total consecration to Jesus Christ.*[53] In his apostolic letter *Mulieris Dignitatem* he asserted Mary's primacy as the perfect creaturely model of consecration in the context of "union with God" (which, of course, is completely equivalent to "union with Jesus and his redeeming consecration"):

The dignity of every human being and the vocation corresponding to that dignity find their definitive measure in *union with God.* Mary, the woman of the Bible, is the most complete expression of this dignity and vocation. For no human being, male or female, created in the image and likeness of God, can *in any way* attain fulfillment apart from this image and likeness.[54]

[51] *Inseg* VII:1 (1984), 816, 842; *ORE* 828:16 (emphasis in original).

[52] *Inseg* XI:2 (1988), 1601, 1612; *ORE* 1043:3.

[53] *Inseg* II:2 (1979), 676; *U.S.A.*, 242 (my emphasis).

[54] *Inseg* XI:3 (1988), 252, 324; *ORE* 1058:2.

Mary's spiritual maternity willed by Christ

Thus far it is sufficiently clear that what one might call the "nucleus" of the acts of consecration/entrustment which the Pope made in 1982 and 1984 is Christocentric. Why then does he go on to consecrate and entrust to Mary? This is a question to which the Holy Father is tireless in responding and the response virtually always refers to the words of the dying Christ to His Mother with reference to the disciple whom He loved: "Woman, behold, your son!" (Jn 19:26). In these words he finds a confirmation of Mary's spiritual maternity which began "with the consent she trustingly gave at the Annunciation." [55]

Theologically, a distinction is frequently made with regard to the beginning of Mary's spiritual maternity and its "promulgation". Father Otto Semmelroth, S.J., puts it this way: "When Mary conceived the God-man, she became ontologically the Mother of the Mystical Christ. This element had to receive the addition of moral completion at Christ's sacrifice on the Cross." [56] Father Wenceslaus Sebastian, O.F.M., differentiates these two "moments" analogously with the Redemption wrought by Christ:

> The Incarnation may be considered as the Redemption in potency or "in actu primo," and the sacrifice on Calvary, as the Redemption in act, or in "actu secundo." Mary's co-operation in the production of the supernatural life follows a similar pattern. At the Incarnation, in virtue of her Divine Maternity, she conceives us to the supernatural life, whereas on Calvary she begets us. . . .
>
> The act of Divine Motherhood is related to Christ as the Man-God and to Christ as Head of the Mystical Body. By engendering the Man-God she became the Mother of God; by begetting the Head of the Mystical Body she became the Spiritual Mother of mankind, receiving from the grace of Headship her fullness of

[55] *LG*, no. 13.

[56] Otto Semmelroth, S.J., *Mary, Archetype of the Church,* trans. Maria von Eroes and John Devlin (New York: Sheed and Ward, 1963), 132.

grace to be transmitted to men. Yet, her Spiritual Motherhood and her plenitude of grace at the Incarnation are such only *in actu primo*. They are not realized completely and effectively *in actu secundo* until Mary has co-operated with her divine Son in the Redemption. . . . That is why theologians commonly say that she conceived us at Nazareth and bore us on Calvary.[57]

While it is true that virtually all of the popes since Benedict XIV have cited the pericope of John 19:25–27 in support of Mary's spiritual maternity,[58] one of the clearest statements of its inception was made by Pope Saint Pius X in his encyclical *Ad Diem Illum*:

For is not Mary the Mother of Christ? She is, therefore, our Mother also. Indeed everyone must believe that Jesus, the Word made Flesh, is also the Saviour of the human race. Now, as the God-Man He acquired a body composed like that of other men, but as the Saviour of our race He had a kind of spiritual and mystical Body, which is the society of those who believe in Christ. "We, the many, are one body in Christ" (*Romans* 12:5). But the Virgin conceived the Eternal Son not only that He might be made man by taking His human nature from her, but also that by means of the nature assumed from her He might be the Saviour of men. For this reason the angel said to the shepherds, "Today in the town of David a Saviour has been born to you, Who is Christ the Lord" (*Luke* 2:11). So in one and the same bosom of His most chaste Mother, Christ took to Himself human flesh and at the same time united to Himself the spiritual body built up of those "who are to believe in Him" (*John* 17:20). Consequently Mary,

[57] Wenceslaus Sebastian, O.F.M., "Mary's Spiritual Maternity", in *Mariology*, 2:331, 335–36. Eschewing the distinction between Mary's spiritual maternity *in actu primo* and *in actu secundo* as an unnecessary "hardening of formulas", Père Salgado prefers, following the lead of Pius XII, to speak of Mary's "double title to motherhood in the supernatural order": her divine maternity and her association with the sacrifice of Calvary; cf. Jean-Marie Salgado, O.M.I., "La Visitation de la Sainte Vierge Marie: Exercice de sa Maternité Spirituelle", *Divinitas* 16 (1972): 448–49, and *La Maternité Spirituelle de la Très Sainte Vierge Marie* (Vatican City: Libreria Editrice Vaticana, "Studi Tomistici", no. 36, 1990), 192–95.

[58] Cf. Salgado, *La Maternité Spirituelle,* 154–59.

bearing in her womb the Saviour, may be said to have borne also all those whose life was contained in the life of the Saviour. All of us, therefore, who are united with Christ and are, as the Apostle says, "Members of His body, made from His flesh and from His bones" (*Ephesians* 5:30), have come forth from the womb of Mary as a body united to its head. Hence, in a spiritual and mystical sense, we are called children of Mary, and she is the Mother of us all.[59]

Even though John Paul's primary emphasis, following his predecessors, is on the "promulgation" or "revelation"[60] of Mary's spiritual maternity on Calvary, he nonetheless acknowledges that this "service" of Mary to the Church began from the first moment of the conception of Christ. Here is how he put it in Ephesus on November 30, 1979:

Uttering her "fiat," Mary does not . . . become Mother of [just] the historical Christ; her gesture sets her as Mother of the total Christ, as "Mother of the Church." "From the moment of the 'fiat'—St. Anselm remarks—Mary began to bear us all in her womb." That is why "the birth of the Head is also the birth of the Body," St. Leo the Great proclaims. On his part, St. Ephrem has a very beautiful expression on this subject: Mary, he says, is "the ground in which the Church was sown."

In fact, from the moment when the Virgin becomes Mother of the Incarnate Word, the Church is constituted secretly, but perfectly in its germ, in its essence as the Mystical Body: there are present, in fact, the Redeemer and the first of the redeemed. Henceforth incorporation into Christ will involve a filial relationship not only with the heavenly Father, but also with Mary, the earthly Mother of the Son of God.[61]

In Fatima on May 12, 1991, he expressed this same truth thus: "Since she [Mary] gave birth to Christ, the Head of

[59] Quoted in Sebastian, 350 (also in *OL,* nos. 229–30).

[60] Cf. Clément Dillenschneider, C.SS.R., *La Mariologie de S. Alphonse de Liguori: Sources et Synthèse Doctrinale* (Fribourg: Studia Friburgensia, 1934), 159.

[61] *Inseg* II:2 (1979), 1289; *Turkey—Ecumenical Pilgrimage* (Boston: St. Paul Editions, 1980), 76–77.

the Mystical Body, she also had to have given birth to all the members of that one Body. Therefore, 'Mary embraces each and every one *in* the Church, and embraces each and every one *through* the Church' " (*Redemptoris Mater,* 47).[62]

It remains true, however, that his almost constant point of reference for Mary's spiritual maternity as well as the basis for his program of entrustment is Calvary. Let us listen to a catechesis on this point given in a general audience on May 11, 1983.

> "Jesus said to his mother, 'Woman, there is your son.' In turn he said to the disciple, 'There is your mother' " (Jn. 19:26, 27).
>
> In this Holy Year, we turn more ardently to Mary, because a very special sign of mankind's reconciliation with God was *the role entrusted to her on Calvary to be the mother of all the redeemed.*
>
> The circumstances under which this motherhood of Mary's was proclaimed show the importance that the Redeemer attributed to it. At the very moment when he was completing his sacrifice, Jesus spoke those basic words to his mother: "Woman, there is your son;" and to the disciple: "There is your mother" (Jn. 19:26-27). And the Evangelist notes that after saying these words Jesus realized that everything was now finished. *The gift of his mother was the final gift that he was giving mankind as the fruit of his sacrifice.*
>
> It is a question then of a gesture intended to crown his redemptive work. *Asking Mary to treat the beloved disciple as her son, Jesus invites her to accept the sacrifice of his death and, as the price of this acceptance, he invites her to take on a new motherhood. As the Saviour of all mankind, he wants to give Mary's motherhood the greatest range. He therefore chooses John as the symbol of all the disciples whom he loves, and he makes it understood that the gift of his mother is the sign of a special intention of love, with which he embraces all who want to follow him as disciples, that is, all Christians and all men.* Besides giving this motherhood an individual form, Jesus manifests the intention to make Mary not merely the mother of his disciples taken as a whole, but of each one of them in particular, as though each were her only son who is taking the place of her Only Son.

[62] *ORE* 1191:5.

This universal motherhood in the spiritual order was the final consequence of Mary's cooperation in the work of her divine Son, a cooperation begun in the fearful joy of the Annunciation and carried through right to the boundless sorrow of Calvary. This is what the Second Vatican Council stressed when it showed the role that Mary was destined to fulfill in the Church. [Here he cites *Lumen Gentium*, nos. 61 and 62.] . . . Mary's mediation constitutes a singular sharing in the unique mediation of Christ, which does not become in the least overshadowed, but rather endures as the central fact in the whole work of salvation.

Devotion to Our Lady therefore is not opposed to devotion to her Son. Rather it can be said that by asking the beloved disciple to treat Mary as his mother Jesus founded Marian devotion.[63] John was quick to carry out the will of his Master: from that hour onward the disciple took her into his care, showing her filial affection that corresponded to her motherly affection, *thus beginning a relationship of spiritual intimacy that contributed to deepening his relationship with his Master, whose unmistakable traces he found on his mother's face. . . .*

The words addressed by the crucified Christ to his mother and to the beloved disciple brought a new dimension to man's religious condition. The presence of a mother in the life of grace is a source of comfort and joy. On Mary's motherly face Christians recognize a most particular expression of the merciful love of God, who with the mediation of a maternal presence has us better understand the Father's own care and goodness. Mary appears as the one who attracts sinners and reveals to them, with her sympathy and her indulgence, the divine offer of reconciliation. . . .

It is to this perfect mother that the Church has recourse in all its difficulties: *it entrusts to her its plans, because in praying to her and loving her it can respond to the wish expressed by the Saviour on the cross, and it is certain it will not be disappointed in its prayers.*[64]

Here again we notice that he invokes the great Marian treatise of the Second Vatican Council explicitly by citing

[63] Père Salgado says that this simple, but striking affirmation had never been made by the magisterium before John Paul II; cf. *La Maternité spirituelle*, 169.

[64] *Inseg* VI:1 (1983), 1200–1202; *ORE* 784:1 (my emphases).

numbers 61 and 62 of *Lumen Gentium* on Mary's spiritual maternity and mediation, which is to be "understood in such wise that it does not derogate from the dignity and efficacy of Christ, the one Mediator, nor does it add anything."[65] We notice his emphasis on the fact that this maternal role is *entrusted* to Mary by Christ, that it is "the final gift that he was giving mankind as the fruit of his sacrifice". Delicately he underscores the fact that the beloved disciple's new relationship with Mary "contributed to deepening his relationship with his Master".

Among many frequent references to Mary's spiritual maternity in homilies and addresses,[66] he devoted numbers 20 through 24 and 44 through 45 of *Redemptoris Mater* to this topic. In the encyclical he developed the concept that the Gospel brings a radically "new dimension" to every relationship, hence also to motherhood, and therefore to the Motherhood of Mary:

> He [Jesus] announced the Kingdom, the "Kingdom of God" and "his Father's business," which add a new dimension and meaning to everything human, and therefore to every human bond, insofar as these things related to the goals and tasks assigned to every human being. Within this new dimension, also a bond such as that of "brotherhood" means something different from "brotherhood according to the flesh" deriving from a common origin from the same set of parents. "*Motherhood,*" too, *in the dimension of the Kingdom of God and in the radius of the fatherhood of God himself, takes on another meaning.*[67]

[65] *LG,* no. 62; Unger, 13.

[66] Cf. *Inseg* V:2 (1982), 1800; *ORE* 736:14; *Inseg* V:2 (1982), 2201; *Pope John Paul II in Argentina* (Boston: St. Paul Editions, 1983), 23 (hereafter cited as *Argentina*); *Inseg* V:3 (1982), 1181; *Inseg* VI:1 (1983), 966; *Inseg* VII:1 (1984), 851; *Inseg* VIII:2 (1985), 262; *ORE* 901:2; *Inseg* X:3 (1987), 859–60; *ORE* 1025:14; *Inseg* XI:1 (1988), 975; 1038:11; 1201:1; 1205:3; 1206:9; 1207:4.

[67] *Inseg* X:1 (1987), 701; St. Paul ed., 28.

He went on to illustrate this "new dimension of Mary's motherhood" (and also her "maternal mediation") by the incident of the wedding at Cana (Jn 2:1–11):

> In John's text . . . the description of the Cana event outlines what is actually manifested as a new kind of motherhood according to the spirit and not just according to the flesh, that is to say *Mary's solicitude for human beings,* her coming to them in the wide variety of their wants and needs. At Cana in Galilee there is shown only one concrete aspect of human need, apparently a small one of little importance ("They have no wine"). But it has a symbolic value: this coming to the aid of human needs means, at the same time, bringing those needs within the radius of Christ's messianic mission and salvific power. Thus there is a mediation: Mary places herself between her Son and mankind in the reality of [its] wants, needs and sufferings. *She puts herself "in the middle,"* that is to say *she acts as a mediatrix not as an outsider, but in her position as mother.* She knows that as such she can point out to her Son the needs of mankind, and in fact, she "has the right" to do so. Her mediation is thus in the nature of intercession: Mary "intercedes" for mankind. And that is not all. As a mother she also *wishes the messianic power of her Son to be manifested,* that salvific power of his which is meant to help man in his misfortunes, to free him from the evil which in various forms and degrees weighs heavily upon his life.[68]

Finally, of course, he made his commentary on the classic text of John 19:25–27, and, although having commented on this famous theme hundreds of times, he presented a new theological synthesis:

> One can say that if Mary's motherhood of the human race had already been outlined, now it is clearly stated and established. It *emerges* from the definitive accomplishment of *the Redeemer's Paschal Mystery.* The Mother of Christ, who stands at the very center of this mystery—a mystery which embraces each individual and all humanity—is given as mother to every single individual and all mankind. The man at the foot of the Cross is John, "the disciple

[68] *Inseg* X:1 (1987), 704; St. Paul ed., 30–31.

> whom he loved." But it is not he alone. Following tradition, the Council does not hesitate to call Mary "*the Mother of Christ and mother of mankind*": since she "belongs to the offspring of Adam she is one with all human beings. . . . Indeed she is 'clearly the mother of the members of Christ . . . since she cooperated out of love so that there might be born in the Church the faithful'."
>
> And so this "new motherhood of Mary," generated by faith, is *the fruit of the "new" love* which came to definitive maturity in her at the foot of the Cross, through her sharing in the redemptive love of her Son.[69]

One might be inclined to think that having offered such a remarkable synthesis on Our Lady's spiritual maternity which is at once completely consistent with the tradition and at the same time extraordinarily rich and fresh, one should not expect any further notable insights from John Paul II on this topic, but this would be to commit a serious error. Here is the conclusion which he drew on Mary's Motherhood of the Church in a general audience of November 23, 1988, which Père Salgado describes as the most beautiful catechesis on the text of John 19:25–27 which he has come across in pontifical documents:[70]

> Jesus does not want his mother to remain alone. In place of himself he leaves to her as a son the disciple whom Mary knows as the beloved one. Thus Jesus entrusts to Mary a new motherhood, asking her to treat John as her son. But the solemnity of that act of entrustment ("Woman, behold, your son!"), its situation at the very heart of the drama of the Cross, the sobriety and pithiness of the words which could be described as proper to an almost sacramental formula, suggest that over and above family relationships, the fact should be considered in the perspective of the work of salvation, where the woman Mary was engaged with the Son of Man in the mission of redemption. At the conclusion of this work, Jesus asks Mary to accept definitively the offering which he makes of himself as the victim of expiation, by now considering John as her

[69] *Inseg* X:1 (1987), 706; St. Paul ed., 33.

[70] Salgado, *La Maternité Spirituelle,* 171.

son. It is at the price of her maternal sacrifice that she receives that new motherhood.

However, that filial gesture, full of messianic meaning, goes far beyond the person of the beloved disciple, designated as the son of Mary. Jesus wishes to give Mary the mission of accepting all his followers of every age as her own sons and daughters. Jesus's gesture has therefore a symbolic value.

It is not merely a gesture of a family nature, as of a son making provision for his mother, but it is a gesture of the world's Redeemer who assigns to Mary, as "woman", a role of new motherhood in relation to all those who are called to membership in the Church. In that moment, therefore, Mary is constituted—one might almost say "consecrated"—Mother of the Church by her Son on the Cross.[71]

To one outside the immediate "household of the faith" this highly developed interpretation of John 19:25–27 can seem to be *eisegesis* rather than *exegesis*. Thus even a student of the Pope's thought as sympathetic as George Huntston Williams of Harvard can say:

In what always seems an uncharacteristically and unnecessarily harsh statement of Jesus to his mother (Jn. 19:26), "Woman, behold your son!" Pope John Paul has obviously for a long time found the inference that Jesus sanctioned a universalization of her [Mary's] maternal role: "In these words I always found the place for every human being and the place for myself." [72]

It ought to be noted that Williams is surely not trying to be polemical here and that he is willing to put the best construction on the Pope's understanding of what he himself has come to see as "an uncharacteristically and unnecessarily harsh statement of Jesus to his mother". This is an illustra-

[71] *Inseg* XI:4 (1988), 1635–36; *ORE* 1066:1. In the second to last sentence I have changed "membership of the Church" to "membership in the Church". Père Salgado lists nine fundamental points which the Pope made in this catechesis in his book *La Maternité Spirituelle,* 171–73.

[72] Williams, 284. The reference is from the Act of Consecration to the Mother of God made at Jasna Góra on June 4, 1979, *Inseg* II:1 (1979), 1417; *Poland,* 110–11.

tion of the difference between reading a given text within the Catholic tradition and outside of it, an illustration of why the Fathers of the Extraordinary Synod of 1985 found it necessary to state even for the benefit of Catholic scholars that "the exegesis of the original meaning of Sacred Scripture, most highly recommended by the Council (cf. *DV* 12), cannot be separated from the living tradition of the Church (cf. *DV* 9) *nor from the authentic interpretation of the Magisterium of the Church* (cf. *DV* 10)." [73]

One such scholar, Canon John McHugh, had already noted in the preface to his book *The Mother of Jesus in the New Testament* ten years earlier "that differences concerning Marian doctrine are to a large extent a consequence of much deeper differences [between Catholics and Protestants] concerning the relationship of Scripture and tradition." [74]

The perspective of Professor Williams is represented even more sharply in the treatment of John 19:25–27 by the scholars of the ecumenical task force of the American Lutheran–Catholic dialogue. They concede by way of footnote that Roman Catholics would make a distinction between Church teaching on Mary's spiritual Motherhood and the teaching of Scripture. "They may accept the spiritual motherhood of Mary without claiming that it is taught by the Scriptures." [75] One could possibly understand how

[73] Final Report (*Relatio Finalis*) II. B. a. 1., *OR,* December 10, 1985, supplemento, II; *The Extraordinary Synod of 1985* (Boston: St. Paul Editions, 1986), 49. The italicized section translates "*neque ab authentica interpretatione magisterii Ecclesiae*" which has been inexplicably omitted in both the English and Italian translations, cf. Msgr. John F. McCarthy, "An Assessment of the Recent Extraordinary Synod", *The Wanderer,* 119, no. 11 (1986): 3. The reference to *Dei Verbum* (Vatican II Dogmatic Constitution on Divine Revelation), no. 9 (hereafter cited as *DV*) is also missing in the English text.

[74] John McHugh, *The Mother of Jesus in the New Testament* (Garden City, N.Y.: Doubleday & Co., 1975), xiii.

[75] Raymond E. Brown, S.S., et al., eds., *Mary in the New Testament* (Philadelphia: Fortress Press; New York: Paulist Press, 1978), 215; cf. entire section,

Lutheran scholars might come to such a conclusion without a thorough knowledge of the Catholic tradition; it is more difficult to grasp how Catholic scholars on the task force could have concurred.

The consensus of the ecumenical task force is certainly out of harmony with the above quoted statement of the Extraordinary Synod and the careful discussion on Scripture and tradition in Canon McHugh's book.[76] Catholic scholars willingly grant that the earliest exegesis of John 19:25–27 did not explicitly find therein the doctrine of Mary's spiritual maternity which in the patristic era was based much more on the understanding of Mary as the New Eve.[77] They do hold, however, that this is an instance of the development of doctrine and a subsequent discovery of the implications contained in this passage from the beginning.[78] They

---

206–18. Cf. the extreme Protestant position which assumes that "death ends all human relationships", that "there is no husband and wife in heaven . . . no mother and son either" and that therefore "there is no authoritative teaching anywhere to show that she [Mary] stands today in any relation towards God in heaven and man on earth different from that in which any other departed saint stands", in William J. Bridcut, "Our Lord's Relationship with His Mother", *One in Christ* 22 (1986): 368–70.

[76] McHugh, xxiii–xlviii.

[77] Cf. *Theotokos,* 139–41; Salgado, *La Maternité Spirituelle,* 57–123. On page 128 of this remarkably well-researched book Père Salgado points out that the first author in the whole Church to base Mary's spiritual maternity on John 19:25–27 as far as we presently know was George of Nicomedia (d. 860); cf. also *Theotokos,* 154–55.

[78] Cf. *Theotokos,* 253–56, 373–75; Théodore Koehler, S.M., "Les principales interprétations traditionelles de Jn. 19, 25–27 pendant les douze premiers siècles", *Études Mariales* 16 (1959): 119–55, and "Mary's Spiritual Maternity after the Second Vatican Council", *Marian Studies* 23 (1972): 39–68; the following contributions to the Mariological Congress held in Santo Domingo in 1965: André Feuillet, P.S.S., "De muliere parturiente et de maternitate spirituali Mariae secundum evangelium sancti Johannis (16, 21; 19, 25–27)", in *De Beata Virgine Maria in Evangelio S. Ioannis et in Apocalypsi*, vol. 5 of *Maria in Sacra Scriptura: Acta Congressus Mariologici-Mariani in Republica Dominicana Anno 1965 Celebrati* (Rome: Pontificia Academia Mariana Internationalis, 1967), 111–22 (latter hereafter cited as *MSS*); Alphonsus Mercado, O.F.M., "De verbis Jesu ad Matrem et Discipulum (Io. 19, 26–27a) iuxta

see it neither as a superimposition of an element alien to the original datum nor a denial of the nucleus of that original datum, but an organic development, a deeper awareness of ramifications in the text itself which were gradually brought to light over a period of time under the guidance of the Holy Spirit.[79] Father Domenico Bertetto, S.D.B., did not hesitate to conclude in his presentation to the Mariological Congress of Santo Domingo that the "testament of the Lord", i.e., the willing of the gift of His Mother to the Church, is established by the ordinary magisterium of the Church.[80]

It is interesting to note that in the course of the Lenten retreat preached to Pope Paul VI and the Roman Curia in 1976 Cardinal Karol Wojtyła used the very same term employed by Father Bertetto: "And even from the cross Jesus once again firmly asserted his mother's role in the mystery of redemption and of the Church, saying to John:

---

genus ioanneum. Adnotationes", in *MSS* 5:123–37; Pastor Gutierrez Osorio, S.J., " 'Ecce Mater tua' (Jn. 19, 25–27): Maternitas spiritualis Mariae in luce exegeseos SS. Patrum et scriptorum posteriorum", in *MSS*, 5:151–60; Henri Barré, C.S.Sp., "Exégèse de Jean 19, 25–27 et développement doctrinal", in *MSS*, 5:161–71; Pierre-Reginald Masson, O.P., " 'Ecce mater tua' (Jn. 19, 25–27) selon l'interprétation des théologiens", in *MSS*, 5:201–23; Jean-Marie Salgado, O.M.I., "La Maternité Spirituelle de la très Sainte Vierge Marie: Bilan Actuel", *Divinitas* 16 (1972): 17–102, and "Mise à Jour d'un Bilan: La Maternité Spirituelle de la Sainte Vierge Marie dans l'Écriture Sainte", *Divus Thomas (Piacenza)* 87 (1984): 289–323; Aristide Serra, O.S.M., *Maria a Cana e presso la croce* (Rome: Centro di Cultura Mariana, "Mater Ecclesiae", 1985), 81–121, and *Maria secondo il Vangelo* (Brescia: Editrice Queriniana, 1988), 149–72; Giuseppe Segalla, Luigi Gambero, and Théodore Koehler, S.M., *Maria ai piedi della Croce* (Casale Monferrato: Edizioni Piemme, 1989); Stefano M. Manelli, F.F.I., *Mariologia Biblica* (Frigento: Casa Mariana Editrice, 1989), 355–71.

[79] Cf. *DV*, no. 8.

[80] Domenico Bertetto, S.D.B., "Beata Virgo Maria et testamentum Domini in Cruce", in *MSS*, 5:197, cf. entire study 181–99. On what constitutes the "ordinary magisterium", cf. *LG*, no. 25.

'Behold your mother' and to the Mother, 'Behold your son' (Jn. 19, 26–27). *These words belong in his testament."* [81]

All of the modern Popes from Leo XIII onward have repeatedly taught that the beloved disciple represented all the faithful and indeed the whole human race.[82] Here is a representative text from Pius XII which exemplifies the ordinary magisterium of the modern papacy on Mary's spiritual Motherhood:

> Jesus Himself from His Cross on high ratified by means of a symbolic and efficacious gift the spiritual motherhood of Mary toward men when He pronounced the memorable words: "Woman, behold thy son." *He thus entrusted all Christians, in the person of the beloved disciple, to the most Blessed Virgin.*[83]

Of this patrimony of growth in insight and appreciation of the *testamentum Domini* John Paul II has surely made his own significant contribution[84] and will undoubtedly continue to do so. This is yet another factor which enters into the rationale of his "program of consecration and entrustment" to Mary and manifests its solid basis from the perspective of Scripture and tradition.

[81] *Sign of Contradiction,* 71 (my emphasis). He had also spoken of the gift of Mary's spiritual maternity as "the testament of Christ" in his homily of May 3, 1968, at Jasna Góra (*Omelie,* 23, 27) and has done so as Pope many times, e.g., at Fatima (*Inseg* V:2 [1982], 1567, 1578; *Portugal,* 72), at Luján in Argentina (*Inseg* V:2 [1982], 2201, 2205; *Argentina,* 23), and in *Redemptoris Mater,* no. 45 (*Inseg* X:1 [1987], 734–35; St. Paul ed., 64).

[82] Bonaventura Duda, O.F.M., "'Ecce mater tua' (Jo. 19, 26–27) in documentis Romanorum Pontificum", in *MSS,* 5:235–89.

[83] *AAS* 46 (1954): 494; *OL,* no. 648.

[84] Fr. Koehler, in Segalla et al., *Maria ai piedi della Croce,* 77–78, briefly calls attention to the contribution which John Paul II has made in expounding this text and notes that his treatment of John 19:25–27 in *Redemptoris Mater* is the most developed that any pope has yet made.

7

ENTRUSTMENT TO MARY

If from the pontificate of Benedict XIV, whose text on Mary's spiritual maternity was incorporated almost verbatim into *Lumen Gentium*, number 53,[1] John 19:25–27 has been reckoned as one of the primary factors in establishing the doctrine of Mary's spiritual maternity, then it would seem as if John Paul II is continuing the process of mining the hidden riches of this text (and consequently the development of doctrine) in finding in it the theological justification of, indeed the mandate for, entrustment/consecration to Mary. Here is a very interesting passage from a homily preached on July 2, 1979, during the first year of his pontificate, in which he rehearses some of the major elements to be derived from the text and points to the first intuition of its bearing on Mary's spiritual maternity in patristic exegesis:

> There is, in the first place, before our eyes the scene vividly described by the evangelist John: we are on Mount Calvary, there is a cross, and Jesus is nailed to it; and there is, close by, the mother of Jesus, surrounded by some women; there is also the beloved disciple, John himself. The Dying Man speaks, breathing with difficulty in the death agony: "Woman, behold, your son!" The intention is evident: Jesus wants to entrust his mother to the care of his beloved disciple.
>
> Is this all? The ancient Fathers of the Church caught sight of a deeper theological meaning behind this episode, which is appar-

[1] *Theotokos,* 374.

ently so simple. *Already Origen identifies the apostle John with every Christian* and, after him, the reference to this text becomes more and more frequent to justify Mary's universal motherhood.

It is a conviction that has a precise foundation in revelation: how can we fail to think, in fact, on reading this passage of Jesus' mysterious words during the wedding at Cana (cf. Jn. 2:4) when, to Mary's request, he replies calling her "woman"—as now—and postponing the beginning of his collaboration with her in favour of men to the moment of the Passion, his "hour," as he is accustomed to call it? (cf. Jn. 7:30; 8:20; 12:27; 13:1; Mk. 14:35, 41; Mt. 26:45; Lk. 22:53.)

Mary is fully conscious of the mission which has been entrusted to her; we find her at the beginning of the life of the Church, together with the disciples who are preparing for the imminent event of Pentecost, as the first lesson of the Mass reminds us. In this narration by Luke, her name stands out among those of the other women; the early community, gathered "in the Upper Room" in prayer, presses around her, "the mother of Jesus," as if seeking protection and comfort before the risks of a future overhung by threatening shadows. . . .

Now let us continue the celebration of Mass. In this liturgical assembly of ours, the experience of the Upper Room lives again mystically. Mary is with us. *We invoke her, we entrust ourselves to her.* May she help us in the resolution, which we renew here, to wish to imitate her generously.[2]

The text of Origen to which the Pope refers is this:

> The Gospels are the first fruits of all Scripture and the Gospel of John is the first of the Gospels. No one can understand the meaning of this Gospel if he has not reclined on the breast of Jesus, if he has not received from Jesus, Mary to be his Mother also. . . . In fact, every man who has become perfect no longer lives, but Christ lives in him and, because Christ lives in him, it is said of him to Mary: Behold your son Christ.[3]

[2] *Inseg* II:2 (1979), 12–13, 14; *ORE* 592:11 (my emphases).

[3] Greek text in Cipriano Vagaggini, O.S.B., *Maria nelle Opere di Origene* (Rome: Pont. Institutum Orientalium Studiorum, "Orientalia Christiana Analecta", no. 31, 1962), 177; Latin text in *PG,* 14, 31 A–B. This translation partially adapted from versions given in *Theotokos,* 254, 275.

Many commentators deny that it is possible to deduce Mary's spiritual maternity as a solid conclusion from this very evocative text. The underlying logic of Origen, they argue, runs like this: in order to understand the fourth gospel well each one ought to aspire to such perfection that he becomes in effect "another Christ" about whom Christ Himself could say to Mary, "Behold your son", namely, behold Jesus whom you bore, behold another Christ.[4] On the other hand, Father F. M. Braun, O.P., holds that "it appears clear that Origen was at least admitting a certain maternity in Mary towards John and those like him. . . . As inexact as the passage remains, it contains a first indication of the spiritual maternity of Mary." [5]

Father Jean-Marie Salgado, O.M.I., whose magisterial work, *La Maternité Spirituelle de la Très Sainte Vierge Marie*, takes account of all the major treatments on Mary's spiritual maternity until 1990, also maintains that, far from excluding Origen's principal idea of identification with Christ, the doctrine of Mary's universal spiritual maternity is implicitly required by such identification. He further holds that an unprejudiced reading of this text is sufficient to establish the conclusion that perfect and total identification with Christ, according to Origen, requires the acceptance of Mary's spiritual Motherhood.[6] Following this same line of reasoning, I would argue that Origen, consciously or not, was also laying the groundwork for the theology of entrustment or consecration to Mary.

While the Pope does not enter directly into the scholarly controversy about what Origen intended, nor does he

[4] Bertetto, "Beata Virgo Maria", 186; Koehler, "Maternité Spirituelle", 582; cf. also Gutierrez, 156; *Theotokos,* 254.

[5] F. M. Braun, O.P., *Mother of God's People,* trans. John Clarke, O.C.D. (New York: Alba House, 1967), 99–100.

[6] Jean-Marie Salgado, O.M.I., "La maternité spirituelle de la Sainte Vierge chez les Pères durant les quatre premiers siècles", *Divinitas* 30 (1986): 58–61, and *La Maternité Spirituelle,* 63–65.

declare that Origen definitively established the link between John 19:26–27 and Mary's spiritual maternity (even if he seems to imply it), he does point out that Origen identifies the apostle John with every Christian and that subsequently this text is referred to more and more frequently as an indication of Mary's universal Motherhood. In this sense, he, too, like Origen, is being evocative, suggesting that already Origen grasped a "spiritual sense"[7] in this text by his extraordinary intuition[8] even if he did not develop it further. Interestingly the Holy Father cites Origen again on this topic in the same evocative way in *Redemptoris Mater.*[9]

The above cited homily was preached on John 19:25–27 and Acts 1:12–14. In it John Paul also stated that "Mary is fully conscious of the mission which has been entrusted to her: we find her at the beginning of the life of the Church, together with the disciples who are preparing for the imminent event of Pentecost."[10] In fact just two months prior to that significant statement about Mary's consciousness of her mission, he had spoken of her as the one "to whose loving patronage God himself willed to entrust, through her obedient 'Yes', the fate of the whole of mankind."[11]

Christ's entrustment to Mary of every human being ("descending" entrustment)

Without fear of exaggeration we may speak of a "theology of entrustment" to Mary in the mind of John Paul II which is frequently expressed in his preaching. Here the word is particularly appropriate because it is, in fact, often used to describe what Jesus did from the Cross: He entrusted John

[7] Gutierrez, 152.

[8] Duda, 289.

[9] *Inseg* X:1 (1987), 706, n. 147; St. Paul ed., 76, n. 47.

[10] *Inseg* II:2 (1979), 13; *ORE* 592:11.

[11] *Inseg* II:1 (1979), 1054; *ORE* 582:3.

to Mary and Mary to John.[12] "Notice, finally," says Father Lucien Deiss, C.S.Sp., "that it is not Mary who is first entrusted to John, but John who is first entrusted to Mary. The accent is placed on the solicitude with which Mary is to surround the disciple, a solicitude to which the disciple is to respond with the tenderness of a son." [13]

Already in a homily at Jasna Góra on the Feast of Our Lady, Queen of Poland, in 1968, Cardinal Wojtyła had spoken similarly, both in terms of the act of "entrusting" by Christ and of the "mission" of Mary: "From the height of the Cross *the Son of God entrusted to the Mother a great mission*: to express the love of the Father, to express His own love linked to His martyrdom and to His death on the Cross, linked to His Resurrection." [14]

Countless numbers of times[15] John Paul emphasizes that in John, the beloved disciple, "every man [or woman] discovers that he [or she] is a child of the one who gave the world the Son of God." [16] Here is a particularly beautiful instance of this "theology of entrustment" which was spoken to youth at Jasna Góra in 1983 with reference to John 19:26:

[12] In *Redemptoris Mater,* no. 45, the Pope says: "Ut Redemptor Mariam Ioanni committit, ita simul Ioannem concredit Mariae" (*Inseg* X:1 [1987], 735). The English translation has: "The Redeemer entrusts Mary to John because he entrusts John to Mary" (St. Paul ed., 64), but, in fact, the Latin text suggests no such causal link; it merely asserts that "as the Redeemer entrusts Mary to John, he thus at the same time entrusts John to Mary." The Italian text is equally neutral, having "Il Redentore affida Maria a Giovanni in quanto affida Giovanni a Maria" (*Inseg* X:1 [1987], 795).

[13] Lucien Deiss, C.S.Sp., *Mary, Daughter of Sion,* trans. Barbara T. Blair (Collegeville, Minn.: Liturgical Press, 1972), 195. Don Giuseppe Segalla argues in the same vein in *Maria ai piedi della Croce,* 17–18.

[14] *Omelie,* 24 (my trans. and emphasis).

[15] One has only to look up the references to John 19:25–27 given in the volumes of the *Insegnamenti* to discover the frequency with which John Paul refers to the action of Christ as "entrustment".

[16] *Inseg* XII:1 (1989), 552; *ORE* 1081:1. The words in brackets do not appear in the original Italian text.

> We believe that, in that one man [John], Christ entrusted to her [Mary] every human being, and at the same time awoke in her heart a love which is a maternal reflection of his own redemptive love.
>
> We believe that we are loved by this love, surrounded by it, that is, by the love of God, which was revealed in the Redemption by means of the Cross, and finally by the love of the Mother, who stood beneath the Cross and who from the Heart of her Son accepted into her heart every human being.[17]

The poetic and delicate, even mystical, references to the Hearts of Jesus and Mary will be seen subsequently to be a further dimension of the Pope's thought on Marian consecration.

In a prayer for vocations in Bologna less than a month before his pilgrimage to Fatima in 1982, he coupled the notion of the "mission" entrusted to Mary from the Cross with what he would request at the great Portuguese shrine: that Mary unite our consecration to that of Jesus and to her own.

> We entrust our life to you, to you who welcomed the Word of God with absolute fidelity and *dedicated yourself to his plan of salvation and grace*, acceding to the action of the Holy Spirit with total docility; *to you who had from your Son the mission of receiving and caring for the disciple whom he loved (cf. Jn. 19:26); to you, each and every one of us repeats, "Totus tuus ego sum" (I am all yours), that you may take our consecration and unite it to that of Jesus and yours, as an offering to God the Father for the life of the world.*[18]

It will be recalled that in the solemn Acts of Consecration of 1982 and 1984, after citing the text about Christ's self-consecration (Jn 17:19) and our desire to unite ourselves to it, the Pope entrusted to Mary the world and "the [very] consecration itself, for the world's sake, placing it in your

[17] *Inseg* VI:1 (1983), 1563; *ORE* 791:3.

[18] *Inseg* V:1 (1982), 1217; *ORE* 731:6.

motherly Heart".[19] Notice, too, that the concepts expressed in the prayer said in Bologna are closely allied to that description of Mary in the Fatima consecration as "wholly united to the redeeming consecration of your Son".

Arguably the most authoritative, and possibly the most comprehensive, exposition of his "theology of entrustment" to date occurs in number 45 of *Redemptoris Mater*:

> The Redeemer entrusts his mother to the disciple, and at the same time he gives her to him as his mother. Mary's motherhood, which becomes man's inheritance, is a gift: *a gift which Christ himself makes* personally to every individual. As the Redeemer entrusts Mary to John, he thus at the same time entrusts John to Mary. At the foot of the Cross there begins that special *entrusting of humanity to the Mother of Christ,* which in the history of the Church has been practiced and expressed in different ways. [*Iuxta Crucem ille actus incipit peculiaris, quo homo Matri Christi committitur, quique postea in Ecclesiae historia variis modis exercebatur.*] The same Apostle and Evangelist, after reporting the words addressed by Jesus on the Cross to his Mother and to himself, adds: "And from that hour the disciple took her to his own home" (Jn. 19:27). This statement certainly means that the role of son was attributed to the disciple and that he assumed responsibility for the Mother of his beloved Master. And since Mary was given as a mother to him personally, the statement indicates, even though indirectly, everything expressed by the intimate relationship of a child with its mother. And all of this can be included in the word "entrusting." [*Totum hoc contineri potest verbo "commendationis".*] Such entrusting is the response to a person's love, and in particular to *the love of a mother.*[20]

In the strictest sense, of course, it is not man who initiates the act of consecration or entrusting, but God. In commenting on the Fatima consecration Father Eamon Carroll says:

[19] Cf. above, 192. This entrusting of our union with the consecration of Christ is also a feature of his Letter to the Bishop of Leiria of April 16, 1983, *Inseg* VI:1 (1983), 967.

[20] *Inseg* X:1 (1979), 735; St. Paul ed., 64 (alt).

> The pope's words make clear that consecration, as an act of religion, is properly directed to God alone, and that consecration is not simply a human act of religion, not something we do, or can do, independently of God's call, of the divine initiative. In the Bible, man never consecrates himself, for he is incapable of so doing. God calls the human being; the election and vocation come from God.[21]

The truth of this statement is borne out and supported by Father Stefano De Fiores in his article on consecration in the *Nuovo Dizionario di Mariologia:*

> It is God who predestines, calls, justifies, and glorifies (Rom 8:30). In particular, sanctification or consecration (*hagiazein*) is a divine act, which renders Christians "holy", or rather sanctified (1 Cor 1:2; Rom 15:16). This passive sense is expressed by Paul with an affirmation which is at base Trinitarian: "You were washed, you were sanctified, you were justified in the name of the Lord Jesus Christ and in the Spirit of our God" (1 Cor 6:11; cf. 2 Tim 2:13; Eph 2:1-6). Christians are not consecrated by themselves, but by virtue of baptism administered "in the name of the Father and of the Son and of the Holy Spirit" (Mt 28:19).[22]
>
> First as a commitment or ideal to actualize, consecration is a call, a grace, an action of God which touches and transforms human existence in its deepest reality.[23]
>
> Every Christian is consecrated by God and to God insofar as he is a member of the Church, the people of God who belong to Him and who ought to live for Him. In fact "Christ loved the Church and gave Himself up for her, that He might sanctify her (= consecrate her) having cleansed her by the washing of water with the word" (Eph 5:25–26). The titles of "spouse" and "virgin" attributed to the Church indicate that she ought to respond to the

[21] Carroll, "Mary: the Woman Come of Age", 153.

[22] "Cons.", 396 (my trans., *Revised Standard Version of the Holy Bible* [hereafter cited as *RSV*]).

[23] "Cons.", 408 (my trans.).

love of Christ with the yes of faith and consecration to Him of her entire life.[24]

The late Father Domenico Bertetto, S.D.B., attempted a further clarification of God's initiative in consecrating by distinguishing between "descending" and "ascending" consecration:

> Consecration is above all *descending*, or rather the action of God, who communicates His perfections, His authority, His holiness, His powers to His creatures. . . .
>
> The consecration *descending* from God implies also on that account a consecration *ascending* from the creature, conscious and free, who recognizes his belonging to God and therefore commits himself to be God's, entrusted to God, put at the service of God, according to the requirement of the consecration received, under the efficacious influence of the Spirit.
>
> Every ascending consecration, which John Paul II likes to call *entrustment* in order to distinguish it from descending consecration, sets out from the recognition of the relations which link the consecrated person to the One to whom he is consecrated.[25]

While one may find Bertetto's distinction helpful in emphasizing God's initiative in the "descending" consecration and ours in the "ascending" one, his contention that Pope John Paul II makes such a real distinction between consecration and entrustment is simply contrary to the facts. In both the major acts of 1982 and 1984 he uses the terms synonymously in the body of the text and as a title of the latter in the covering letter sent to the bishops of the world.[26] But, of even greater significance is the fact which we have seen the Pope emphasizing here, namely that *in the first*

[24] "Cons.", 411–12 (my trans., *RSV*).

[25] Domenico Bertetto, S.D.B., "Consacrazione e affidamento: Senso ed esigenze dell' affidamento a Maria", in *L'Affidamento a Maria,* ed. Bertetto (Rome: Libreria Ateneo Salesiano, 1984), 75–76 (my trans.). This thesis is also espoused by other members of the Salesian family including its Rector Major, Egidio Viganò, see De Fiores, *Maria nella Teologia Contemporanea,* 331–33.

[26] *Inseg* VII:1 (1984), 417; *ORE* 823:2. Cf. also our discussion above, 143–52.

instance it is Christ Himself who entrusts us to Mary. In John Paul's exegesis of John 19:25–27 he repeats over and over again that it is Christ who, by entrusting John to Mary, has entrusted us all to her.

The theme of entrusting to Mary, particularly as a response to her motherly love, which we have seen referred to in *Redemptoris Mater*, number 45,[27] is a fascinating one. The Pope further states that "the figure of Mary of Nazareth sheds light on *womanhood as such* by the very fact that God, in the sublime event of the Incarnation of his Son, entrusted himself to the ministry, the free and active ministry of a woman." [28] In this regard I would like to present some of the reflections of Dr. Joyce A. Little of the University of Saint Thomas, Houston, which were presented at the Annual Convention of the Mariological Society of America in June of 1988, which had *Redemptoris Mater* as its theme.

Dr. Little asks, "Why does the Pope identify 'entrusting' as that which defines the importance not only of Mary, but of women in general? " [29] and again,

[27] Cf. above, 225.

[28] St. Paul ed., 65. Curiously, the Latin text is more sober and does not speak of God's entrusting Himself to Mary: "Hic solum animadvertere placet Mariam Nazarethanam lucem effundere in mulierem ut talem eo ipso quod Deus, in praecelso eventu Incarnationis Filii, ministerio libero et actuoso mulieris est usus" (*Inseg* X:1 [1987], 736–37). However, the Italian translation, which may well represent the Pope's thought more accurately here, is: "Qui desidero solo rilevare che la figura di Maria di Nazareth proietta luce sulla *donna in quanto tale* per il fatto stesso che Dio, nel sublime evento dell' incarnazione del Figlio, si è affidato al ministero, libero e attivo, di una donna" (*Inseg* X:1 [1987], 796). I retain the Vatican English translation here, as well, because it conforms sufficiently to other statements of the Pope on the matter of God's entrusting of Himself to Mary (cf. *Inseg* III:1 [1980], 414; *ORE* 623:8) and His "entrusting to women" in a special way (cf. *Mulieris Dignitatem,* nos. 30–31, *Inseg* XI:3 [1988], 311–16, 374–76; *ORE* 1058:13; and *Christifideles Laici,* no. 51, *Inseg* XI:4 [1988], 2056–60, 2154–57; *ORE* 1075:17).

[29] Joyce A. Little, "*Redemptoris Mater:* The Significance of Mary for Women", *Marian Studies* 39 (1988): 140.

> Why is it that entrusting does not, at least in its most basic form, refer to the relationship which exists between a father and a child, or, more specifically, between the Eternal Father in heaven and his children here on earth? To put it another way, what is the difference between fatherhood and motherhood which requires that we identify "entrusting" more with the love of a mother than with the love of a father? The answer, I believe, lies in the difference between that distancing which is implied by fatherhood, as contrasted with the immediacy which is associated with motherhood.[30]

She goes on, then, to justify this identification of distance with fatherhood by citing first Father Walter J. Ong who says that "Masculinity stands in the human psyche for a kind of otherness, difference" and that, therefore, God

> is likened to the masculine not because he has a masculine physical constitution, but because he is a source of existence that is other, different, separated (*kadosh,* the Hebrew word translated *sanctus, hagios,* "holy," means at root "separated") from all his creation, even from human beings, though they are "made in his image and likeness". . . . The male reproductive cell becomes effectively reproductive when it is totally detached from the male's body and joins the cell that, in the higher forms of life, remains attached to the female. Fathers are essentially distant from offspring physically. They can even be dead and buried when the child is being formed and is born.[31]

With regard to identifying immediacy with motherhood, she cites the psychiatrist Karl Stern who says that "Woman, in her being, is deeply committed to *bios,* to nature itself. The words for *mother* and *matter,* for *mater* and *materia* are etymologically related."[32]

[30] Little, 141–42.

[31] Walter J. Ong, S.J., *Fighting for Life* (Ithaca, N.Y./London: Cornell University Press, 1981), 175–76.

[32] Karl Stern, *The Flight from Woman* (New York: Farrar, Strauss and Giroux, 1965), 23.

Dr. Little proceeds, then, to theologize about these distinctions between the role of father and mother in a way that very interestingly links "entrusting" to mothers and to Mary.

> Motherhood lies at the center of the New Covenant, because the Father entrusts his Son to a mother. But, in point of fact and as noted earlier, God entrusts every child of his making to a mother. Each of us, by our very creation, is forced, as it were, to trust the mother to whom God has entrusted us. As Stern has observed, the paradox of being human resides in the fact that, while we are the summit of God's creation, each one of us must, in order to enter this life, pass through a period of "utter helplessness and dependence." We must trust our mothers for the simple reason that we are given, literally, no alternatives. For that reason alone, as Stern points out, "faith grows out of the relation of child and mother."[33] Father, whether divine or human, lies off in the distance, beyond mother.
>
> If our relationship with God the Father does not supply the most basic instance of "entrusting," it is because we are material beings who must first be "entrusted" to a mother before there is any possibility of our coming to know our father, whether human or divine. And, for the same reason, of course, our relationship with Christ also cannot supply the most basic instance of "entrusting," inasmuch as we must also necessarily trust our mothers before we are in a position to entrust ourselves to Christ. We must, in other words, be born of flesh and blood before we can be born of water and the Spirit. No one can enter into the New Covenant by way of baptism who has not first entered into the world by way of a woman.[34]

Inter alia, she draws this very obvious conclusion, which is nonetheless hardly sufficiently appreciated with regard to its applications on the divine or human levels:

> Mothers are therefore the first, and generally, the most influential guide children are given in this world. *Children are entrusted to*

[33] Stern, 188–89.

[34] Little, 144–45.

> *mothers, in order that mothers might enable children to entrust themselves to others, initially their fathers, and, of course, ultimately their Eternal Father.* And, since not all people or things are trustworthy, children also depend on their mothers to inform them of and protect them from anyone or anything which might harm them. The child is entrusted to his mother in order that he might know, beyond her, what can and cannot be trusted.[35]

I have taken note of and referred to the arguments of Dr. Little at some length because I believe that they illustrate and provide further context for the thought of John Paul II.

In his apostolic letter *Mulieris Dignitatem*, On the Dignity and Vocation of Women, on the occasion of the Marian Year he says:

> The moral and spiritual strength of a woman is joined to her awareness that *God entrusts the human being to her in a special way*. Of course, God entrusts every human being to each and every other human being. But this entrusting concerns women in a special way—precisely by reason of their femininity—and this in a particular way determines their vocation.
>
> The moral force of women, which draws strength from this awareness and this entrusting, expresses itself in a great number of figures of the Old Testament, of the time of Christ, and of later ages right up to our own day.
>
> *A woman is strong because of her awareness of this entrusting,* strong because of the fact that God "entrusts the human being to her", always and in every way, even in the situations of social discrimination in which she may find herself. This awareness and this fundamental vocation speak to women of the dignity which they receive from God himself, and this makes them "strong" and strengthens their vocations.[36]

Evidently assuming as a foundation what he had already asserted in *Redemptoris Mater* and *Mulieris Dignitatem,* the Pope simply stated in his post-synodal apostolic exhortation *Christifideles Laici* that "two great tasks entrusted to women

[35] Little, 146 (my emphasis).

[36] *Inseg* XI:3 (1988), 313, 375–76; *ORE* 1058:13.

merit the attention of everyone": "the task of *bringing full dignity to conjugal life and to motherhood*" and "the task of *assuring the moral dimension of culture*".[37] Again in Vicenza on the Feast of Our Lady's Nativity in 1991 he spoke thus: "Mothers who are listening to me, how great is the task which God entrusts to you! How important is your role in the education of your children, the fruit of your family's love."[38] Undoubtedly the theme of "entrusting to women", even if the Pope doesn't speak on it with great frequency, is an important point of reference for him and a further basis for this theology of "entrustment to Mary".

We have noted above Father Stefano De Fiores' comment that entrustment "includes an attitude of interior trust. . . . In order to make an act of entrustment it is necessary to have trust in the person to whom one entrusts himself."[39] Dr. Little's last lines quoted above also recognize the link between "entrusting" and "trust". Let us hear her further on this topic.

> Mothers, it might therefore be said, stand for the realm of trust, first, in the sense that the survival of children depends primarily on the trustworthiness of mothers, and second, in the sense that mothers, more than any other person in our lives, are expected to be able to distinguish, beyond themselves, what can be trusted from what cannot. Indeed, in a larger sense, the female per se would seem to stand for the realm of trust.[40]

It is in this sense, she points out, that Mary has a crucial role to play in our lives. She assures us that her Son is worthy of all trust and that we will not be misled in entrusting ourselves totally to Him.

> Mary is our most reliable guide to Christ, the person in the best position to attest to the truth of Christ, precisely because she is his

[37] *Inseg* XI:4 (1988), 2058–59, 2156; *ORE* 1075:17.

[38] *ORE* 1207:1.

[39] Cf. above, 146–47.

[40] Little, 146–47.

> mother. She knows him as no one else among us possibly can. And because God was able to entrust his only Son to her, her Son has been able to entrust us to her guidance. When Mary counsels every one of us to "Do whatever he tells you," she is assuring us that we can entrust ourselves to him. By so doing, she is inviting every one of us to do what is, in the created order, the supremely female thing, namely to surrender ourselves to another. . . .
>
> If Christ is the truth, then Mary is the trust. And the truth, because personal and material, cannot be efficacious in our world unless we entrust ourselves to him. For that reason, Christ requires the female mediation of his mother, for only a mother can offer us the assurance we require that we not only can believe what he says, but can also safely entrust ourselves to the Person he is.[41]

Hardly surprisingly, we find this dimension of trust in Mary as a frequent motif in the Marian teaching of John Paul II. Perhaps what might be described as his two principal catecheses on this subject were both appropriately given in the chapel of the Roman Major Seminary whose sanctuary features a beautiful depiction of Our Lady under the title of *La Madonna della Fiducia* (Our Lady of Confidence). The first of these was given on February 16, 1980.

> Mary's joy was . . . joy for the trust that God had shown in her by entrusting himself to her in the person of his Only Son. Bearing in her womb the Word incarnate, and giving him to the world, *she became the extraordinary depositary of God's trust in man,* so that Mary is rightly honoured as the Mother of divine confidence. . . .
>
> Dear seminarians and dear youths, to respond to such divine trust, that is, to the grace of vocation, it is necessary above all to have confidence; the grace of the Lord is greater than our weakness, it is greater than our unworthiness, precisely as St. John expresses: "By this we shall . . . reassure our hearts before him whenever our hearts condemn us; for God is greater than our hearts" (1 Jn. 3:19–20). We must have invincible confidence, so as always to deserve the trust of the Lord; and *Mary who is mother of God's trust in us, will thus become, at the same time, mother of our trust in him.*

[41] Little, 148–49.

The pious invocation "Mater mea, fiducia mea", so dear to all those who have been formed in this Seminary, contains the deepest and fullest sense of our relationship with Mary, who is praised and venerated precisely by means of such regard of confidence, esteem and hope. In fact, "the Father's eternal love, which has been manifested in the history of mankind through the Son . . . comes to each of us through this Mother and thus takes on tokens that are of more easy understanding and access by each person. Consequently, Mary must be on all the ways for the Church's daily life" (*Redemptor Hominis,* no. 22).[42]

The second was given on February 12, 1983, and was a kind of homiletic response to a musical setting of the Gospel passage on the wedding feast of Cana (Jn 2:1–11) which had just been performed in the Pope's presence for the Feast of Our Lady of Confidence.

What were the newly-weds feeling in their hearts at the moment that the wine ran out, as they approached the Mother of Jesus? Confidence, precisely. They had confidence in her. They had a spontaneous confidence, a confidence that said: "She can help us". Why? Maybe they did not think it, maybe they did not know it, but they felt it: "She can help us because she is the Mother, and being a mother she can understand us, she can understand our difficulties and this is the first step to helping: understanding the difficulties. And then, after having understood our difficulties, she will be able to help us".

They were not thinking about *how* she could help them, but they were convinced that she *would* help them. So in the Gospel about Cana in Galilee, one discovers human confidence and at the same time the Mother of Confidence, because Mary did not disappoint the newly-weds, but rather did what they wanted: she helped them. . . .

If we have confidence in the Mother of Christ as the newly-weds at Cana did, we can entrust our worries to her, as they did. We can also entrust to her our decisions, the interior torments which sometimes afflict us; *we can entrust all this to her, to Our Lady of Confidence, that is, to the Mother of our trust: I place my trust in you,*

[42] *Inseg* III:1 (1980), 414–16; *ORE* 623:8–9 (my emphasis).

> *I wish to dedicate myself to Christ, but I entrust myself to you, just as the newly-weds did.* They did not go directly to Christ to ask for a miracle, they went to Mary; they entrusted their worries, their difficulties to Mary. *In so doing, they naturally wanted to arrive at Christ,* they wanted to provoke Christ—if one can say so—and his messianic power. And thus we too, in our vocation which is a path, a spiritual walk toward Christ, *in order to be Christ's, to be an* alter Christus, *we too must find this Mother of our trust and we must entrust ourselves to her in order to entrust ourselves to Christ, to dedicate ourselves to Christ, to give ourselves to Christ. We must entrust ourselves to her because there is but a single course, and if we turn to her we turn to Christ,* just as the newly-weds turned to her and arrived at Christ. Thus is Mary united to her Son.[43]

On many occasions, as well, the Pope has also given clear indications that entrustment to Mary implies trust in her motherly concern for her children, that it is an act of trust, even of "abandonment"[44] to her. Here are some instances. In his first major act of entrustment outside of Rome, that of Mexico and Latin America, made in Guadalupe on January 27, 1979, he prayed:

> We offer and entrust to you everybody and everything for which we have pastoral responsibility, *confident that you will be with us and will help us* to carry out what your Son has told us to do (cf. Jn. 2:5). *We bring you this unlimited trust; with this trust I, John Paul II, with all my Brothers in the Episcopate of Mexico and Latin America, wish to bind you still more strongly to our ministry, to the Church and to the life of our nations.* We wish to place in your hands the whole of our future, the future of evangelization in Latin America.[45]

Again that same year at Jasna Góra he spoke of the 1966 act of servitude to the Mother of God in these terms:

> Love constitutes the fulfillment of freedom, yet at the same time "belonging," and so not being free is part of its essence. However,

[43] *Inseg* VI:1 (1983), 409–11; *ORE* 775:10–11 (alt.), (my emphases).

[44] Cf. above, 149, n. 42.

[45] *Inseg* II:1 (1979), 165; *Messages,* 238 (my emphases).

> this "not being free" in love is not felt as slavery but rather as an affirmation and fulfillment of freedom. The act of consecration in slavery indicates therefore a unique dependence and a limitless trust.[46]

And then he added just before he renewed this consecration himself:

> Consent that I should bring here, as I did already in the Basilica of St. Mary Major in Rome and later in the shrine of Guadalupe in Mexico, the mysteries of the hearts, the sorrow and suffering, and finally *the hope and expectation of this final period of the twentieth century of the Christian era.*
>
> Consent that I should *entrust* all this to Mary.
>
> Consent that I should *entrust* it to her in a new and solemn way.
>
> I am a man of great trust.
>
> I learnt to be so here.[47]

Again he prefaced the entrustment of Ireland to Mary on September 30, 1979, with these words: "I pronounce, at the close of this homily, the following words of trust and consecration." [48] Likewise on the occasion of the centenary of the evangelization of Zaire and of its consecration to Mary by the first missionaries he prayed:

> I entrust to you . . . the whole nation, which is living its own independent life today. I do so in the *same spirit of faith* and with the same *trust* as the first missionaries, and I do so at the same time *with all the greater joy since the act of consecration and abandonment* that I make now, is made with me at the same time by all the *pastors* of this Church and also by the whole *People of God*: this People of God that wishes to assume and continue with its pastors, in love and apostolic courage, the work of the construction of the Body of Christ and the approach of the kingdom of God on this earth.
>
> Accept, O Mother, *this act of trust* of ours.[49]

[46] *Inseg* I:1 (1979), 1414; *Poland,* 106.

[47] *Inseg* I:1 (1979), 1416; *Poland,* 109.

[48] *Inseg* II:2 (1979), 468; *Ireland,* 88.

[49] *Inseg* III:1 (1980), 1069–70; *Africa Ap,* 41–42 (my emphases).

Again on the occasion of the consecration of Brazil he prayed:

> I wish to entrust to you particularly this people and this Church, this whole great and hospitable Brazil, all your sons and daughters, with all their problems and their worries, their activities and their joys. I wish to do so as Successor of Peter and Pastor of the universal Church, *entering into this heritage of veneration and love, dedication and trust,* which for centuries has been part of the Church of Brazil and of all those who form it.[50]

And, perhaps most significantly, he prayed in the course of his Act of Entrustment of the world to Mary at Fatima on May 13, 1982: "Accept our humble trust—and our act of entrusting!"[51] It should be fairly clear, then, after reviewing these representative texts, that in the mind of John Paul II entrusting to Mary necessarily implies trust in her and is predicated upon such confidence.[52]

What Dr. Little has articulated in terms of anthropology, John Paul has fleshed out in the exercise of his teaching office: *we entrust ourselves to Mary because we trust her as a mother and in order to entrust ourselves ever more completely to Christ.* In an address to the male religious of Guatemala on March 7, 1983, he said, "I entrust you to her, to preserve and increase your fidelity to Christ and to the Church."[53] In a prayer before the statue of Our Lady of Fatima which had been brought into Saint Peter's Basilica after the Act of Entrustment on March 25, 1984, he said: "Today we have wanted to entrust the fate of the world, of individuals, of peoples, to your Immaculate Heart in order to arrive at the

[50] *Inseg* III:2 (1980), 106; *Brazil,* 185 (my emphasis).

[51] *Inseg* V:2 (1982), 1587; *ORE* 735:12.

[52] That this relationship between trust in Mary and entrustment to her has been a consistent theme in the teaching of Karol Wojtyła may be observed in a sermon he gave on December 31, 1966 (*The Word Made Flesh: The Meaning of the Christmas Season,* trans. Leslie Wearne [San Francisco: Harper & Row, 1985], 81–82) and in *Sources of Renewal,* 422.

[53] *Inseg* VI:1 (1983), 637; *ORE* 779:12.

very centre of the mystery of the Redemption."[54] He puts it with great clarity in *Redemptoris Mater* that entrustment to Mary is not only willed by Christ but also has Him as its final end; He is both its *terminus a quo* and its *terminus ad quem*:

> This filial relationship, this self-entrusting of a child to its mother, not only has its *beginning in Christ* but can also be said to be *definitively directed towards him*. Mary can be said to continue to say to each individual the words which she spoke at Cana in Galilee: "Do whatever he tells you." For he, Christ, is the one Mediator between God and mankind; he is "the way, and the truth, and the life" (Jn. 14:6); it is he whom the Father has given to the world, so that man "should not perish but have eternal life" (Jn. 3:16). The Virgin of Nazareth became the first "witness" of this saving love of the Father, and she also wishes to *remain* its *humble handmaid always and everywhere*. For every Christian, for every human being, Mary is the one who first "believed," and *precisely with her faith as Spouse and Mother she wishes to act upon all those who entrust themselves to her as her children. And it is well known that the more her children persevere and progress in this attitude, the nearer Mary leads them to the "unsearchable riches of Christ"* (Eph. 3:8).[55]

This, indeed, is a beautifully rich yet concise statement on the rationale of Marian entrustment.

Our considerations about the divine initiative in consecration/entrustment, about what Father Bertetto calls "descending" consecration and the appropriateness of the word *entrust* to express the disciple's relationship to Mary all serve to reinforce this fundamental insight: *the principal Christological foundation of Marian consecration is that it is the express will of Christ as stated in John 19:26–27. Jesus Himself entrusts us to Mary*. The primary Marian entrustment, then, is a "descending" one; it comes from Him, but it is meant by Him to be complemented by an "ascending" one on our part.

[54] *Inseg* VII:1 (1984), 779; *ORE* 828:10.

[55] *Inseg* X:1 (1987), 736; St. Paul ed., 65 (final emphasis mine).

This, as we have already seen, is a fundamental perspective of John Paul II. Let us listen to how he relates the "descending" to the "ascending" entrustment in his words outside the Cathedral of Turin on April 13, 1980.

> Our hearts do not forget that she was standing by the cross of Jesus (cf. Jn. 19:25): *stabat Mater dolorosa.* Nor can we forget that, from the Cross, *Jesus looked at his mother and John,* the disciple whom he loved, and, as to a special witness, indicated to the disciple Mary, as Mother, *and entrusted the disciple to his Mother:* "Behold, your mother!" "Woman, behold your son!" (Jn. 19:27, 26). We believe that in this one man, precisely in John, Jesus indicated Mary as Mother of every man—*He entrusted everyone to her, as if every man were her child, her son or her daughter.*
>
> *From this fact is derived the particular necessity that we—obedient to these words of Christ's testament—should entrust ourselves and everything that belongs to us, to Mary.*
>
> Letting myself be guided by this faith and at the same time by this hope, today I wish to renew what is part of Christ's paschal testament and entrust to the Mother of God this city and this Church which welcomes me as a pilgrim today. . . .
>
> O Mother, may this prayer and this abandonment, which we renew once more, tell you everything about us.[56]

Again, in an even more emphatic way he underscored the necessity of the "ascending" entrustment on our part in his Angelus address of January 3, 1988.

> What, then, should be our attitude towards her whom Jesus himself gave us as our mother? Our attitude cannot be other than that of the Apostle John, of whom it was said, "From that moment the disciple took her to his own house" (Jn. 19:27). To accept Mary in our lives, entrusting ourselves totally to her: this is what Our Lady expects of each of us. Entrustment is the only response adequate to the love of a person, in particular to the love of a mother.[57]

[56] *Inseg* III:1 (1980), 891–93; *ORE* 629:2 (my emphasis).

[57] *Inseg* XI:1 (1988), 14; *ORE* 1021:3.

The "ascending" entrustment is derived from the "descending" entrustment and necessitated by it. What Jesus has done for us in principle, we must ratify and appropriate both individually as well as collectively. On May 12, 1991, during a prayer vigil held in Fatima, Portugal, the Holy Father summarized his understanding of this exigency once again in a way that is particularly striking:

> During this journey [Mary's life on earth] of collaboration in the work of the redemption, her motherhood "itself underwent a singular transformation, becoming ever more imbued with 'burning charity', towards all those to whom Christ's mission was directed" (*Redemptoris Mater,* 39) and whose Mother he consecrated her at the foot of the cross: "Behold your son!" In fact, since she gave birth to Christ, the Head of the Mystical Body, she also had to have given birth to all the members of that one Body. Therefore, "Mary embraces each and every one *in* the Church, and embraces each and every one *through* the Church" (*Redemptoris Mater,* 47). *The Church, for her part does not cease consecrating herself to Mary.*[58]

The Church does not cease consecrating herself to Mary who was consecrated her Mother at the foot of the Cross, says John Paul II. And never, would it seem, has there been a Pope who has been so intrepid in giving voice to this ceaseless consecration.

Welcoming/receiving Mary ("ascending" entrustment)

"Entrusting oneself totally to Mary", then, according to Pope John Paul II, means "accepting Mary into our lives". And, indeed, according to the best insights into the fourth gospel, this is precisely the response of the beloved disciple to his being entrusted by Jesus to Mary. "And from that hour the disciple took her to his own home" (Jn 19:27).

[58] *ORE* 1191:5 (final emphasis mine).

Thus the rendition of the usually very dependable Revised Standard Version. "But", says Canon McHugh,

> if we take careful notice of John's vocabulary, a more meaningful rendering emerges. In the Fourth Gospel, the verb *lambáno* has two senses. When applied to material things, it means simply "to take hold of," "to pick up," "to grasp," etc. (*e.g.* 6:11; 12:13; 13:12; 19:23, 40); when applied to immaterial things, it means "to accept" or "to welcome," usually as a gift from God (*e.g.* his witness, 3:11; his word, 17:8; his Spirit, 14:17; I Jn. 2:27). Secondly, the words *'eis tà 'ídia,* which certainly can mean "to one's own home" (in a purely physical sense), can also mean "among one's own spiritual possessions" (compare Jn. 8:44 and 15:19, in the Greek). The phrase is found in the prologue with this double meaning of "physical home" and "spiritual possession," and in close conjunction with the verb "to accept or welcome." "He came to *what was his own* . . . and to all who *accepted* him, he gave the power to become children of God" (Jn. 1:12–13). Jn. 19:27 seems to demand a translation which includes both the purely physical and the deeper, spiritual sense. "And from that hour the disciple took her into his own home, and accepted her as his own mother, as part of the spiritual legacy bequeathed to him by his Lord." [59]

"To receive Jesus and to receive His Mother are, definitively, two equivalent gestures", says Father Ignace de la Potterie, S.J., quoting Father André Feuillet, P.S.S.[60] In another place he says: "This relation to Christ is prolonged now in a new relationship of the disciple to the Mother of Jesus. In other words, the welcome which the disciple accords to the Mother of Jesus maintains a Christological

[59] McHugh, 378. (In the seventh line of this quotation I have given the reference to John 17:8 rather than to 17:18 which seems to be a typographical error in the book.) Cf. also Braun, 119–24; Aristide Serra, O.S.M., *Contributi dell'antica letteratura giudaica per l'esegesi di Giovanni 2, 1–12 e 19, 25–27* (Rome: Herder, 1977), 217, 226; *Maria a Cana,* 106–15; *Maria secondo il Vangelo,* 165–66.

[60] Ignace de la Potterie, S.J., "La maternità spirituale di Maria e la fondazione della chiesa", in *Gesù verità: Studi di cristologia giovannea* (Turin: Marietti, 1973), 160, n. 17 (my trans.).

significance."[61] Father de la Potterie, who has become an authority on the text of John 19:27b, traces the concept of receiving or welcoming Mary[62] through the Spanish Renaissance Cardinal Toleto back to Saint Ambrose[63] and indicates that the Greek words *'eis tà 'ídia* were understood by the late Cardinal Charles Journet in a manner similar to that expounded by Canon McHugh:

> "He took her [let us say rather: "he welcomed her"] *into his intimacy*", into his interior life, *into his faith life.* This interiority of the disciple is none other than his availability to open himself in faith to the last words of Jesus and to carry out His spiritual testament, becoming the son of the Mother of Jesus, welcoming her as his Mother in his life as a disciple: the Mother of Jesus, henceforth, is also *his Mother.*[64]

Father Stefano De Fiores provides an appropriate practical summary of the exegetical positions which we have just presented with regard to the concept of "welcoming Mary" in his article on consecration in the *Nuovo Dizionario di Mariologia*[65] as well as in *Maria nella Teologia Contemporanea.*[66] We cited material from the latter source above together with the apposite comments of Bishop Franzi.[67]

[61] Ignace de la Potterie, S.J., "La parole de Jésus", 37–38 (my trans.). Fr. de la Potterie further defended this position in the light of a controversy with F. Neirynck with " 'Et à partir de cette heure, le Disciple l'accueillit dans son intimité' (Jn. 19, 27b)", *Marianum* 42 (1980): 84–125.

[62] Cf. Ignace de la Potterie, S.J., *Maria nel mistero dell' alleanza* (Genoa: Marietti "Dabar", 1988), 243, in which he, like McHugh, makes an excellent case for translating the Greek verb *lambáno* in this instance, by the Italian word *accogliere* (to receive, to accept, to welcome) or the French word *accueillir* (to receive, to receive graciously, to welcome).

[63] Serra, in *Maria a Cana,* 111–12, provides brief texts on this topic from St. Ambrose and Toleto.

[64] De la Potterie, *Maria nel mistero dell' alleanza,* 245 (my trans.).

[65] "Cons.", 398, 409, 410, 413.

[66] See 326–28.

[67] Cf. above, 152–53.

In his constant and consistent treatment of John 19:25–27 the Holy Father has shown himself to be in complete accord with this exegetical position. Already in his first encyclical *Redemptor Hominis* he said:

> Her Son [Jesus] explicitly extended His Mother's maternity in a way that could easily be understood by every soul and every heart by designating, when He was raised on the cross, His beloved disciple as her son. . . . Later, all the generations of disciples, of those who confess and love Christ, like the apostle John, spiritually took this Mother to their own homes.[68]

In his homily at Fatima on May 13, 1982, which is a theological as well as pastoral masterpiece, he begins by citing John 19:27, developing first its literal meaning and then drawing out its "spiritual sense" with particular regard to Marian sanctuaries:

> The words "he took her to his own home" can be taken in the literal sense as referring to the place where he lived.
>
> Mary's motherhood in our regard is manifested in a particular way in the places where she meets us: her dwelling places; places in which a special presence of the mother is felt.
>
> There are many such dwelling places. They are of all kinds: from a special corner in the home or little wayside shrines adorned with an image of the Mother of God, to chapels and churches built in her honor. However, in certain places the Mother's presence is felt in a particularly vivid way. These places sometimes radiate their light over a great distance and draw people from afar. Their radiance may extend over a diocese, a whole nation, or at times over several countries and even continents. These places are the Marian sanctuaries or shrines.
>
> In all these places that unique testament of the crucified Lord is wonderfully actualized: in them man feels that he is entrusted and confided to Mary; he goes there in order to be with her, as with his Mother; he opens his heart to her and speaks to her about everything: he *"takes her to his own home," that is to say, he brings her into all his problems, which at times are difficult. His own problems and*

[68] *Inseg* II:1 (1979), 607; St. Paul ed., 56.

those of others. The problems of the family, of societies, of nations, and of the whole of humanity.[69]

Just two weeks earlier he developed this same theme with a large group of priests who work with the Focolari Movement (also known as "Opera di Maria"). This time he drew out the meaning of John 19:27 with particular reference to priests.

> The Gospel text just cited offers us the model for our devotion to Mary. "And from that hour the disciple took her to his own home" (Jn. 19:27). Can the same be said of us? *Do we also welcome Mary into our homes? Indeed, we should grant her full rights in the home of our lives, of our faith, of our affections, of our commitments, and acknowledge the maternal role that is hers, that is to say, her function as guide, as adviser, as encourager, or even merely as a silent presence which at times may of itself be enough to infuse us with strength and courage.* On the other hand, the first Scripture reading reminded us that the first disciples, after Jesus' ascension, were gathered with "Mary, the Mother of Jesus" (Acts 1:14). She was, therefore, also a part of their community; in fact, perhaps it was she who gave it cohesion. And the fact that she is specified as "the Mother of Jesus" shows how closely she was linked to the figure of her son; it tells us that Mary recalls always and only the salvific value of what Jesus did, our only Saviour, and on the other hand *it likewise tells us that to believe in Jesus Christ cannot dispense us from including also in our act of faith the one who was his mother.* In God's family, and so much more in the priestly family, Mary watches over the diversity of each one within the communion of all. *And at the same time she can teach us to be open to the Holy Spirit, to share anxiously Christ's total dedication to the will of the Father; above all she can teach us to participate deeply in the passion of the Son and carry out our ministry with assured spiritual fruitfulness. "Behold, your mother!" (Jn. 19:27). Everyone feels that these words are addressed to him, and therefore draws faith and enthusiasm from*

[69] *Inseg* V:2 (1982), 1568, 1578; *Portugal*, 73 (my emphasis). In his Letter to the Bishop of Leiria of April 16, 1983, he took up the theme again of Marian sanctuaries as special places of encounter with Our Lady, but expanded also on the need of each pilgrim to open his heart to her, to receive her even into his problems and preoccupations, cf. *Inseg* VI:1 (1983), 968.

them for an always more determined and serene journey along the committed road of his priestly life.[70]

To welcome, to receive Mary "as guide, as adviser, as encourager, or even merely as a silent presence" is a concrete translation of what the text *'élaben autèn ho mathètes 'eis tà 'ídia,* "to receive Mary as one of his spiritual goods" (Jn 19:27), means. It is an exhortation to which the Holy Father likes to return, especially with priests, since the "beloved disciple" represents not only all the faithful, but as a member of the Apostolic College, priests in a special way.[71] To ordinands in Valencia on November 8, 1982, he said, "Welcome her [Mary] as a Mother as John welcomed her at the foot of the Cross",[72] and he took up the theme explicitly in his Holy Thursday Letter to Priests of March 25, 1988.[73]

On May 8, 1983, at the Marian Shrine of Suyapa, Honduras, Pope John Paul II even more explicitly made his own the interpretation of *'eis tà 'ídia* proposed by the exegetes cited above. Here is what he said on that occasion:

> In the hour of Jesus, of his Mother and of the Church, the words of the Redeemer are solemn and they make real what they proclaim: Mary is made the mother of Christ's disciples, of all men. Whoever welcomes in faith the doctrine of the Teacher has the privilege, the fortune, of welcoming the virgin as mother, *of receiving her with faith and love among his most beloved goods,* with the security that she who has faithfully carried out the word of the

[70] *Inseg* V:1 (1982), 1370–71; *ORE* 736:12 (my emphases).

[71] While there continues to be a great deal of speculation on the identity of the "beloved disciple" as to whether he is John, the son of Zebedee, and also the author of the fourth gospel (cf. Brown, *John, I–XII,* lxxxvii–cii), the Holy Father continues to follow the tradition in assuming him to be John the Apostle (cf. *Inseg* X:3 [1987], 1377; *ORE* 1020:11; *Inseg* XI:1 (1988), 724, 736; *ORE* 1032:6) and Evangelist (cf. *Inseg* X:1 [1987], 735; St. Paul ed., 64).

[72] *Inseg* V:3 (1983), 1224 (my trans.).

[73] *ORE* 1032:6–7. He also quoted from the section of this letter on the welcoming of Mary at an Ordination Mass in Florida, Uruguay, see *Inseg* XI:2 (1988), 1224; *ORE* 1041:5–6.

> Lord has lovingly accepted the task of always being the mother of whoever follows Christ. Thus, from the dawn of faith and at every stage in the preaching of the Gospel, in the birth of every particular Church, the Virgin occupies the place which belongs to her as mother of the imitators of Jesus who make up the Church. . . .
>
> "Behold your mother;" the pilgrim Pope repeats Jesus' words to you. Welcome her into your home: accept her as mother and model. She will make you know Christ and love the Church; she will show you the path of life; she will encourage you during difficulties. In her the Church and the Christian find reason for consolation and hope, because she "shines forth on earth, until the day of the Lord shall come, as a sign of sure hope and solace for the pilgrim People of God" (*Lumen Gentium,* 68).[74]

He has continued to preach the importance and necessity of welcoming Mary into our lives with great conviction. There need be no hesitation about Mary ever usurping the place of Christ, he told a neocatechumenal group from Madrid in March of 1984: "Welcome her as a true mother, as a teacher, as a guide and example in your entire life because far from eclipsing the necessary Christological orientation of your life, she will facilitate it." [75] In the context of the Consecration of Togo to Our Lady he prayed: "We feel the need to receive you—still more—as our Mother. To take you with us down the days and down the years in a deeper way! In order that you may keep us close, ever closer to Jesus the Savior, ever more faithful in the service of all his brethren." [76]

[74] *Inseg* VI:1 (1983), 649, 653; *ORE* 781:9–10 (my emphasis). Fr. Ignazio Calabuig Adan, O.S.M., made explicit recognition of the Pope's adoption in this homily of the exegesis of de la Potterie, Serra et al. in a 1985 typescript publication of the Congregation for Divine Worship which was preparing for the publication of the *Collectio Missarum Beatae Mariae Virginis*. This appropriation was likewise acknowledged by Fr. de la Potterie in a conversation with the writer on October 14, 1985.

[75] *Inseg* VII:1 (1984), 750 (my trans.).

[76] *Inseg* VIII:2 (1985), 265; *ORE* 901:2.

As we have already noted with regard to other themes which had previously characterized the Pope's Marian catechesis, so here also he presented the theme of "welcoming Mary" with particular solemnity and clarity in *Redemptoris Mater* in the context of his teaching on entrusting as "the response to the love of a mother":

> The Marian dimension of the life of a disciple of Christ is expressed in a special way precisely through this filial entrusting to the Mother of Christ, which began with the testament of the Redeemer on Golgotha. Entrusting himself to Mary in a filial manner, the Christian, like the Apostle John, "welcomes" the Mother of Christ "into his own home" and brings her into everything that makes up his inner life, that is to say, into his human and Christian "I": he "*took her to his own home.*" Thus the Christian seeks to be taken into that "maternal charity" with which the Redeemer's Mother "cares for the brethren of her Son," "in whose birth and development she cooperates" in the measure of the gift proper to each one through the power of Christ's Spirit. Thus also is exercised that motherhood in the Spirit which became Mary's role at the foot of the Cross and in the Upper Room.[77]

Let us conclude the treatment of this rich theme of the "welcome" of Mary with the conclusion of the magnificent catechesis on the words of Christ, "Behold your Mother", which the Pope gave on November 23, 1988.

> John's action [of taking Mary into his own home] was the execution of Jesus' testament in regard to Mary; but it had a symbolic value for each one of Christ's disciples, who are asked to make room for Mary in their lives, to take her into their own homes. By virtue of these words of the dying Christ, every Christian life must offer a "space" to Mary and provide for her presence.
>
> We can then conclude this reflection on the message of the Cross with an invitation which I address to each one, namely, to ask oneself how one accepts Mary into one's home, into one's life;

[77] *Inseg* X:1 (1987), 735–36; St. Paul ed., 64–65.

> and with an exhortation to appreciate to an ever greater extent the gift which Christ Crucified made to us by leaving us his own Mother as our mother.[78]

Remarkably, his variations on the theme continue to offer new insights and provide an indication of the ongoing development of the doctrine of Marian consecration in the life of the Church.

Why to Mary's Immaculate Heart?

Shortly before the visit of Pope John Paul II to France in October of 1986, an excellent article appeared in the Belgian Jesuit theological journal, *Nouvelle Revue Théologique,* entitled "John Paul II at Paray-le-Monial or Why the 'Heart'? "[79] The question was raised with regard to the *cultus* of the Sacred Heart of Jesus and its meaning since the Pope was scheduled to visit the sanctuary of Paray-le-Monial, the site of the apparitions to Saint Margaret Mary Alacoque. The question was answered largely in terms of the history of seventeenth-century French spirituality, particularly the seldom recognized link between Saint Margaret Mary Alacoque and Saint John Eudes.

In our particular context we might raise the query, "Why the Heart?" from the perspective of the papal magisterium of Pope John Paul II since many of his acts of consecration and entrustment to Mary are addressed to her Immaculate Heart. We have already treated the magisterial development of the theology of the Hearts of Jesus and Mary as it pertains to the history of consecration and the specific questions

[78] *Inseg* XI:4 (1988), 1638; *ORE* 1066:16.

[79] Édouard Glotin, S.J., "Jean-Paul à Paray-le-Monial ou Pourquoi le 'Coeur'? " *Nouvelle Revue Théologique* 108 (1986): 685–714. This is condensed from a larger study which appeared in *Jésus-Christ Rédempteur de l'Homme* (Venasque: Éditions du Carmel, 1986) under the title "Le centre de l'âme et l'Icône sacrée du Coeur. De Thérèse d'Avila à Marguerite-Marie", 103–54.

about the objects of these devotions.[80] Now let us examine briefly some of the particular nuances and developments which he has contributed to the magisterium on the Hearts of Jesus and Mary.[81]

We have already briefly noted the basis for the Holy Father's "theology of the heart" as he gave expression to it in the extraordinarily insightful homily which he gave in Rome on June 28, 1984, to the associated Faculty of Medicine at the Gemelli Polyclinic.[82] Here I would like to return to another passage of it:

> We know the richness of anthropological resonance which in biblical language the word "heart" awakens. This word evokes not only sentiments proper to the affective sphere, but also all those memories, thoughts, reasonings, plans, that make up man's innermost world. The heart in biblical culture, and also in a large part of other cultures, is that essential center of the personality in which man stands before God as the totality of body and soul, as I who am thinking, willing and loving, as the center in which the memory of the past opens up to the planning of the future.[83]

From the anthropological exposition contained in that highly significant and concentrated discourse as well as from other statements of a phenomenological nature which he has made on this topic, Paul L. Peeters does not hesitate to speak of "the Pope's theology of the heart".[84] The first thing to be noted in the above passage is that the heart

[80] See above, chapter 2.

[81] Canon Laurentin treated this matter briefly from the perspective of the "alliance of the two Hearts" in his paper, "The Magisterium of the Church on the Alliance of the Hearts of Jesus and Mary", trans. Srs. Edita Telan, M.I.C., and Rachel de Mars, M.I.C., in *The Alliance of the Hearts of Jesus and Mary,* 169–84. I have also considered some of the Pope's fundamental contributions in my article, "Why the Heart? " The most detailed treatment of the Pope's Sacred Heart doctrine thus far to appear in English is in O'Donnell, 225–55.

[82] Cf. above, 76–77.

[83] *Inseg* VII:1 (1984), 1974; *ORE* 843:9.

[84] Paul L. Peeters, "*Dominum et Vivificantem:* The Conscience and the Heart", *Communio* 15 (1988): 148.

stands for the whole person, but particularly "the essential center of the personality". In this he certainly stands in the Church's great tradition which has been brought into ever clearer focus by the Holy Spirit as the magisterium has had to deal with the development of the *cultus* of the Hearts of Jesus and Mary.

Very significantly, in fact, in the pages of the gospels the word *heart* is used quite often, but in only two cases is the heart of a particular person indicated: Jesus (Mt 11:29) and Mary (Lk 2:19, 51).[85] Surely this is not without import. In both cases this usage constitutes an invitation to ponder a profound mystery. In the Gemelli homily the Pope said:

> In the Heart of Christ, therefore, there meet divine richness and human poverty, the power of grace and the frailty of nature, an appeal from God and a response from man. In the Heart of Christ the history of mankind has its definitive place of arrival, because "the Father has assigned all judgment to the Son" (Jn. 5:22). *Therefore, willing or not, every human heart must refer to the Heart of Christ.*[86]

In the Heart of the God-Man there is present simultaneously, according to the words of the Pope, "an appeal from God and a response from man". This is a wonderful way of describing the unique mediation of Jesus (cf. 1 Tim 2:5–6) who in His divinity presents the call from God to mankind and in His humanity makes the perfect response to God in His earthly life and the sacrifice thereof.

All of this is symbolized in His pierced Heart. Every disposition of His human soul, every state through which He passed in His earthly life is encapsulated in His Heart. By analogy the same can be said of the Heart of Mary. The

[85] Cf. Ignace de la Potterie, S.J., "L'Alleanza dei Cuori di Gesù e di Maria", in *Il Mistero del Cuore Trafitto: Fondamenti biblici della spiritualità del Cuore di Gesù* (Bologna: Edizioni Dehoniane, 1988), 159; "The Alliance of the Hearts of Jesus and Mary: A Biblical Approach", trans. Sr. Rosario de Veyra, R.A., in *The Alliance of the Hearts of Jesus and Mary,* 85.

[86] *Inseg* VII:1 (1984), 1976; *ORE* 843:9 (my emphasis).

theology of the "states" or "mysteries" of Jesus and Mary as comprised of the interior dispositions of their souls and most perfectly represented by their Hearts is a major contribution of the "French School" of spirituality which developed under the impetus of the illustrious Cardinal Pierre de Bérulle.[87] The insights of Bérulle and his disciples, Charles de Condren, the Venerable Jean-Jacques Olier, Saint John Eudes, together with the doctrine of Saint Francis de Sales set the stage for the revelations to Saint Margaret Mary.[88]

So devoted is Pope John Paul II to this mystery of the Heart of Jesus that, besides numerous other references to the Sacred Heart, in 1985 he gave twelve Angelus addresses on the Heart of Jesus (virtually always with reference to Mary and her Heart),[89] culminating in a marvelous exhortation inviting his hearers to unite with the "admirable alliance" of the Hearts of Jesus and Mary.[90] In 1986 he dedicated the same number of Angelus messages to this theme[91] and concluded a third cycle of eleven such reflections in 1989.[92] In

[87] See above, 56–58.

[88] Cf. Marie-Odile and Jean-Hughes Marquis, *Spiritualità del Cuore di Cristo*, trans. Sr. Clemente Moro (Milan: Editrice Ancora, 1986), 55–95. On Margaret Mary's relationship to the French School, cf. Glotin, "Le centre de l'âme", 110–36.

[89] *Inseg* VIII:1 (1985), 1703–4, 1758–59, 1856–57, 1951–52, 2037–38; *Inseg* VIII:2 (1985), 125–26, 146–47, 169–71, 195–96, 526–27, 545–46, 670–71; *ORE* 889:1, 890:1, 891:1, 892:1, 893:7, 895:1, 896:2, 897:2, 898:2, 901:9, 902:8, 904:1.

[90] Angelus Address of September 15, 1985, *Inseg* VIII:2 (1985), 670–71; *ORE* 904:1. It should be noted that this was on the traditional date of the Feast of Our Lady of Sorrows, but since the date occurred on a Sunday there was no liturgical observance. The Pope, however, did not wish to let the date pass unobserved.

[91] *Inseg* IX:1 (1986), 1788–89, 1839–40, 1904–5; *Inseg* IX:2 (1986), 253–54, 277–78, 294–95, 315–16, 358–59, 391–92, 405–6, 501–2, 836–37; *ORE* 941:5, 942:11, 943:12, 946:2, 947:5, 948:1, 949:11, 950:2, 951:2, 952:2, 953:2, 960:4. It might be noted that the last of these addresses was not a part of the series, but an Angelus message given at Paray-le-Monial with the Hearts of Jesus and Mary as major points of reference.

[92] *Inseg* XII:2 (1989), 8–9, 60–61, 138–40, 159–60, 192–94, 393–95, 430–31, 498–99, 534–35, 1159–61, 1224–25; *ORE* 1097:12, 1098:12, 1100:1, 1101:2, 1103:7, 1105:8, 1106:8, 1107:1, 1108:1, 1115:11, 1116:1.

1991 he devoted two Angelus addresses to the Heart of Jesus in the month of June.[93]

On the occasion of his visit on October 5, 1986, to Paray-le-Monial, site of the apparitions of the Lord to Saint Margaret Mary, he personally presented a letter to Father Peter-Hans Kolvenbach, the superior general of the Jesuits, encouraging the members of the Society of Jesus to continue promoting this devotion whose "essential elements", he said,

> belong in a permanent fashion to the spirituality of the Church throughout her history; for since the beginning, the Church has looked to the Heart of Christ pierced on the Cross, from which blood and water flowed forth as symbols of the sacraments that constitute the Church; and, in the Heart of the Incarnate Word, the Fathers of the Christian East and West saw the beginning of all the work of our salvation, fruit of the love of the divine Redeemer. This pierced Heart is a particularly expressive symbol of that love.[94]

If His Heart synthesizes the redemptive sacrifice, man's perfect reparation to God, it is nonetheless also "an appeal from God". In fact, this is precisely what John Paul II chose to underscore in Vancouver when he said: *"The Heart of Jesus Christ is a great and unceasing call from God, addressed to humanity, to each human heart!"* [95] Obviously, the first human heart to respond fully to this call was Mary's. Her *fiat* at Nazareth (Lk 1:38) made possible the formation of His human heart (and all that it represented) beneath hers, a theme which the Pope never tires of alluding to.[96]

Mary's Heart, by virtue of her Immaculate Conception, is from the first moment of her existence totally open to the call of God, and from the moment of her *fiat* she is in com-

[93] *ORE* 1196:11, 1198:10.

[94] *Inseg* IX:2 (1986), 843; *ORE* 960:7.

[95] *Inseg* VII:2 (1984), 603; *ORE* 855:17.

[96] Cf. *Redemptor Hominis*, no. 22 (*Inseg* II:1 [1979], 608; St. Paul ed., 57).

munion with the "forming" Heart of Jesus. Her Heart is the first to enter into the dialogue of salvation, that "alliance of hearts" [97] to which we are all called. Here is how the Pope put it in a letter addressed to Cardinal Sin:

> We can say that just as the mystery of Redemption began in the womb of the Virgin of Nazareth, so did that splendid union of the hearts of Christ and his Mother. From the very moment when the Word was made flesh beneath the heart of Mary, there has existed, under the influence of the Holy Spirit, an enduring relationship of love between them. The heart of the Mother has always followed the redemptive mission of her Son. As Jesus hung on the Cross in completion of his salvific work, Simeon's prophecy foretelling the definitive alliance of the hearts of the Son and of the Mother was fulfilled: "And a sword will pierce your own soul too" (Lk 2:25). Indeed the centurion's lance that pierced the side of Christ also penetrated the heart of his sorrowful Mother and sealed it in sacrificial love.[98]

If Jesus' Heart "is a great and unceasing call from God, addressed to humanity", then Mary's Heart is the perfect response of humanity to the "call from God". If, "when we say 'Heart of Jesus Christ,' we address ourselves in faith to the whole Christological mystery: the mystery of the God-Man", as the Holy Father asserted at Vancouver's Abbotsford Airport on September 18, 1984,[99] then by analogy when we say "Heart of Mary", we might say that we address ourselves to the whole Mariological *and* ecclesiological mystery. For as the perfect human response to the "call from God", as that powerful symbol which evokes the whole mystery of Mary, especially with reference to her

[97] Cf. Angelus address of September 15, 1985, cf. *Inseg* VIII:2 (1985), 671; *ORE* 904:1.

[98] From Letter to Cardinal Jaime L. Sin, president of the International Theological Symposium on the Alliance of the Hearts of Jesus and Mary, September 8, 1986, *Miles Immaculatae* 23 (1987): 42–43.

[99] *Inseg* VII:2 (1984), 600. It should be noted that John Paul's insight is in total harmony with the French School on this point.

maternity,[100] her Heart also summarizes all that the Church is meant to be in responding to the "call from God" which the Vatican Council refers to as "the universal call to holiness".[101]

Hence, when in his exceptional Angelus address of September 15, 1985, the Pope spoke of "that admirable alliance of" the Hearts of Jesus and Mary, he was speaking of the union of the Hearts of Jesus and Mary as paradigmatic of the synergy of divine and human, grace and nature, salvific initiative of God and cooperative response of man, Redemption by the God-Man and "co-redemption" by Mary in the sense of Saint Paul's words to the Colossians: "In my flesh I complete what is lacking in Christ's afflictions for the sake of his body, that is, the Church" (Col 1:24). The response of Mary's Heart became the first answer of the Church to the "call from God" and remains its most perfect reply. It also becomes the model for our response.

In this sense, then, it is not surprising that on at least two occasions the Pope has indicated that consecrating the world to the Immaculate Heart of Mary means effectively consecrating it to the pierced Heart of the Savior. Here, then, is a highly significant passage which he spoke in Fatima on May 13, 1982, as a prelude to consecration of the world to the Immaculate Heart of Mary:

> On the cross Christ said: "Woman, behold your son!" With these words He opened in a new way His Mother's heart. A little later, the Roman soldier's spear pierced the side of the Crucified One.

[100] In this regard note the words of the Sacred Congregation of Rites in the Decree establishing the Feast of the Immaculate Heart of Mary: "With this devotion the Church renders the honor due to the Immaculate Heart of the Blessed Virgin Mary, since under the symbol of this heart she venerates with reverence the eminent and singular holiness of the *Mother of God* and especially her most ardent love for God and Jesus her Son and moreover *her maternal compassion for all those redeemed by the divine Blood*" (Decree of May 4, 1944, *AAS* 37 [1945]: 50; *ORE* 959:12), (my emphasis).

[101] *LG,* nos. 39–42. This theme was singled out for special attention at the Extraordinary Synod of 1985, cf. *Relatio Finalis,* II.A.4.

That pierced heart became a sign of redemption achieved through the death of the Lamb of God.

The Immaculate Heart of Mary opened with the words "Woman, behold, your son!" is spiritually united with the heart of her Son opened by the soldier's spear. Mary's heart was opened by the same love for man and for the world with which Christ loved man and the world, offering Himself for them on the cross, until the soldier's spear struck that blow.

Consecrating the world to the Immaculate Heart of Mary means drawing near, through the Mother's intercession, to the very Fountain of life that sprang up from Golgotha. This Fountain pours forth unceasingly redemption and grace. In it reparation is made continually for the sins of the world. It is a ceaseless source of new life and holiness.

Consecrating the world to the Immaculate Heart of the Mother means returning beneath the cross of the Son. It means consecrating this world to the pierced heart of the Savior, bringing it back to the very source of its redemption.[102]

Again on September 22, 1986, he said of this act carried out most solemnly on May 13, 1982, and March 25, 1984:

Our act of consecration refers ultimately to the Heart of her son, for as the Mother of Christ she is wholly united to his redemptive mission. As at the marriage feast of Cana, when she said "Do whatever he tells you", Mary directs all things to her Son, who answers our prayers and forgives our sins. *Thus by dedicating ourselves to the heart of Mary we discover a sure way to the Sacred Heart of Jesus, symbol of the merciful love of our Savior.*

The act of entrusting ourselves to the Heart of Our Lady establishes a relationship of love with her in which we dedicate to her all that we have and are. This consecration is practised essentially by a life of grace, of purity, of prayer, of penance that is joined to the fulfillment of all the duties of a Christian, and of reparation for our sins and the sins of the world.[103]

[102] *Inseg* V:2 (1982), 1573; *Portugal,* 79–80.

[103] From an address to participaants in the International Theological Symposium on the Alliance of the Hearts of Jesus and Mary, held in Fatima under the patronage of Cardinal Jaime L. Sin, archbishop of Manila, from September 14 to 19, 1986, *Inseg* IX:2 (1986), 700 (beginning emphasis mine).

There is a profound inner logic to all of this which may well escape the worldly-wise (cf. 1 Cor 1:18–2:16). *To respond to the "call from God" symbolized in the pierced Heart of Jesus, we must belong to Mary that she might teach us the dispositions of her Heart and become our tutor in the spiritual life.* As we learn from her, we take on her characteristics and become ever more perfectly that immaculate spouse "without spot or wrinkle" (Eph 5:27) which the Church has already become in the person of Mary.[104]

[104] *LG*, no. 65.

PART THREE

ASSESSMENT

8

Pope John Paul II's Thought in Perspective

Recapitulation

In the first part of this study we considered the Pope's "program of Marian consecration and entrustment" in the context of the evolution of the very ancient practice of the giving of oneself into the protection of Mary as this tradition has continued to flourish in every era of the Church's life. We have also noted the development of the concomitant theology implied in this praxis, especially as it has reached its highest dogmatic expression in the various acts of the pontifical magisterium. We have further taken account of the unique flowering of this custom as it has unfolded in twentieth-century Poland, the providential matrix of Karol Wojtyła. We have observed how thoroughly all of the various elements of the tradition—ecclesial, pontifical, and specifically Polish—have been integrated into the "program" of John Paul as it has been manifested in the course of his pontificate thus far. Finally, we have considered various representative strains of contemporary thought on the question of "the total gift of oneself [to Mary] for life and for eternity",[1] as this topic has continued to be deliberated subsequent to the Second Vatican Council's monumental eighth chapter of *Lumen Gentium* and the guidelines

[1] This is the classic definition of Marian consecration as given by Pope Pius XII on January 21, 1945; cf. above, 142.

of *Marialis Cultus*. We have seen that the sometimes vexing and occasionally heated debate over the terminology of "consecration" as opposed to "entrustment" does not seem to be envisioned as a matter of opposition in the thought of the Pope, but rather that he employs both terms as well as many others in order to draw out the various nuances of what it means to belong to Mary.

In the second part we carried out an extended analysis of the thought of Pope John Paul II on the question of Marian consecration. Although he has nowhere presented a fully developed treatise on this issue as a bishop or as pope, he has treated the subject and its ramifications with sufficient frequency and depth to make it possible for one to follow the major outlines of his thought.

We began our analysis by asking the classical question: "How can consecration to Mary be legitimate in light of the fact that consecration in the strict sense pertains only to God?" We presented the classical response to this query by having recourse to the principle of analogy and noted the frequently implicit analogous use of the term "to entrust" by the Pope which fully respects the distinction between *latria* and *hyperdulia*. We further noted that in his own usage of the terms "consecration", "entrustment", and their cognates he effectively takes the position that consecration is in the first instance an elicited act of religion (*latria*) directed to God or Christ without ceasing to be an act of *hyperdulia* directed to Mary.

The Holy Father in effect frequently speaks of consecrating or entrusting oneself to Christ through Mary. This, again, is in accord with the classical theological treatment of the matter. For example, it underlies the entire theology of Saint Louis-Marie Grignion de Montfort,[2] whose influence on his own spiritual formation the Pope readily acknowledges, and it finds, moreover, its most developed explanation

[2] Cf above, 170–71; *True Devotion*, no. 121; *God Alone*, 327; "Cons.", 404–5.

in the section on "Mary's Maternal Mediation" in *Redemptoris Mater*, numbers 38–41. The principle of Mary's secondary and subordinate, but nonetheless real, mediation is neatly synthesized in that same encyclical in his endorsement of "the figure of Saint Louis-Marie Grignion de Montfort, who proposes consecration to Christ through the hands of Mary, as an effective means for Christians to live faithfully their baptismal commitments." [3]

Next we came to examine a question fundamental to our study, the Christological foundation of the two great public consecrations of the world to the Immaculate Heart of Mary and, in effect, of the Pope's whole program of entrustment. We noted that the core of the acts of 1982 and 1984 is the reference to the self-consecration of Christ (Jn 17:19) as victim, which further implies His prior consecration as priest by the Father in the Incarnation (Jn 10:36). Jesus' self-consecration becomes paradigmatic of the Christian's desire to unite himself with the sacrifice of Jesus for the sake of His Body, the Church (Col 1:24) and as a ratification of the fundamental consecration accomplished in him by God in baptism. This desire to be united with the redemptive consecration of Christ is then *entrusted* by the Pope to Our Lady along with the whole world, a further emphasis on the crucial role of her maternal mediation.

Then we further focused on the way the Pope linked Mary with Christ's consecration by describing her as "wholly united to the redeeming consecration of her Son". We also noticed how the Pope's emphasis on Mary as a "co-victim" with Christ, consecrated under Him, with Him, and for the sake of the Redemption, is deeply rooted in the eighth chapter of *Lumen Gentium*. This recognition of Mary as the human being most "wholly united to the redeeming consecration of Christ" readily leads to her being proposed as the model of consecrated souls. This, we noted,

[3] Cf. above, 187–88.

is a special emphasis of the Holy Father in his exhortations to religious.

After the establishment of this Christological foundation of John Paul's two great acts of consecration, we asked, "Why, then, should there be explicit entrustment to Mary?" The Pope's constant and consistent response is "the entrustment scene" on Calvary (Jn 19:25–27). He teaches that Mary's spiritual maternity is confirmed by the dying Christ as the fruit of His sacrifice and the final consequence of Mary's cooperation in it. He points to her maternal mediation as deepening, but never interfering with or inhibiting, one's relationship with Christ. We also noted here his continuity with the teaching of the popes since Benedict XIV on Mary's spiritual maternity.

If his predecessors have invoked John 19:25–27 as a principal scriptural basis for Mary's spiritual maternity, John Paul II has further found in the episode of Christ's entrustment of John to Mary the rationale for the entrustment of all of Christ's disciples to her. The Pope's thought in this area is particularly rich and deep.

The word *trust* is linguistically associated with the word *entrust* (at least in Italian and English), and so it is in the Pope's mind. Children are entrusted by God to mothers even more than to fathers in the sense that in the ordinary course of events mothers are the first objects of their children's trust and become bridges by which their children can learn to trust their fathers and the world outside of themselves. It is in this sense that Mary is both the Mother of our trust in God and also intended by Him as the Mother of His trust in us. The unique linking of a mother to her child is implied in the word "entrusting" which is in a special way the response to a mother's love.[4]

Without using the terminology proposed by Father Bertetto, John Paul effectively upholds the principle that the

[4] Cf. *Redemptoris Mater*, no. 45.

"descending" entrustment to Mary, which was accomplished by Christ on Calvary, should be ratified by the Church's and our own "ascending" acts of entrustment. This understanding is further complemented by the exegesis of John 19:27b by de la Potterie, McHugh, Serra, and others on the meaning of the beloved disciple's "welcome" or "reception" of Mary. It confirms the profound intuition of Origen, the first of the Fathers to speak of the "receiving" or "acceptance" of Mary by John, and has been readily appropriated by the Holy Father who speaks of welcoming Mary "among our most beloved goods" and "as guide, adviser, encourager, or even merely as a silent presence which at times may be enough to infuse us with strength and courage".[5]

Finally, we pondered the unique relationship between Jesus and Mary in terms of John Paul's "theology of the heart", which builds upon the accumulated pontifical magisterium on this subject while developing his own theological and anthropological insights. Here Mary's subordinate, but nonetheless very real, cooperation in the work of our Redemption is described as an "admirable alliance" with the Heart of Jesus.[6] Because of the singular nature of this "alliance" or "covenant" specifically willed by God, consecration to the Immaculate Heart of Mary is the chosen means of approaching the Heart of the Savior, the "Fountain of Salvation". Hence the Pope can declare the ultimate equivalence of "consecration to the Immaculate Heart of Mary" and "consecration to the pierced Heart of the Savior".[7]

The Pope's contributions to the theology of Marian consecration

At first sight it might appear that Pope John Paul II has simply consolidated the teaching of his predecessors on the

[5] Cf. above, 244.
[6] Cf. above, 251.
[7] Cf. above, 254–55.

question of Marian consecration. Indeed, it is an important function of the office of Peter to hand on intact the teachings of the *depositum fidei* to the next generation and, given the tendencies toward "revisionism" which are present in every era, this in itself would constitute no small blessing. But John Paul has done much more than this. He has made his own significant contributions to the development of the body of doctrine on this subject which is so obviously close to his heart, and, of course, the final chapter cannot be written on this topic until the conclusion of his pontificate. Nonetheless, even at this point in his papal service to the Church it is possible, I believe, to enumerate his distinctive contributions to the subject.

UNIQUE EMPHASIS ON CHRIST'S SELF-CONSECRATION

The first of these, his unique emphasis on Christ's self-consecration (Jn 17:19), was well-signaled in the theological world after his acts of consecration to the Immaculate Heart of Mary in Fatima on May 13, 1982, and in Rome on March 25, 1984.[8] It was a reaffirmation in an original way that all consecration is ultimately accomplished by and oriented to the Father.[9] Consecrated by the Father at the moment of His conception, Christ, when His supreme sacrifice becomes imminent, consecrates Himself to the Father for the sake of humanity. The consecration of Christians, then, must participate in the self-consecration of Jesus, their Head.

[8] Cf. J. Patrick Gaffney, S.M.M., "Changing the I to We", *Queen of All Hearts* 35 (September–October 1984): 19; Eamon R. Carroll, O. Carm., "A Survey of Recent Mariology", 167–69, "Mary: the Woman Come of Age", 150–55, and "The New Testament Charisms of the Blessed Virgin Mary", *One in Christ* 22 (1986): 361; Alfredo Marranzini, S.J., "L' 'Atto di Affidamento' ", 12–17.

[9] Cf. René Laurentin, "Bulletin sur la Vierge Marie", *Revue des Sciences Philosophiques et Théologiques* 70 (1986): 115–17.

INVOCATION OF MARY AS "WHOLLY UNITED TO THE REDEEMING CONSECRATION OF HER SON"

Intimately related to the self-consecration of Christ in those acts of 1982 and 1984 is his identification of Mary and calling upon her as "wholly united to the redeeming consecration of your Son". By virtue of her Immaculate Conception, Mary is the most perfectly consecrated human being, consecrated by the Holy Spirit, as was Christ, from the first moment of her conception. She who had been predestined in the same divine decree with her Son,[10] was to associate herself freely with his redemptive sacrifice.[11]

THE THEOLOGY OF ENTRUSTMENT—A DEVELOPMENT OF DOCTRINE

Perhaps the major contribution of John Paul II to the discussion of Marian consecration is what I have characterized as his "theology of entrustment". While it is true that the term was in use much earlier,[12] he has made it his own with all of its Polish resonances[13] and has used it consistently in interpreting the text of John 19:25–27.[14] It might well be argued that the applications which he has drawn from this text constitute a genuine development of doctrine which flows from the teaching on Mary's spiritual maternity.

Having established the will of Christ with regard to every Christian's being entrusted to Mary with such emphasis, he never fails to point to the exigence on the part of the Christian to appropriate that entrustment by one's own deliberate act and to welcome her into one's own life with all that that

[10] Cf. above, 201.

[11] Cf. *LG*, no. 61.

[12] Cf. above, 98–99, where Pius XII uses the term *affidiamo* along with *consacriamo* in his famous Act of Consecration to the Immaculate Heart of October 31, 1942.

[13] Cf. above, 149–50.

[14] Cf. above, 207–40.

implies.[15] If de Montfort argues in favor of Marian consecration that Mary is the most direct way to Jesus and Kolbe argues that going through Mary maximizes the values of all our acts, John Paul continues the argument by insisting that this is expressly the will of Christ.

On July 19, 1987, in the course of an Angelus address on the sanctuary at Lourdes the Pope said:

> Mary is . . . an excellent and unique vehicle of Christ's redemption. She is a most privileged channel of his grace, a chosen path by means of which grace comes to mankind with an extraordinary and marvellous abundance. Where Mary is present, grace abounds and people are healed both in body and soul.[16]

Without even a further word about the desirability of entrustment or consecration to her he has said enough for the discerning listener. Mary shares in Jesus' mediation to the greatest extent possible for a creature and He desires that we belong to her. To go to Jesus, then, through Mary is not to take a roundabout route, but the one that He has ordained. To consecrate ourselves to her is to consecrate ourselves to Him by the means which He has designated.

Magisterial value of this teaching

It will have been noted that there is a profound continuity between what Karol Wojtyła taught as archbishop of Krakow and what he continues to teach as Pope with regard to consecration/entrustment to Our Lady. His commentaries on the various acts of consecration of Poland to the Mother of God bear this out. Nevertheless, what merits our special attention is what he has presented as Supreme Pontiff and therefore chief teacher of the Church. While it is true that he has presented nothing about consecration/entrustment to Mary in terms of a solemn *ex cathedra* definition on the level

[15] Cf. above, 240–48.

[16] *Inseg* X:3 (1987), 98; *ORE* 998:2.

of the proclamation of Mary's Immaculate Conception by the Venerable Pius IX or the definition of her corporeal Assumption into heaven by the Servant of God Pius XII, it can certainly be argued that his "habitual acts of entrustment", his more solemn consecrations of the world and of individual nations to Our Lady, his frequent commentaries expounding the "theology of entrustment", especially his authoritative presentation on this matter in his encyclical letter *Redemptoris Mater*, constitute an authentic exercise of the "ordinary magisterium" of the Roman Pontiff.

Here is what the Dogmatic Constitution on the Church, *Lumen Gentium*, says about such an exercise in its twenty-fifth article:

> In matters of faith and morals, the bishops speak in the name of Christ and the faithful are to accept their teaching and adhere to it with a religious assent [*religioso animi obsequio*]. This religious submission of mind and will must be shown in a special way to the authentic magisterium of the Roman Pontiff, even when he is not speaking ex cathedra [*Hoc vero religiosum voluntatis et intellectus obsequium singulari ratione praestandum est Romani Pontificis authentico magisterio etiam cum non ex cathedra loquitur*]; that is, it must be shown in such a way that his supreme magisterium is acknowledged with reverence, the judgements made by him are sincerely adhered to, according to his manifest mind and will. His mind and will in the matter may be known either from the character of the documents, from his frequent repetition of the same doctrine, or from his manner of speaking [*sive indole documentorum, sive ex frequenti propositione eiusdem doctrinae, sive ex dicendi ratione*].[17]

In this exposition the Fathers of the Council were making more explicit what Pius XII had already taught in his encyclical letter *Humani Generis* on the "ordinary magisterium" of the Roman Pontiff.[18]

[17] NCWC trans. (St. Paul ed., 1965), 24.
[18] *AAS* 42 (1950): 568–69.

THE CHARACTER OF THE DOCUMENTS

The first of the three criteria offered by *Lumen Gentium* has to do with the nature of the documents themselves. Clearly, the most formal and explicit teaching of John Paul II thus far on the matter of Marian consecration/entrustment is to be found in *Redemptoris Mater*, numbers 45–46 and 48. However, it would seem that the Act of Consecration and Entrustment of March 25, 1984, would be equally on the most solemn level of the "ordinary magisterium" as a text of the *Ecclesia orans* used throughout the entire Catholic world and promulgated by the Supreme Pontiff in his capacity as Universal Bishop and not only of the Diocese of Rome [*in quantum Orbis et non tantum Urbis Episcopus*].[19] Although this latter text was not explicitly proposed as an instrument of teaching, it may certainly be taken as an instance of the axiom that the faith of the Church may be ascertained by her prayer [*Lex orandi statuat legem credendi*] and surely many of the Church's beliefs about Mary, such as her spiritual maternity and mediation, may be deduced from this prayer.

FREQUENT REPETITION OF THE SAME DOCTRINE

The second of the criteria proposed by *Lumen Gentium* is the "frequent repetition of the same doctrine". So frequent are the major and minor instances of entrustment to Mary on the part of the Pope that they ordinarily tend to occur in speeches, Angelus addresses, homilies, and prayers several times in a given week.[20] Every time the Pope addresses a

[19] Conradus M. Berti, Salvator M. Meo, Hermannus M. Toniolo, O.S.M., *De Ratione Ponderandi Documenta Magisterii Ecclesiastici* (Rome: Edizioni Marianum, 1961), 42.

[20] For instance, for the fifth year of his pontificate (October 22, 1982, to October 21, 1983) I count 116 references to entrustment in the "log" of papal statements on Mary chronicled by Bertetto in *Maria nel Magistero, Quinto Anno*, and have found six others for that year myself. That averages a reference to Marian entrustment about every third day.

group, whether a small gathering of bishops on the "ad limina" visit or an assembly of thousands of the faithful in Saint Peter's Square, or anywhere throughout Italy or the world and simply says: "I entrust you to the Mother of God", this surely constitutes an exercise of his "ordinary magisterium" and is thus a powerful reinforcement of the importance of the Christian's putting his life in Mary's hands. If the Montfort Fathers were able to put together an anthology of texts from Pius XII on Marian consecration,[21] there is no doubt that a similar and immensely larger compilation could be made from the texts of John Paul II.

THE MANNER OF SPEAKING

The third criterion presented in *Lumen Gentium* for recognizing the mind and will of the Pontiff is his manner of speaking [*ratio dicendi*]. Very frequently these acts of commendation take place within the context of prayer, an obvious indication of the great seriousness with which they are made. References to the "theology of entrustment" are often also found in homilies, general audiences, and Angelus addresses where the Pope is always careful to present the doctrine of the Church in an unadulterated and integral form as an explicit exercise of his pastoral office.

The "why" of consecration to Mary

One might well wonder why the Pope has made the subject of consecration/entrustment to Mary such a consistent point of reference in his ordinary magisterium. I believe that he has given the explanation for his preoccupation in the retreat which he preached for Pope Paul VI and the members of the Roman Curia in Lent of 1976:

[21] Cf. Pocock, *Pius XII on Consecration to Mary*.

Both holy scripture, so rich in metaphor as we have just found, and the experience of the faithful see the Mother of God as the one who in a very special way is united with the Church at the most difficult moments in her history, when the attacks on her become most threatening. And this is in full accord with the vision of the woman revealed in Genesis and Revelation. Precisely in periods when Christ, and therefore his Church, Pope, bishops, priests, religious and all the faithful become the sign which provokes the most implacable and premeditated contradiction, Mary appears particularly close to the Church, because the Church is always in a way her Christ, first the Christ-child and then the crucified and risen Christ.

If in such periods, such times in history, there arises a particular need to entrust oneself to Mary—as the Holy Father did on 8th December 1975, the 10th anniversary of the end of the Council—that need flows directly from the integral logic of the faith, from rediscovery of the whole divine economy and from understanding of its mysteries.

The Father in heaven demonstrated the greatest trust in mankind by giving mankind his Son (cf. Jn. 3:16). The human creature to whom he first entrusted him was Mary, the woman of the *proto-evangelium* (cf. Gen. 3:15), then Mary of Nazareth and Bethlehem. And until the end of time she will remain the one to whom God entrusts the whole of his mystery of salvation.[22]

A NEED FLOWING "FROM THE INTEGRAL LOGIC OF THE FAITH"

The answer then, quite simply, is that he sees a great need at this particular moment in the life of the Church to entrust her to Mary. She, "the woman of the proto-evangelium" and "the woman clothed with the sun", is involved by God's will in all the struggles of the Church against the powers of darkness. This is part of "the integral logic of the faith". The more the Church belongs to her and is conformed to her the more she will belong to Christ and be

[22] *Sign of Contradiction*, 205.

conformed to Him, and the more she is conformed to Christ in His humiliation the more she will be conformed to Christ in His victory.

ENMITY BETWEEN "THE WORLD AND THE WOMAN"

The very "framework" of *Redemptoris Mater* in effect speaks of the enmity between the world and "the woman". At the beginning of the encyclical, with bold and deliberate strokes, the Pope presents Mary as "the woman of Genesis" and "the woman of the Apocalypse":

> In the salvific design of the Most Holy Trinity, the mystery of the Incarnation constitutes the superabundant *fulfillment of the promise* made by God to man *after original sin*, after that first sin whose effects oppress the whole earthly history of man (cf. Gen. 3:15). And so, there comes into the world a Son, "the seed of the woman" who will crush the evil of sin in its very origins: "he will crush the head of the serpent." As we see from the words of the Protogospel, the victory of the woman's Son will not take place without a hard struggle, a struggle that is to extend through the whole of human history. The "enmity," foretold at the beginning, is confirmed in the Apocalypse (the book of the final events of the Church and the world), in which there recurs the sign of the "woman," this time "clothed with the sun" (Rev. 12:1).
>
> Mary, Mother of the Incarnate Word, is placed *at the very center of that enmity*, that struggle which accompanies the history of humanity on earth and the history of salvation itself. In this central place, she who belongs to the "weak and poor of the Lord" bears in herself, like no other member of the human race, that "glory of grace" which the Father "has bestowed on us in his beloved Son," and this *grace determines the extraordinary greatness and beauty* of her whole being. Mary thus remains before God, and also before the whole of humanity, as the unchangeable and inviolable sign of God's election, spoken of in Paul's letter: "in Christ . . . he chose us . . . before the foundation of the world . . . he destined us . . . to be his sons" (Eph. 1:4, 5). *This election is more powerful than any*

> *experience of evil and sin, than all that "enmity" which marks the history of man.* In this history Mary remains a sign of sure hope.[23]

At the end of the encyclical he presents Mary in the same way.

> Thanks to this special bond linking the Mother of Christ with the Church, there is further *clarified the mystery of that "woman"* who, from the first chapters of the Book of *Genesis* until the Book of *Revelation*, accompanies the revelation of God's salvific plan for humanity. For Mary, present in the Church as the Mother of the Redeemer, takes part, as a mother, in that "monumental struggle against the powers of darkness" which continues throughout human history. And by her ecclesial identification as the "woman clothed with the sun" (Rev. 12:1), it can be said that "in the Most Holy Virgin the Church has already reached that perfection whereby she exists without spot or wrinkle." Hence, as Christians raise their eyes with faith to Mary in the course of their earthly pilgrimage, they "strive to increase in holiness". Mary, the exalted Daughter of Sion, helps all her children, wherever they may be and whatever their condition, *to find in Christ the path to the Father's house.*[24]

Both of these splendid passages which "frame" the encyclical speak of the struggle, "the hard struggle . . . that is to extend through the whole of human history", "that 'monumental struggle against the powers of darkness' which continues throughout human history".

ACCORDING TO GOD'S ETERNAL PLAN

In the first of the above quotations Mary is portrayed as "at the very center of that enmity . . . which accompanies the history of humanity on earth and the history of salvation itself", but her election by God (which implies her Immaculate Conception) "is more powerful than any experience

[23] *Inseg* X:1 (1987), 689–90; St Paul ed., 16 (final emphasis mine).
[24] *Inseg* X:1 (1987), 738; St. Paul ed., 66.

of evil and sin, than all that 'enmity' which marks the history of man." Hence in the two most solemn acts of consecration to the Immaculate Heart of Mary, John Paul says that

> the power of this consecration [which is meant to be an identification with the self-consecration of Christ and entrusted to Mary] lasts for all time and embraces all individuals, peoples and nations. It overcomes every evil that the spirit of darkness is able to awaken, and has in fact awakened in our times, in the heart of man and in his history.[25]

John Paul wrote to his brother bishops on the Feast of the Immaculate Conception in 1983, in preparation for the second of these solemn acts, that it was through the Immaculate Heart of Mary—the "woman of the Apocalypse" in whom "the salvific power of the Redemption" had already triumphed—that he wished to profess this "power of the Redemption" again with the entire Church.[26] He spoke similarly on March 17, 1984, at the close of his annual retreat[27] and on the Feast of the Immaculate Conception in 1985 at the conclusion of the Extraordinary Synod.[28] Clearly in his mind consecration/entrustment to her is intended by God and necessary in the struggle against the evils which threaten to engulf the world.

The second text from *Redemptoris Mater* which we cited above might be said to speak in terms of that "integral logic of the faith" that holds consecration to Mary is necessary in order to be ever more fully consecrated to Christ in order to belong ever more completely to the Father. This is a manifestation of God's eternal plan (cf. Eph 1:10–11) and Mary's place in it which the Pope so beautifully considers in the first part of the encyclical.[29]

[25] *Inseg* V:2 (1982), 1588; *ORE* 735:12; *Inseg* VII:1 (1984), 776; *ORE* 828:9.

[26] *Inseg* VII:1 (1984), 417; *ORE* 823:2.

[27] *Inseg* VII:1 (1984), 691; *ORE* 827:5.

[28] *Inseg* VIII:2 (1985), 1460; *ORE* 917:10.

[29] *Inseg* X:1 (1987), 684–85; St. Paul ed., 12–13.

Clarifications from the magisterium of John Paul II about Marian consecration

In his noted encyclical letter *Humani Generis* of August 12, 1950, Pope Pius XII spoke with precision on the value of the "ordinary magisterium" of the Supreme Pontiff:

> It is true that Popes generally leave theologians free in those matters which are disputed in various ways by men of very high authority in this field; but history teaches that many matters that formerly were open to discussion, no longer now admit of discussion.
>
> Nor must it be thought that what is expounded in Encyclical Letters does not of itself demand consent, since in writing such Letters the Popes do not exercise the supreme power of their Teaching Authority. For these matters are taught with the ordinary teaching authority [*Magisterio enim ordinario haec docentur*], of which it is true to say: "He who heareth you, heareth me"; and generally what is expounded and inculcated in Encyclical Letters already for other reasons appertains to Catholic doctrine. But if the Supreme Pontiffs in their official documents purposely pass judgment on a matter up to that time under dispute, it is obvious that that matter, according to the mind and will of the same Pontiffs, cannot be any longer considered a question open to discussion among theologians.[30]

We have already considered how John Paul II's teaching on Marian consecration fulfills the criteria laid down in *Lumen Gentium*, number 25, for being considered part of the ordinary magisterium. The extent to which this same teaching, at least in its broad outlines, also fulfills the above-stated teaching of *Humani Generis* is a more delicate question.

While contemporary theologians, especially Mariologists, have espoused various contrary opinions on the question of Marian consecration,[31] it would be virtually untenable to state *prima facie* that the Pope has taken note of all of these

[30] *AAS* 42 (1950): 568; NCWC trans., 9–10.

[31] Cf. above, 144–49.

and wished to settle various of these theological disputes (such as to whether one should employ the term "entrust" instead of "consecrate") definitively. This is so especially because when Pius XII, the formulator of this principle, wished to settle matters which had previously been *quaestiones disputatae*, he did so in such a way that his magisterial intervention could be readily acknowledged and adhered to, as, in fact, he did in *Humani Generis*. The style or *modus operandi* of John Paul II tends to differ from that of his predecessor and perhaps he has not deemed it necessary up to this point in his pontificate to make such deliberate interventions on theological questions.

On the other hand, even if he has not specifically intended to settle disputes among theologians on matters pertaining to Marian consecration, I submit that by his consistent teaching, which is also an exercise of the ordinary magisterium, he has nonetheless done so. What, then, are some of the questions to which he has brought clarification?

MARY'S MEDIATION

I would hazard to say that the first of these is that of Mary's mediation. Without the foundational principles of analogy and mediation, which I illustrated at length throughout chapter five, no orthodox theology of Marian consecration could be elaborated. Now without a doubt the theology of Mary's mediation had already been firmly established in the magisterium from the middle of the eighteenth century up until the Second Vatican Council.[32]

Nonetheless there was a certain revisionist tendency at work in the Council which wished, primarily seemingly for ecumenical reasons,[33] to avoid any statement on Mary's

[32] Cf. above, 184–85, n. 69.

[33] Cf. René Laurentin, *The Question of Mary*, trans. I. G. Pidoux (New York: Holt, Rinehart and Winston, 1965), 138; Salvatore Meo, O.S.M., "La 'Mediazione materna' di Maria nell' Enciclica 'Redemptoris Mater' ", in *Redemptoris Mater:*

mediation even though in a preconciliar consultation 382 bishops asked for a statement on Mary's mediation and 266 of them expressed a desire that the matter be defined.[34] The statement which did emerge in numbers 60 through 62 of *Lumen Gentium*, while theologically sound, did not advance the question as far as the previous papal magisterium had done, and reference to Mary as mediatrix was deliberately attenuated by apposition with more indeterminate titles such as advocate, helper, and benefactress [*advocata, auxiliatrix, adiutrix*]. This text of the Council was further very often subject to a "minimizing" interpretation.

The genius of John Paul II's treatment of Mary's maternal mediation in *Redemptoris Mater*, numbers 21 through 22 and 38 through 41, is that it gave the Council's handling of the matter a "maximizing" interpretation, a veritable *tour de force*.[35] This matter is crucial because the Pope, as well as all reputable theologians before him, readily admits that Mary is not the *terminus ad quem* of consecration,[36] rather she is the one *through whom* [*per manus Mariae*] we may renew our consecration to Christ.[37] While this point itself does not represent a specific advance on the part of the magisterium, it may be seen as a salutary reaffirmation of the Church's

---

Contenuti e Prospettive Dottrinali e Pastorali (Rome: Pontificia Accademia Mariana Internazionale, 1988), 150, 154.

[34] Cf. O'Carroll, "Still Mediatress?", 122.

[35] Cf. the interesting conclusions drawn about John Paul's development and deepening of the Council's teaching in Meo, "La 'Mediazione materna' ", 155–57.

[36] *Redemptoris Mater*, no. 46: "This filial relationship, this self-entrusting of a child to its mother, not only has its *beginning in Christ* but can also be said to be *definitively directed towards him*" (*Inseg* X:1 [1987], 736; St. Paul ed., 65).

[37] *Redemptoris Mater*, no. 47: "I would like to recall, among the many witnesses and teachers of this spirituality, the figure of Saint Louis-Marie Grignion de Montfort, who proposes consecration to Christ through the hands of Mary, as an effective means for Christians to live faithfully their baptismal commitments" (*Inseg* X:1 (1987), 739; St. Paul ed., 68).

teaching after more than twenty years of hesitance on this issue among theologians.[38]

LEGITIMACY OF SPEAKING OF "CONSECRATION TO MARY"

While it is true that Mary is not the *terminus finalis ad quem* of any consecration, the Pope's scripturally rooted and very original teaching on entrustment (especially as concentrated in *Redemptoris Mater*, nos. 21–22, 44–46) as well as his use of the term "consecration to Mary" or "to her Immaculate Heart", make it clear that Mary is an "intermediate end" of the act of entrustment, commendation, or consecration. Hence the magisterial tradition, especially as it developed under Pius XII, never invalidated or rescinded, which spoke freely of consecration to Mary, receives a further endorsement from John Paul II. This is important because, following upon the unwillingness of some theologians in the years since the Council to accept Mary's maternal mediation as an active principle or as analogous to that of Christ (always understanding thereby its secondary and subordinate position),[39] they have manifested strong resistance to the use of such terminology as well as what it stands for.[40]

Now, of course, the term "consecration to Mary" is only one option among a number, and I believe that Don Gabriele Amorth puts the matter well when he says:

[38] Cf. René Laurentin, *Queen of Heaven: A Short Treatise on Marian Theology*, trans. Gordon Smith (Dublin: Clonmore & Reynolds; London: Burns Oates & Washbourne, 1956), 123–24, *Question of Mary*, 43–46, and *A Year of Grace with Mary*, 154–55; De Fiores, *Maria nella Teologia Contemporanea*, 248–50.

[39] Cf. the excellent pastoral treatment of the analogous nature of Mary's mediation where the word "analogous" is not used, but the meaning is beautifully explained in Gabriele Amorth, S.S.P., *Dialoghi su Maria* (Padua: Edizioni Messagero Padova, 1987), 320–21.

[40] Cf. Laurentin, *Question of Mary*, 67, "Consecration and Entrustment", 238–45, *A Year of Grace with Mary*, 126–31, and "Bulletin sur la Vierge Marie", 115–17.

> If we reflect on the contents and on the consequences of the consecration, we see that we find ourselves before a complex act which cannot be defined in a few words nor can it be expressed with only one term. When Pius XII, in 1942, consecrated the world to the Immaculate Heart of Mary, he had recourse to three verbs: "I consecrate, I entrust, I commit". Also the present Pontiff, who wherever he goes never omits consecration to Mary, shows great liberty in the use of words, even if, most of the time he limits himself to coupling the terms "I entrust and I consecrate". It seems to me that, for one's personal consecration or that of a community of believers, the more strong and compelling term is "consecration"; in other cases the term "entrustment". But I believe that we should not be bound to words: many priests have recourse to those terms which they find more adapted to the understanding of their parishioners. What is important is to make them understand the value of the consecration.[41]

While we have already seen that the word "consecrate" has been used in this context since the time of Saint John of Damascus[42] and "consecrated by consistent use" since early in the seventeenth century,[43] what is of utmost importance is the concept that belonging to Mary is a privileged means of belonging to Christ.

Possible areas for future development

While we have taken into consideration the cumulative teaching on Marian consecration/entrustment of the first thirteen years of the pontificate of Pope John Paul II and have noted the extraordinarily rich developments of his thought in this area, there is every reason to expect that he will continue to bring forth from his treasury "what is new and what is old" (cf. Mt 13:52). While he has never set out to present an *ex professo* treatise on Marian consecration, through his accumulated addresses, homilies, and documents

[41] Amorth, 303–4 (my trans.).

[42] Cf. above, 47–48.

[43] Cf. above, 54.

he has nevertheless developed a remarkably thorough treatment of the topic.

That he has not dealt exhaustively with what might be considered all of the traditional factors of Marian consecration should not be surprising; that he has treated so many with the unique hallmark of his own originality is truly astonishing. The previous teaching of the magisterium and the perennial tradition of the Church are always to be assumed as supplementing what he has not yet presented with his accustomed thoroughness. However, given sufficient time to develop and augment what he has thus far presented with the stamp of his own personality, one might reasonably expect the Pope to continue unfolding and expanding his teaching along the following lines.

THE QUEENSHIP OF MARY

It might be recalled that the rationale of the magisterium as it developed under Leo XIII, Pius XI, and Pius XII has linked consecration to the Most Sacred Heart of Jesus with his Kingship and consecration to the Immaculate Heart of Mary with her Queenship.[44] The emphasis of John Paul II has been to relate consecration to Mary and her Immaculate Heart much more to her Motherhood. One can readily recognize this as a development of the magisterial tradition and a more direct appeal to the human heart, but, of course, this does not detract or derogate from the connection between consecration and Mary's royalty which is already established by Saints Ildephonsus of Toledo and John of Damascus[45] and a frequent theme in de Montfort's exposition of Marian consecration.[46] Perhaps among his most evocative remarks

[44] Cf. above, 102–5.

[45] Cf. above, 46–47.

[46] One need only recognize that the term "slave" so dear to him is correlative to "Queen" and then check the references to Mary's Queenship in his *Oeuvres complètes*.

on the subject of Mary's Queenship thus far are those made in relation to the crowning of four Marian images at Jasna Góra on June 19, 1983, when he said: "To the kingdom of the Son is linked the reign of his Mother", and

> His Kingdom—and her kingdom—is not of this world. Yet it is rooted in human history, in the history of the whole human race—above all because of the fact that the Son of God, of the same substance as the Father, was made man by the power of the Holy Spirit in the womb of Mary. And that kingdom is definitively rooted in the history of humanity through the Cross, at the foot of which the Mother of God stood as the "Socia Redemptoris". And, in this rooting, that kingdom endures. It endures on earth. It endures in different places on earth. Different human communities experience the maternal reign of Mary, which brings near to them the Kingdom of Christ.[47]

Of course, one could also cite his treatment of Mary's royalty in *Redemptoris Mater,* number 41.

THE THEOLOGY OF "COLLECTIVE" CONSECRATION

It will be remembered that when the question arose of consecrating the entire world to the Most Sacred Heart of Jesus, Pope Leo XIII had had the matter studied to determine in what sense he could consecrate the unbaptized.[48] The formula which he used with regard to non-Christians, "with all Our soul We commend them, and as far as in us lies We consecrate them to the Sacred Heart of Jesus",[49] provided the basis on which Pius XII would consecrate the entire world to the Immaculate Heart of Mary in his capacity as "the common father of the vast Christian family" and "the Vicar of Him to whom was given 'all power in heaven and on earth' ".[50]

[47] *Inseg* VI:1 (1983), 1580, 1582; *ORE* 791:6.
[48] Cf. above, 83–84.
[49] Cf. above, 87.
[50] Cf. above, 98–99.

The dogmatic basis already established by his predecessors is certainly a sufficient justification for John Paul's consecration of the world to Mary and her Immaculate Heart as well. But the further question remains, however: "What is achieved by such all-inclusive acts of consecration? What is the point of them?" [51] In his frequent emphasis on Mary's unique role in the Redemption, the Pope comes close to suggesting that Mary's mediatorial function is not limited to either Catholics or Christians, but that all humanity has been committed *modo tacito* to her maternal mediation. Should the Pope's reflection continue to develop in this direction, such would be a further substantiation of the doctrine[52] that every grace comes through Mary [53] and a further justification for seeking her intercession that Christ may be known and received through such "collective" consecrations.[54]

THE ALLIANCE OF THE HEARTS OF JESUS AND MARY

The linking of the Hearts of Jesus and Mary in the thought of Pope John Paul II and his frequent references to them are notable. He showed particular interest in an International Theological Symposium on the Alliance of the Hearts of Jesus and Mary,[55] which was held in Fatima, Portugal, from

[51] Cf. Luis, "La consagración a María", 105–6.

[52] To a request for the dogmatic definition of Mary's universal mediation made by the late dean of the Sacred College of Cardinals, Carlo Confalonieri, in the name of the chapter of Saint Mary Major on March 2, 1984, Cardinal Joseph Ratzinger, prefect of the Congregation for the Doctrine of the Faith, replied that he did not consider such a solemn definition necessary because "la dottrina sulla mediazione universale di Maria santissima si trova giá adeguatamente proposta nei diversi documenti del magistero della chiesa" [the doctrine on the universal mediation of Mary Most Holy has already been sufficiently proposed in the documents of the Church's magisterium] (Amorth, 325).

[53] Cf. Roschini, *Dizionario di Mariologia*, 344–54; Armand J. Robichaud, S.M., "Mary, Dispensatrix of All Graces", in *Mariology*, 2:426–60.

[54] Cf. Amorth, 302.

[55] Cf. Michael O'Carroll, C.S.Sp., "The Alliance of the Two Hearts", *Doctrine and Life* 38 (1988): 234–41; *Veni Creator Spiritus*, 4–5.

September 14 to 19, 1986, under the presidency of Cardinal Jaime L. Sin,[56] by addressing a letter to the participants[57] and by delivering a special address to them on September 22, 1986, after the conclusion of the symposium.[58] Similarly he sent a letter to the participants in an International Theological/Pastoral Conference on the Alliance of the Hearts of Jesus and Mary which was held in Manila, Philippines, from November 30 to December 3, 1987, as a follow-up to the previous symposium. In that letter he said: "It is altogether fitting . . . that your Conference should seek to deepen the awareness of the intimate relationship between the two Hearts and *the value for our own day of authentic devotion and consecration to the Hearts of Jesus and Mary*." [59] Clearly he traced out a new theological pathway by his celebrated Angelus address of September 15, 1985, and by his multiple and evocative references to the Hearts of Jesus and Mary, a path which remains to be further explored, developed, and related to the theology of consecration to the Most Sacred Heart of Jesus and to the Immaculate Heart of Mary.

THE RELATIONSHIP BETWEEN MARY AND THE HOLY SPIRIT

The exploration of the relationship between the Virgin Mary and the Holy Spirit has been rich and fruitful for theology[60] and the devotional life of the faithful and has shed no little light on the theology of Marian consecration

[56] Cf. *Miles Immaculatae* 23 (1987): 178–79; *Marian Studies* 39 (1988): 182–83.

[57] *Miles Immaculatae* 23 (1987): 42–43.

[58] *Inseg* IX:2 (1986), 698–700; *ORE* 959:12–13.

[59] *Alliance of the Hearts of Jesus and Mary*, 2 (emphasis mine).

[60] Cf. O'Carroll, *Veni Creator Spiritus*, 101–3, 145; *Theotokos*, 329–33; Peter Damian Fehlner, O.F.M. Conv., "The Immaculate and the Mystery of the Trinity in the Thought of St. Maximilian Kolbe", in *La Mariologia di S. Massimiliano M. Kolbe* (Rome: Ed. Miscellanea Francescana, 1985), 391–400; Jean-Marie Salgado, O.M.I., "Les appropriations trinitaires et la théologie mariale", *Marianum* 49 (1987): 430–48.

from the days of Saint Ildephonsus of Toledo.[61] While the Pope has not hesitated to speak of Mary as "Spouse of the Holy Spirit",[62] a title which came into use at least by the beginning of the ninth century,[63] and while he has used this title precisely when others have refrained from so doing for fear of suggesting "theogamy"[64] or of saying too much about Mary,[65] he has not notably amplified this relationship with regard to the theology of consecration.

The two great proponents of Marian consecration among the saints, Louis-Marie Grignion de Montfort and Maximilian Maria Kolbe, have propounded their doctrine with reference to Mary, "Spouse of the Holy Spirit". De Montfort says:

> God the Holy Spirit, who does not produce any divine person, became fruitful through Mary whom he espoused. It was with her, in her and of her that he produced his masterpiece, God-made-man, and that he produces every day until the end of the world the members of the body of this adorable Head. For this reason the more he finds Mary his dear and inseparable spouse in a soul the more powerful and effective he becomes in producing Jesus Christ in that soul and that soul in Jesus Christ.

[61] Cf. the text of the prayer in which Ildephonsus prays: "I beg you, O holy Virgin, that I may have Jesus from the Spirit from whom you conceived Jesus . . ." in *Theotokos*, 330.

[62] Cf. for instance the Apostolic Letter to Religious on the occasion of the Marian Year (*Inseg* XI:2 [1988], 1602, 1613; *ORE* 1043:3) and also *Inseg* XII:1 (1989), 1775; *ORE* 1096:2, 1106:4, 1139:11, 1148:11, 1201:1, 1204:6.

[63] Cf. Salgado, "Les appropriations trinitaires", 440–48. In times past it was thought that St. Francis was the first to use this title. Like Fr. Salgado other scholars have also demonstrated its existence prior to this saint's usage of it in the well-known Antiphon from his *Office of the Passion*. Its usage, however, by St. Francis in this *Office* was and still is particularly significant for the Marian piety and thought distinctive of the Franciscan Order, and the widespread diffusion of that *Office* in the 13th century contributed greatly to its general use in the Church.

[64] Cf. Laurentin, *A Year of Grace with Mary*, 77–78.

[65] Cf. the excellent article by Fr. Edward D. O'Connor, C.S.C., "Mary and the Holy Spirit", *Homiletic & Pastoral Review* 90, no. 8 (1990): 21–30, which defends retaining this title in the Catholic lexicon.

> This does not mean that the Blessed Virgin confers on the Holy Spirit a fruitfulness which he does not already possess. . . . But it does mean that the Holy Spirit chose to make use of our Blessed Lady, although he had no absolute need of her, in order to become actively fruitful in producing Jesus Christ and his members in her and by her. [66]

It might be argued that, following in the centuries-long Franciscan tradition, the position of Mary as collaborator with the Holy Spirit, Immaculate Mediatrix in the plan of God, is even more explicit in the theology of Saint Maximilian.[67] Let this excerpt serve as an example:

> The soul is regenerated in the sacred waters of baptism and thus becomes God's child.
>
> Water, which purifies everything over which it runs, is a symbol of her who purifies every soul that draws near to her. It is a symbol of the Immaculate, of her who is without stain; upon whoever is washed in this water the grace of the Holy Spirit descends. The Holy Spirit, the divine Spouse of the Immaculate, acts only in her and through her; he communicates supernatural life, the life of grace, the divine life, the sharing in divine love, in the divinity itself.[68]

Pope Paul VI, who called for theological and pastoral meditation on "the hidden relationship between the Spirit of God and the Virgin of Nazareth" [69] in number 27 of his apostolic exhortation *Marialis Cultus* of February 2, 1974, wrote to Cardinal Leo Jozef Suenens on May 13, 1975:

> We must consider, therefore, that the activity of the Mother of the Church for the benefit of the redeemed does not replace, or compete with, the almighty and universal action of the Holy Spirit. Rather, the former implores and prepares for the latter, not only

[66] *True Devotion*, nos. 20–21; *God Alone*, 295–96.

[67] Cf. Henri-Marie Manteau-Bonamy, O.P., *Immaculate Conception and the Holy Spirit: The Marian Teachings of Father Kolbe*, trans. Br. Richard Arnandez, F.S.C. (Kenosha, Wis.: Franciscan Marytown Press, 1977), passim.

[68] Kolbe, *Scritti*, no. 1326 (3:769); Romb, 199.

[69] *AAS* 66 (1974): 139; *Mary—God's Mother and Ours*, 126.

by prayer of intercession, in harmony with the divine plans which Mary contemplates in the beatific vision, but also with the direct influence of her example, in particular the extremely important one of her supreme docility to the inspirations of the Divine Spirit. It is, therefore, always in dependence on the Holy Spirit that Mary leads souls to Jesus, forms them in her image, inspires them with good advice and serves as a bond of love between Jesus and the faithful.

To confirm these reflections, we are happy to recall the testimony of the Fathers and Doctors of the Eastern Church. They are models of belief in and worship of the Holy Spirit; they have also witnessed to the Church's belief in and veneration of the Mother of Christ as the mediatrix of divine favors . . . They take it for granted and sometimes expressly declare that the Virgin's mediative activity depends upon and has its source in that of the Spirit of God.[70]

While Pope John Paul II has made literally hundreds of references to Our Lady's relationship to the Holy Spirit, the only one of which I am aware which has a bearing on the question of Marian consecration occurs in the Act of Consecration of June 7, 1981,[71] which became the archetype of the 1982 Act of Consecration in Fatima and that of March 25, 1984, in Rome. Here are the salient passages:

Mother of all individuals and peoples, you know all their sufferings and hopes. In your motherly heart you feel all the struggles between good and evil, between light and darkness, that convulse the world: accept the plea which we make in the Holy Spirit directly to your heart, and embrace with the love of the Mother and Handmaid of the Lord those who most await this embrace, and also those whose act of dedication you too await in a particular way. Take under your motherly protection the whole human family, which with affectionate love we entrust to you, O Mother.

[70] *AAS* 67 (1975): 358; English trans. in Edward D. O'Connor, C.S.C., *Pope Paul and the Spirit: Charisms and Church Renewal in the Teaching of Paul VI* (Notre Dame, Ind.: Ave Maria Press, 1978), 222.

[71] Cf. above, 31–32.

> God the Holy Spirit! who with the Father and the Son are adored and glorified! Accept these words of humble dedication addressed to you in the heart of Mary of Nazareth, your Spouse and the Mother of the Redeemer, whom the Church too calls Mother, for since the Upper Room of Pentecost the Church learns from her her own vocation as a mother! [72]

It is to be hoped that the relationship of the Holy Spirit to the Virgin Mary, insofar as this pertains to the theology of Marian consecration, may be further developed by the Holy Father on this promising foundation.

THE ULTIMATE FINALITY OF MARIAN CONSECRATION

The intimate relationship of Mary with the Holy Spirit and her collaboration with Him in the application of the fruits of the Redemption lead logically to a consideration of the economy within the Trinity as it pertains to us. The Father sends the Son to become man for our salvation by the power of the Holy Spirit. To complete the work of the Redemption which He has wrought, the Son sends the Holy Spirit upon His followers. By the Holy Spirit we are led to Jesus and through Jesus we are led to the Father. The Father is the *fons et origo* of our salvation and at the same time all is definitively directed toward Him as our final goal.[73]

[72] *Inseg* IV:1 (1981), 1246, 1247; *ORE* 688:10. It will be remembered that this consecration was renewed on the Feast of the Immaculate Conception in 1981 as well, see *Inseg* IV:2 (1981), 878; *ORE* 714:12.

[73] The classic formulations of St. Bonaventure: "Ipse Spiritus Sanctus, cum procedat a Filio, per Filium cum aliis (i.e. creaturis) ad Patrem reducitur" [The Holy Spirit Himself, since He proceeds from the Son, through the Son with others (creatures) returns to the Father], (*I Sent.* d. 31, p. 2, dub. 7). "Unde . . . Pater est principium, ad quod reducimur; Filius forma, quam sequimur; et Spiritus Sanctus gratia, qua reconciliamur. . . ." [Hence . . . the Father is the starting point to which we return; the Son the form which we follow; and the Holy Spirit the grace by which we are reconciled], (*I Sent.* d. 27, p. 2, a. un. 1 q. 2, ad 5).

Since we know that consecration to Mary is willed by God in order that we might achieve a deeper consecration to Christ, we would logically expect that consecration to Christ should lead to a deeper consecration to the Father so that God might be "all in all" (cf. 1 Cor 15:28).[74] This, in fact, is part and parcel of the Franciscan tradition with which Saint Louis-Marie Grignion de Montfort was quite conversant and in which Saint Maximilian Kolbe was formed.[75]

Let us note how the Breton missioner gives expression to this divine economy:

> All this is taken from St. Bernard and St. Bonaventure. According to them, we have three steps to take in order to reach God. The first, nearest to us and most suited to our capacity, is Mary; the second is Jesus Christ; the third is God the Father. To go to Jesus, we should go to Mary, our mediatrix of intercession. To go to God the Father, we must go to Jesus, our Mediator of redemption. This order is perfectly observed in the devotion I shall speak about further on.[76]

> This devotion is a safe means of going to Jesus Christ, because it is Mary's role to lead us safely to her Son; just as it is the role of Our Lord to lead us to the eternal Father.[77]

"Reparatio est operatio primi principii, ita quod ab ipso manat secundum liberalitatem et ad ipsum reducit secundum conformitatem. . . ." [Reparation is the work of the first principle, in such wise that it flows from Him on grounds of His generosity and returns to Him in proportion to its conformity], (*Breviloquium*, p. 4, c. 5).

[74] Cf. above, 273.

[75] Henry of Avranches in a well-known verse of his Legend pinpoints the doctrinal basis of St. Francis' profound devotion to the Virgin Mother, his Lady or Queen: "Mediatrix Virgo beata ad Christum, Christus ad Patrem sit Mediator" [Our Mediatrix may the Blessed Virgin be to Christ, and Christ our Mediator to the Father], (*Legenda Versificata* VII, 8, in *Analecta Franciscana* 10:448).

[76] *True Devotion*, no. 86.

[77] Ibid., no. 164.

Now let us listen to some of the many affirmations of this divine economy as enunciated by the martyr of Auschwitz, keeping in mind in particular his understanding of the relationship between Mary and the Holy Spirit:

> Let us come to realize more deeply every day our belonging to the Immaculate, to Jesus and to God in her and through her, but not parallel to her. We do not serve God the Father, Jesus and the Immaculate as separate objects of worship. We serve God in Jesus and through Jesus. We serve Jesus in the Immaculate and through the Immaculate. In other words, we serve the Immaculate directly, exclusively and without limits, but with her, in her and through her we serve Jesus; and with him, in him and through him we serve God the Father.
>
> And what about the Holy Spirit?
>
> He is in the Immaculate, as the Second Person of the Holy Trinity, the Son of God, is in Jesus, but with this difference: that in Jesus there are two natures, divine and human, in one single Person, the divine Person. The nature and the person of the Immaculate, on the contrary, are distinct from the nature and the Person of the Holy Spirit. But this union is so inexpressible and perfect that the Holy Spirit acts only through the Immaculate, his spouse. Consequently she is the Mediatrix of all the graces of the Holy Spirit. Since every grace is a gift of God the Father through the Son and the Holy Spirit, it follows that there is no grace which does not belong to the Immaculate, which is not offered to her and which does not remain at her free disposal.
>
> So when we venerate the Immaculate we venerate the Holy Spirit in a very special manner, and because grace comes to us from the Father through the Son and the Holy Spirit, so, as is only right, the fruits of this grace arise from us to the Father in the reverse order: through the Holy Spirit and the Son, which means through the Immaculate and Jesus.[78]

Thus, precisely because we are consecrated unreservedly to the Immaculate, with so much the greater fearlessness we, notwithstanding our wickedness, are able to approach the Most Sacred Heart of Jesus.

[78] Kolbe, *Scritti*, no. 634 (2:189); Romb, 128–29.

In reality, therefore, we are entirely, completely and exclusively consecrated to the Immaculate with all our actions, and in her and through her we are consecrated always entirely, completely and exclusively to Jesus Christ; in him, then, and through him we are consecrated entirely, completely and exclusively to our heavenly Father.[79]

The end of every man is to belong to God through Jesus, our Mediator with his Father, and to belong to Jesus through the Immaculate, Mediatrix of all graces. Those who love the Immaculate have at various times, both in public and in private, used various formulas to express their consecration to our Lady. All of them seek to stress the most perfect form of consecration, as far as this is possible, even though in the words used and in the direct meaning of these words there is considerable diversity. . . .

Therefore the Knights [of the Immaculate] seek to become ever more truly the property of the Immaculate; to belong to her in an ever more perfect way and under every aspect without any exception. They wish to develop their understanding of what it means to belong to her so that they may enlighten, reinvigorate and set on fire the souls living in their own milieu, and make them similar to themselves. . . .

In this way, by becoming ever more fully the Immaculate's property, to the point of conquering, as her Knight, ever more numerous throngs of souls, and by becoming through the Immaculate the property of Jesus, and through him in an ever more perfect manner the property of our heavenly Father, a soul becomes ever more truly a Knight of the Immaculate, and penetrates ever more deeply into the essence of the Knights of the Immaculate.[80]

Finally we have the words of Pope Leo XIII's encyclical letter *Octobri Mense* of September 22, 1891, to conclude our citation of sources on the end of Marian consecration: "As no man goes to the Father but by the Son, so no one goes to Christ except through His Mother." [81]

[79] Kolbe, *Scritti*, no. 643 (2:204), (my trans.).

[80] Ibid., no. 1329 (3:776–77, 779); Romb, 158–59, 160.

[81] *AAS* 24 (1891–1892): 195; *OL*, no. 113.

While surely this finality is always presumed by our Holy Father in the consistent carrying out of his program of entrustment to Mary and is explicit in the great acts of consecration of 1982 and 1984, in which he prays that we may identify ourselves with Christ's consecration to the Father and then entrusts this consecration to Mary,[82] this is an area in his teaching on Marian consecration which we might expect him to "flesh out" further in the future.

Let us bring this section to a close with a beautiful line in *Redemptoris Mater* which captures all that we have tried to express under this last heading in a marvelously concise way: "Mary, the exalted Daughter of Sion, helps all her children, wherever they may be and whatever their condition, *to find in Christ the path to the Father's house.*"[83] Very beautifully, Mary is designated as the one who leads to Christ who, in turn, leads to the Father.

Those, then, who, according to John Paul's teaching, accept the gift of the Lord and "take Mary into their own homes" (cf. Jn 19:27), who bring her into everything that makes up their inner lives, who allow themselves to be taken into her maternal charity,[84] may justly appropriate to themselves Saint Paul's statement to the Corinthians with this addition: "You are *Mary's and Mary is* Christ's and Christ is God's" (1 Cor 3:23) because God has willed that we belong to His Son and His Son has willed that we belong to His Mother. As Mary prepares us for the reign of her Son, so He prepares us for the reign of His Father. "When, finally, all has been subjected to the Son, he will then subject himself to the One who made all things subject to him, so that God may be all in all" (1 Cor 15:28).

[82] *Inseg* V:2 (1982), 1587–89; *ORE* 735:12; *Inseg* VII:1 (1984), 775–76; *ORE* 828:9–10.

[83] *Inseg* X:1 (1987), 738; St. Paul ed., 67.

[84] Cf. *Redemptoris Mater*, no. 45.

CONCLUSION

In the course of this study I have done my best to allow Pope John Paul II to speak for himself. If he does not explicitly state on every occasion that consecration or entrustment to Mary is important for every Christian—and, indeed, ultimately for every human being—such a statement is unnecessary because he consistently and undeviatingly proclaims this in his prayers and in his actions. On the other hand, as we have repeatedly seen, he makes such exhortations with amazing frequency.

Entrustment to Mary, then, with all that this implies, has become one of the fixed points of reference of his pontificate. While this may be known in some few circles, it would seem that its significance is barely appreciated. Perhaps never in the entire two-millennia history of the Church has the Successor of Saint Peter emphasized the significance of consecration or entrustment to Mary so much. Surely, then, the first conclusion of this book is that in the mind and teaching of the Pope the importance of consecration to Mary can hardly be overestimated.

This leads to an intimately related conclusion: Marian consecration or the "self-entrustment of a child to its mother", as he refers to it in *Redemptoris Mater*, number 46, "not only has its *beginning in Christ* but can also be said to be *definitively directed towards him*". In this epigrammatic statement, perhaps easy to miss in that densely-packed theological treatise, John Paul states unequivocally that entrustment or consecration to Mary has a Christological foundation as well as finality.

One could say that in that one sentence he answers the "theological problem" which this study has set out to deal with. This is not an insight which he presented for the first time in *Redemptoris Mater*, as the attentive will have recognized, since it is truly a golden thread which runs throughout his papal teaching. But perhaps it is presented there with a conciseness that can only be fully appreciated when one is cognizant of all that it summarizes in terms of Mary's complete identification with the self-consecration of Christ, her mediation, her spiritual maternity, and what I have referred to as the Pope's "theology of entrustment".

I am profoundly convinced that what I have presented has great significance for the Church and for the world, not because *I* have presented it, but because it is the ordinary magisterium of the Vicar of Christ and it meets all the requisite qualifications in order to be recognized as such according to *Lumen Gentium*, number 25. I am grateful to have had the opportunity to undertake this study and the grace to bring it to a conclusion (even if the ultimate evaluation will be able to be written only as an epilogue to this pontificate) because it makes a contribution to Christology, to Mariology, to ecclesiology, and to the study of the papal magisterium which, to my knowledge, has not hitherto been made. I offer it as an act of filial homage to the Mother of God and to the Vicar of her Son.

LAUS JESU ET MARIAE

BIBLIOGRAPHY

I. Works of Pope John Paul II (Karol Wojtyła)

A. PREPAPAL WORKS

Il Buon Pastore: Scritti, Discorsi e Lettere Pastorali. Trans. Elzbieta Cywiak and Renzo Panzone. Rome: Edizioni Logos, 1978.

Chiamati all' Amore: Itinerari di Santità. Trans. Aldo Cantarini. Rome: Edizioni Logos, 1980.

"Inspiracja Maryjna Vaticanum II". *W Kierunku prawdy.* Ed. Bohdan Bejze. Warsaw Catholic Academy of Theology, 1976, 112–21.

"Komentarz teologiczno-diszpasterski do aktu dokonanego na Jansnej Gorze dnia 3 maja 1966 R". *Ateneum Kapłanskie* (Wokławek) 79 (1972): 5–21.

Maria: Omelie. Preface by Stefan Cardinal Wyszyński. Trans. Janina Korzeniewska. Vatican City: Libreria Editrice Vaticana, 1982.

Maximilien Kolbe, Patron de nôtre siècle difficile. Paris: Lethielleux, 1982.

"Oddanie Bogurodzicy w świetle nauki Soboru". *Przewodnnik Katolicki*, no. 26 (1972): 228.

"O Matce i Krolowej Polakow"—Refleksje, modlitwy, piesni. Jasna Góra. Rome: Paulini, 1982, 263–66.

Sign of Contradiction. New York: Crossroad-Seabury Press, 1979.

Sources of Renewal: The Implementation of the Second Vatican Council. Trans. P. S. Falla. San Francisco: Harper & Row, 1980.

"Tysiacleci chrztu a oddanie Matce Boskiej". *Notificationes e Curia Metropolitana Cracoviensi* (1965): 189–95.
The Word Made Flesh: The Meaning of the Christmas Season. Trans. Leslie Wearne. San Francisco: Harper & Row, 1985.
"Znaczenie Kardynała Stefana Wyszyńskiego dla Współczesnego Kościoła". *Zeszyty Naukowe* 3 (1971): 19–37.

B. PAPAL WORKS

Affido a Te, O Maria. Ed. Sergio Trasatti and Arturo Mari. Bergamo: Editrice Velar, 1982.
Africa: Apostolic Pilgrimage. Boston: St. Paul Editions, 1980.
Africa: Land of Promise, Land of Hope. Boston: St. Paul Editions, 1982.
Brazil: Journey in the Light of the Eucharist. Boston: St. Paul Editions, 1980.
The Far East: Journey of Peace and Brotherhood. Boston: St. Paul Editions, 1981.
France: Message of Peace, Trust, Love and Faith. Boston: St. Paul Editions, 1980.
Germany: Pilgrimage of Unity and Peace. Boston: St. Paul Editions, 1981.
Insegnamenti di Giovanni Paolo II (1978–). Vatican City: Libreria Editrice Vaticana, 1979– .
Ireland "In the Footsteps of St. Patrick". Boston: St. Paul Editions, 1979.
Messages of John Paul II: Servant of Truth. Boston: St. Paul Editions, 1979.
Mother of the Redeemer [*Redemptoris Mater*]. Boston: St. Paul Editions, 1987.
L'Osservatore Romano, weekly edition in English.
Pilgrim to Poland. Boston: St. Paul Editions, 1979.
Pope John Paul II in Argentina. Boston: St. Paul Editions, 1983.
Portugal: Message of Fatima. Boston: St. Paul Editions, 1983.

The Redeemer of Man [*Redemptor Hominis*]. Boston: St. Paul Editions, 1979.

Talks of John Paul II. Boston: St. Paul Editions, 1979.

Turkey—Ecumenical Pilgrimage. Boston: St. Paul Editions, 1980.

U.S.A.—The Message of Justice, Peace and Love. Boston: St. Paul Editions, 1979.

II. Magisterial Documents

Acta Apostolicae Sedis (1909–).

Acta Sanctae Sedis (1865–1908).

Bertetto, Domenico, S.D.B., ed. *La Madonna nella Parola di Paolo VI*. 2nd ed. Rome: Libreria Ateneo Salesiano, 1980.

———, *Il Magistero Mariano di Pio XII*. Rome: Edizioni Paoline, 1956.

Carlen, Claudia, I.H.M. *The Papal Encyclicals 1878–1903*. Raleigh, N.C.: McGrath Publishing Co., "Consortium Book", 1981.

———, *The Papal Encyclicals 1903–1939*. Raleigh, N.C.: McGrath Publishing Co., "Consortium Book", 1981.

Congregation for Catholic Education, *The Virgin Mary in Intellectual and Spiritual Formation* (March 25, 1988), no. 14.

Denzinger, Henricus, and Adolfus Schonmetzer, S.J., eds. *Enchiridion Symbolorum Definitionum et Declarationum de Rebus Fidei et Morum*. 32nd ed. Freiburg-im-Breisgau: Herder, 1963.

Dogmatic Constitution on the Church [*Lumen Gentium*]. Boston: St. Paul Editions, 1964.

Flannery, Austin, O.P., ed. *Vatican Council II: The Conciliar and Post Conciliar Documents*. Collegeville, Minn.: Liturgical Press, 1975.

Humani Generis: Encyclical Letter of Pope Pius XII. Washington, D.C.: National Catholic Welfare Conference, 1950.

Insegnamenti di Paolo VI (1963–1978). 15 vols. Vatican City: Libreria Editrice Vaticana, 1965–1979.

Larkin, Francis, SS.CC., ed. *Haurietis Aquas: The Sacred Heart Encyclical of Pope Pius XII.* Orlando, Fl.: Sacred Heart Publication Center, 1974.

Neuner, J., S.J., and J. Dupuis, S.J., eds. *The Christian Faith in the Doctrinal Documents of the Catholic Church.* New York: Alba House, 1982.

Paul VI. *Mary—God's Mother and Ours.* Boston: St. Paul Editions, 1979.

Pocock, Hubert M., S.M.M., ed. *Pius XII on Consecration to Mary.* Bay Shore, N.Y.: Montfort Publications, 1956.

The Pope Speaks (1954–).

Sacrosanctum Oecumenicum Concilium Vaticanum II. *Constitutiones, Decreta, Declarationes.* Cura et studio Secretariae Generalis Concilii Oecumenici Vaticani II. Vatican City: Typis Polyglottis Vaticanis, 1974.

Solesmes, Benedictine Monks of., eds. *Our Lady: Papal Teachings.* Trans. Daughters of St. Paul. Boston: St. Paul Editions, 1961.

Synod of 1985, Extraordinary. Boston: St. Paul Editions, 1986.

Synodus Extraordinaria. Relatio Finalis. L'Osservatore Romano. December 10, 1985, supplement.

Unger, Dominic J., O.F.M. Cap., ed. and trans. *Mary, Christ and the Church.* Bay Shore, N.Y.: Montfort Publications, 1979.

III. Scriptural Studies

Braun, F. M., O.P. *Mother of God's People.* Trans. John Clarke, O.C.D. New York: Alba House, 1967.

Brown, Raymond E., S.S. *The Gospel According to John, I–XII.* Anchor Bible, vol. 29. Garden City, N.Y.: Doubleday & Co., 1966.

———, *The Gospel According to John, XIII–XXI.* Anchor Bible, vol. 29A. Garden City, N.Y.: Doubleday & Co., 1970.

Brown, Raymond E., S.S., et al., eds. *Mary in the New Testament.* Philadelphia: Fortress Press; New York: Paulist Press, 1978.

Cazelles, Henri, P.S.S. "Consécration du Christ et consécration de l'homme". *Cahiers Marials,* no. 86 (1973): 5–13.

———, "L'Esprit qui consacre le Christ, Marie, l'Eglise". *Cahiers Marials,* no. 133 (1982): 131–45.

———, "Note sur le ministère apostolique de consécration". *Bulletin de Saint-Sulpice* 1 (1975): 302–7.

Deiss, Lucien, C.S.Sp. *Mary, Daughter of Sion.* Trans. Barbara T. Blair. Collegeville, Minn.: Liturgical Press, 1972.

De la Potterie, Ignace, S.J. "L'Alleanza dei Cuori di Gesù e di Maria". In *Il Mistero del Cuore Trafitto: Fondamenti biblici della spiritualità del Cuore di Gesù,* 137–80. Bologna: Edizioni Dehoniane, 1988.

———, "The Alliance of the Hearts of Jesus and Mary: A Biblical Approach". Trans. Sr. Rosario de Veyra, R.A. *The Alliance of the Hearts of Jesus and Mary: The International Theological/Pastoral Conference, Manila, Philippines, 30 November–3 December 1987, Texts and Documents,* 68–117. Manila: Bahay Maria, 1988.

———, " 'Et à partir de cette heure, le Disciple l'accueillit dans son intimité' (Jn. 19, 27b)". *Marianum* 42 (1980): 84–125.

———, *Maria nel mistero dell' alleanza.* Genoa: Marietti "Dabar", 1988.

———, "La maternità spirituale di Maria e la fondazione della chiesa". In *Gesù verità: Studi di cristologia giovannea,* 158–64. Turin: Marietti, 1973.

———, "La parole de Jésus 'Voici ta Mère' et l'accueil du Disciple (Jn. 19, 27b)". *Marianum* 36 (1974): 1–39.

———, *La Vérité dans Saint Jean,* vol. 2. Analecta Biblica, no. 74. Rome: Pontificium Institutum Biblicum, 1977.

Delorme, Jean. "Sacerdoce du Christ et Ministère (A propos de Jean 17): Sémantique et théologie biblique". *Recherches de Science Religieuse* 62 (1974): 199–219.

———, "Sacrifice, sacerdoce, consécration". *Recherches de Science Religieuse* 63 (1975): 343–66.

Feuillet, André, P.S.S. "De muliere parturiente et de maternitate spirituali Mariae secundum evangelium sancti Johannis (16, 21; 19, 25–27)". In *De Beata Virgine Maria in Evangelio S. Ioannis et in Apocalypsi*, 111–22. Vol. 5 of *Maria in Sacra Scriptura: Acta Congressus Mariologici-Mariani in Republica Dominicana Anno 1965 Celebrati*. Rome: Pontificia Academia Mariana Internationalis, 1967.

———, *The Priesthood of Christ and His Ministers*. Trans. Matthew J. O'Connell. Garden City, N.Y.: Doubleday & Co., 1975.

Koester, Helmut. "splángchnon, splangchnízomai, 'eúsplangchnos". In *Theological Dictionary of the New Testament*, ed. Gerhard Friedrich, 548–59. Grand Rapids, Mich.: W. B. Eerdmans, 1971.

Lagrange, M. J., O.P. *L'Évangile selon Saint Jean*. Paris: Gabalda et Cie., 1936.

Manelli, Stefano, M., F.F.I. *Mariologia Biblica*. Frigento: Casa Mariana Editrice, 1989.

McHugh, John. *The Mother of Jesus in the New Testament*. Garden City, N.Y.: Doubleday & Co., 1975.

Serra, Aristide, O.S.M. *Contributi dell'antica letteratura giudaica per l'esegesi di Giovanni 2, 1–12 e 19, 25–27*. Rome: Herder, 1977.

———, *Maria a Cana e presso la croce: saggio di Mariologia Giovannea*. Rome: Centro di Cultura Mariana, "Mater Ecclesia", 1985.

———, *Maria secondo il Vangelo*. Brescia: Editrice Queriniana, 1988.

IV. Theological Works Consulted

Alonso, Joaquin Maria, C.M.F. "Her Own Words". *A Heart for All: The Immaculate Heart of Mary in the Apparitions of Fatima*, 23–72. Washington, N.J.: A.M.I. Press, 1972.

Amorth, Gabriele, S.S.P. *Dialoghi su Maria*. Padua: Edizioni Messagero Padova, 1987.

Anderson, Robin. *Between Two Wars: The Story of Pope Pius XI*. Chicago: Franciscan Herald Press, 1977.

Barré, Henri, C.S.Sp. "Exégèse de Jean 19, 25–27 et développement doctrinal". In *De Beata Virgine Maria in Evangelio S. Ioannis et in Apocalypsi*, 161–71. Vol. 5 of *Maria in Sacra Scriptura: Acta Congressus Mariologici-Mariani in Republica Dominicana Anno 1965 Celebrati*. Rome: Pontificia Academia Mariana Internationalis, 1967.

———, *Prières Anciennes de L'Occident à la Mère du Sauveur: Des origènes à saint Anselme*. Paris: Lethielleux, 1963.

Becker, Constantin. "Marie du Divin Cœur". In Marcel Viller, S.J., et al., *Dictionnaire de Spiritualité Ascétique et Mystique*, 10:485–86. Paris: Beauchesne et Ses Fils, 1980.

Bengoechea, I., O.C.D. "Un precursor de la consagración a Maria en el siglo XV: Arnoldo Bostio (1445–1499)". *Estudios Marianos* 51 (1986): 215–29.

Bertetto, Domenico, S.D.B. "Beata Virgo Maria et testamentum Domini in cruce". In *De Beata Virgine Maria in Evangelio S. Ioannis et in Apocalypsi*, 181–99. Vol. 5 of *Maria in Sacra Scriptura: Acta Congressus Mariologici-Mariani in Republica Dominicana Anno 1965 Celebrati*. Rome: Pontificia Academia Mariana Internationalis, 1967.

———, "Consacrazione e affidamento: Senso ed esigenze dell' affidamento a Maria". In *L'Affidamento a Maria*, ed. Domenico Bertetto, S.D.B., 75–85. Rome: Libreria Ateneo Salesiano, 1984.

———, *Maria nel Magistero di Giovanni Paolo II; Primo Anno di Pontificato, 16 ottobre 1978–21 ottobre 1979*. Rome: Libreria Ateneo Salesiano, 1980.

———, *Maria nel Magistero di Giovanni Paolo II; Secondo Anno di Pontificato, 22 ottobre 1979–21 ottobre 1980*. Rome: Libreria Ateneo Salesiano, 1981.

———, *Maria nel Magistero di Giovanni Paolo II; Terzo Anno di Pontificato, 22 ottobre 1980–21 ottobre 1981*. Rome: Libreria Ateneo Salesiano, 1983.

———, *Maria nel Magistero di Giovanni Paolo II; Quarto Anno di Pontificato, 22 ottobre 1981–21 ottobre 1982*. Rome: Libreria Ateneo Salesiano, 1984.

———, *Maria nel Magistero di Giovanni Paolo II; Quinto Anno di Pontificato, 22 ottobre 1982–21 ottobre 1983*. Rome: Libreria Ateneo Salesiano, 1986.

———, *Maria nel Magistero di Giovanni Paolo II; Sesto Anno di Pontificato, 22 ottobre 1983–21 ottobre 1984*. Rome: Libreria Ateneo Salesiano, 1986.

Berti, Conradus M., Salvator M. Meo, Hermannus M. Toniolo, O.S.M. *De Ratione Ponderandi Documenta Magisterii Ecclesiastici*. Rome: Edizioni Marianum, 1961.

Bérulle, Cardinal Pierre de. *La Vie de Jésus*. Paris, 1629.

Besutti, Giuseppe, O.S.M. *Bibliografia Mariana 1967–1972*. Rome: Edizioni Marianum, 1974.

———, *Bibliografia Mariana 1973–1977*. Rome: Edizioni Marianum, 1980.

———, *Bibliografia Mariana 1978–1984*. Rome: Edizioni Marianum, 1988.

"Biography of Card. Stefan Wyszynski: 1901–1981", *ORE* 687:2, 12.

Bittrémieux, J. "Consecratio Mundi Immaculato Cordi B. Mariae Virginis". *Ephemerides Theologicae Lovanienses* 20 (1943): 99–103.

Bossard, Alphonse, S.M.M. "Le don total au Christ par Marie selon Montfort". *Cahiers Marials*, no. 86 (1973): 29–48.

———, "Se consacrer à Marie". *Cahiers Marials*, no. 137 (1983): 95–106.

Bover, José M., S.J. "El Principio Mariológico de Analogía". In *De Mariologia in Genere Nonnullisque Privilegiis ac Muneribus*, 1–13. Vol. 11 of *Alma Socia Christi: Acta Congressus Mariologici-Mariani Romae Anno Sancto MCML Celebrati*. Rome: Pontificia Academia Mariana Internationalis, 1953.

Bradshaw, Robert. *Frank Duff: Founder of the Legion of Mary*. Bay Shore, N.Y.: Montfort Publications, 1985.

Buono, A. "Hyperdulia". In *Dictionary of Mary*, 129–30. New York: Catholic Book Publishing Co., 1985.

Calabuig Adan, Ignazio M., O.S.M. "Liturgia". In *Nuovo Dizionario di Mariologia*, ed. Stefano De Fiores, S.M.M., and Salvatore Meo, O.S.M., 767–87. Milan: Edizioni Paoline, 1985.

———, "Tre Messe in onore della Beata Vergine *Madre della Chiesa*". *Marianum* 36 (1974): 70–78.

Calkins, Arthur Burton. "The Cultus of the Hearts of Jesus and Mary in the Papal Magisterium from Pius IX to Pius XII". To be published in the *Acta* of the Tenth International Mariological Congress, held in Kevelaer, Germany, from September 11 to 17, 1987.

———, "John Paul II's Consecration to the Immaculate Heart of Mary: Christological Foundation". *Miles Immaculatae* 23 (1987): 88–116, 364–417.

———, "Mary's Maternal Mediation and the Practice of Marian Consecration". To be published in the *Proceedings of the National Marian Year Congress*, held in Chicago, August 11–15, 1988.

———, "The Union of the Hearts of Jesus and Mary in St. Francis de Sales and St. John Eudes". *Miles Immaculatae* 25 (1989): 472–512.

———, "Why the Heart?" *Homiletic & Pastoral Review* 89, no. 9 (1989): 18–23.

Calvo Moralejo, Gaspar, O.F.M. "Fray Melchor de Cetina, O.F.M., el primer teólogo de la 'Esclavitud Mariana' (1618)". *Estudios Marianos* 51 (1986): 249–71.

Canal, José María, C.M.F. "La Consagración a la Vírgen y a su Corazón Inmaculado". In *De Virginis Immaculatae Regalitate Eiusque Corde Materno*, 221–348. Vol. 12 of *Virgo Immaculata: Acta Congressus Mariologici-Mariani Romae Anno MCMLIV Celebrati*. Rome: Pontificia Academia Mariana Internationalis, 1956.

Carroll, Eamon R., O. Carm. "Mary: the Woman Come of Age". *Marian Studies* 36 (1985): 136–60.

———, "The New Testament Charisms of the Blessed Virgin Mary". *One in Christ* 22 (1986): 356–64.

———, "A Survey of Recent Mariology". *Marian Studies* 35 (1984): 157–87.

———, *Understanding the Mother of Jesus*. Wilmington, Del.: Michael Glazier, 1979.

Chasle, Louis. *Sister Mary of the Divine Heart*. Trans. by a member of the order. London: Burns & Oates, 1906.

Ciappi, Mario Luigi Cardinal, O.P. *The Heart of Christ, the Centre of the Mystery of Salvation*. Trans. Leslie Wearne and Andrew Wade. Rome: Cuore di Cristo Publishers, 1983.

Cochois, Paul. *Bérulle et l'École française*. No. 31 of "Maîtres Spirituels". Paris: Éditions du Seuil, 1963.

La Consacrazione nella Congregazione Mariana. Trans. of *Quatrième Centenaire des Congrégations Mariales. Documents du Congrès Européen*, held in Rome, September 8–12, 1963. Rome: Edizioni Stella Matutina, 1963.

Cras, Pierre. "Mother Mary of the Divine Heart: A Divine Messenger". In *Divine Masterpieces*. Ed. and trans. John J. Sullivan, S.J. Paterson, N. J.: St. Anthony Guild Press, 1960.

De Becker, Gérald, SS.CC. *Lexique pour la Théologie du Cœur du Christ*. Paris: Téqui, 1975.

———, *Les Sacrés-Cœurs de Jésus et de Marie: Étude Doctrinale*. Rome: Études Picpuciennes no. 5, 1959.

De Finance, Joseph, S.J. "Consécration". In Marcel Viller, S.J., et al., *Dictionnaire de Spiritualité Ascétique et Mystique*, 2:1576–83. Paris: Beauchesne et Ses Fils, 1953.

De Fiores, Stefano, S.M.M. *Itinerario spirituale di S. Luigi Maria de Montfort (1673–1716) nel periodo fino al sacerdozio (5 giugno 1700)*. Marian Library Studies, n.s. 6. Dayton, Oh.: University of Dayton, 1974.

———, "Linee di Sviluppo della Riflessione Teologica sul Ruolo Storico di Maria". In *Il Ruolo di Maria nell'oggi della Chiesa e del Mondo*, 205–18. Rome: Edizioni Marianum, 1979.

———, *Maria nella Teologia Contemporanea*. 2nd ed. Rome: Centro di Cultura Mariana "Mater Ecclesiae", 1987.

———, *Maria: presenza viva nel popolo di Dio*. Rome: Edizioni Monfortane, 1980.

———, "Proposte teologiche circa la consacrazione Mariana". *La Madonna* 30, nos. 3–4 (1982): 3–15.

———, "Questi tuoi figli o Madre". *L'Osservatore Romano* (1981): 1–2.

De Fiores, Stefano, S.M.M., Santino Epis, S.M.M., and Gabriele Amorth S.S.P. *La Consacrazione dell' Italia a Maria: Teologia, storia, cronaca*. Presentation of Cardinal Carlo Maria Martini. Rome: Edizioni Paoline, 1983.

De Fiores, Stefano, S.M.M. and Salvatore Meo, O.S.M., eds. *Nuovo Dizionario di Mariologia*. Milan: Edizioni Paoline, 1985.

Degli Esposti, Francesco. *La Teologia del Sacro Cuore di Gesù da Leone XIII a Pio XII*. Rome: Casa Editrice Herder, 1967.

De Montfort, St. Louis-Marie Grignion. *Oeuvres complètes de saint Louis-Marie Grignion de Montfort*. Paris: Éditions du Seuil, 1982.

———, *God Alone: The Collected Writings of St. Louis Mary de Montfort*. Bay Shore, N.Y.: Montfort Publications, 1987.

Deville, Raymond, P.S.S. *L'école française de spiritualité*. No. 11 of *Bibliothèque d'Histoire du Christianisme*. Paris: Desclée, 1987.

Dillenschneider, Clément, C.SS.R. *La Mariologie de S. Alphonse de Liguori: Sources et Synthèse Doctrinale*. Fribourg: Studia Friburgensia, 1934.

Duda, Bonaventura, O.F.M. "'Ecce mater tua' (Jo. 19, 26–27) in documentis Romanorum Pontificum". In *De Beata Virgine Maria in Evangelio S. Ioannis et in Apocalypsi*, 235–89. Vol. 5 of *Maria in Sacra Scriptura: Acta Congressus Mariologici-Mariani in Republica Dominicana Anno 1965 Celebrati*. Rome: Pontificia Academia Mariana Internationalis, 1967.

Duff, Frank. *The Woman of Genesis*. Dublin: Praedicanda Publications, 1976.

Durwell, F. X., C.SS.R. *The Resurrection: A Biblical Study*. Trans. Rosemary Sheed. New York: Sheed and Ward, 1960.

Elvins, Mark. "The Origin of the Title 'Dowry of Mary' and the Shrines of Our Lady at Westminster". A paper given to the London branch of the Ecumenical Society of the Blessed Virgin Mary on May 18, 1989.

Epis, Santino, S.M.M. "La Consacrazione dell' Italia a Maria: Un Capitolo di Storia e un Impegno Permanente". In *La Consacrazione dell' Italia a Maria*, De Fiores, Epis, Amorth, eds., 65–88. Rome: Edizioni Paoline, 1983.

Études Carmélitaines: Le Coeur. Paris: Desclée de Brouwer, 1950.

Eudes, St. John. *Oeuvres Complètes du Vénérable Jean Eudes*, 12 vols. Vannes: Imprimerie Lafoyle Frères, 1905–1911.

———, *The Life and Kingdom of Jesus in Christian Souls*. Trans. Trappist father. New York: P. J. Kenedy & Sons, 1946.

———, *Letters and Shorter Works*. Trans. Ruth Hauser. New York: P. J. Kenedy & Sons, 1948.

———, *The Sacred Heart of Jesus*. Trans. Richard Flower, O.S.B. New York: P. J. Kenedy & Sons, 1946.

Fehlner, Peter Damian, O.F.M. Conv. "The Immaculate and the Mystery of the Trinity in the Thought of St. Maximilian M. Kolbe". In *La Mariologia di S. Massimiliano Kolbe*, 382–416. Rome: Editrice Miscellanea Francescana, 1985.

———, "Mary Immaculate and St. Francis". *Miscellanea Francescana* 82 (1982): 502–19.

———, "Mulieris Dignitatem". *Miles Immaculatae* 25 (1989): 6–9.

Fernandez, Quirino. "Los Ríos y Alarcón (Bartolomé de)". In Marcel Viller, S.J., et al., *Dictionnaire de Spiritualité Ascétique et Mystique* 9:1013–18. Paris: Beauchesne et Ses Fils, 1976.

Flynn, J. "Mazzella, Camillo". In *New Catholic Encyclopedia*, 9:523–24. New York: McGraw-Hill Book Co., 1967.

Franzi, Francesco M. " 'Consacrazione' o 'affidamento' ? " *Miles Immaculatae* 17 (1981): 216–28.

———, "Per un orientamento sul tema della 'consacrazione a Maria' ". In *Teologia e Pastorale della Consacrazione a Maria*, 7–12. Padua: Edizioni Messagero, 1969.

Frossard, André. *"Be Not Afraid!": Pope John Paul II Speaks out on His Life, His Beliefs, and His Inspiring Vision for Humanity*. Trans. J. R. Foster. New York: St. Martin's Press, 1984.

Gaffney, J. Patrick, S.M.M. "Changing the I to We". *Queen of All Hearts* 35 (September–October 1984): 18–19, 24.

———, "The Holy Slavery of Love". In *Mariology*, ed. Juniper B. Carol, O.F.M., 3:143–61. Milwaukee: Bruce Publishing Co., 1961.

———, "Saint Louis Mary Grignion de Montfort and the Marian Consecration". *Marian Studies* 35 (1984): 111–56.

Galot, Jean, S.J. "The First Act of Consecration". *Queen of All Hearts* 33, no. 2 (July–August 1982): 12–13.

———, *Theology of the Priesthood*. Trans. Roger Balducelli, O.S.F.S. San Francisco: Ignatius Press, 1984.

Gardeil, H. D., O.P. *Introduction to the Philosophy of St. Thomas Aquinas IV: Metaphysics*. Trans. John A. Otto. St. Louis: B. Herder Book Co., 1967.

Garrigou-Lagrange, Reginald, O.P. *The Mother of The Saviour and Our Interior Life*. Trans. Bernard J. Kelly, C.S.Sp. St. Louis, Mo.: B. Herder Book Co., 1957.

———, *Our Savior and His Love for Us*. Trans. A. Bouchard. St. Louis, Mo.: B. Herder Book Co., 1951.

———, *The Three Ages of the Interior Life*, vol. 2. Trans. Sr. Timothea Doyle, O.P. St. Louis, Mo.: B. Herder Book Co., 1948.

Gautier, Jean, P.S.S. *Some Schools of Catholic Spirituality*. Trans. Kathryn Sullivan, R.S.C.J. Tournai: Desclée Co., 1959.

Geenen, G., O.P. "Les Antécédents Doctrinaux et Historiques de la Consécration du Monde au Cœur Immaculé de Marie". In *Maria: Études sur la Sainte Vierge*, ed. Hubert du Manoir, S.J., 1:825–73. Paris: Beauchesne et Ses Fils, 1949.

Gharib, Georges, "La Madonna della Misericordia: 'Sotto la tua protezione' ". *Madre di Dio* 59 (May 1991): 13–16.

Gharib, Georges, et al., eds. *Padri e altri autori bizantini*. Vol. 2 of *Testi Mariani del Primo Millennio*. Rome: Città Nuova Editrice, 1989.

Gherardini, Brunero. *La Madre: Maria in una sintesi storico-teologica*. Frigento: Casa Mariana Editrice, 1989.

Giamberardini, Gabriele O.F.M. *Il culto mariano in Egitto*. Vol. 1 of *Secoli I–VI*. Jerusalem: Franciscan Printing Press, 1975.

Ginn, Roman, O.C.S.O. "Slave Talk in St. Paul and St. Louis de Montfort". *Queen of All Hearts* 39 (March–April 1989): 12–13.

Glotin, Édouard, S.J. "Le centre de l'âme et l'Icône sacrée du Coeur. De Thérèse d'Avila à Marguerite-Marie".

In *Jésus-Christ Rédempteur de l'Homme*, 103–54. Venasque: Éditions de Carmel, 1986.

———, "Jean-Paul à Paray-le-Monial ou Pourquoi le 'Cœur'?" *Nouvelle Revue Théologique* 108 (1986): 685–714.

Gutierrez Osorio, Pastor, S.J. " 'Ecce Mater tua' (Jn. 19, 25–27): Maternitas spiritualis Mariae in luce exegeseos SS. Patrum et scriptorum posteriorum". In *De Beata Virgine Maria in Evangelio S. Ioannis et in Apocalypsi*, 151–60. Vol. 5 of *Maria in Sacra Scriptura: Acta Congressus Mariologici-Mariani in Republica Dominicana Anno 1965 Celebrati*. Rome: Pontificia Academia Mariana Internationalis, 1967.

Iacoangeli, R. "*Sub tuum praesidium*. La più antica preghiera mariana: filologia e fede". In *La mariologia nella catechesi dei Padri (età prenicena)*, ed. Sergio Felici, 207–40. Rome: Libreria Ateneo Salesiano "Biblioteca di Scienza Religiosa" no. 88, 1989.

Jelly, Frederick M., O.P. "The mystery of Mary's mediation". *Homiletic & Pastoral Review* 80, no. 8 (1980): 11–20.

Johnston, Francis. *Alexandrina: The Agony and the Glory*. Rockford, Ill.: Tan Books and Publishers, 1982.

———, *Fatima: The Great Sign*. Washington, N.J.: A.M.I. Press, 1980.

Joseph de Sainte-Marie, O.C.D. *Reflections on the Act of Consecration at Fatima of Pope John Paul II on 13th May 1982*. Trans. William Lawson, S.J. Chulmleigh, Devon.: Augustine Publishing Co.; Rockford, Ill.: Tan Books and Publishers, 1983. Originally published as "Réflexions sur un acte de consécration: Fatima, 13 mai 1982". *Marianum* 44 (1982): 88–142.

———, *Teologia e Spiritualità della Consacrazione a Maria*. Rome: Pontificio Istituto di Spiritualità del Teresianum, lectures, n.d.

Jungmann, J. A., S.J. *Pastoral Liturgy*. New York: Herder and Herder, 1962.

Klubertanz, G. P. "Analogy". In *New Catholic Encyclopedia,* 1:461–65. New York: McGraw-Hill Book Co., 1967.

Koehler, Théodore, S.M. "Maternité Spirituelle, Maternité Mystique". In *Maria: Études sur la Sainte Vierge,* ed. Hubert du Manoir, S.J., 6:552–638. Paris: Beauchesne et Ses Fils, 1961.

———, "Mary's Spiritual Maternity after the Second Vatican Council". *Marian Studies* 23 (1972): 39–68.

———, "Les principales interprétations traditionelles de Jn. 19, 25–27 pendant les douze premiers siècles". *Études Mariales* 16 (1959): 119–55.

———, "Servitude (saint esclavage)". In Marcel Viller, S.J., et al., *Dictionnaire de Spiritualité Ascétique et Mystique,* 14:730–45. Paris: Beauchesne et Ses Fils, 1990.

Kolbe, St. Maximilian, O.F.M. Conv. *Gli Scritti di Massimiliano Kolbe: eroe di Oświęcim e Beato della Chiesa.* 3 vols. Trans. Cristoforo Zambelli. Florence: Città di Vita, 1975–1978.

Kondor, Louis, S.V.D., ed. *Fatima in Lucia's Own Words.* Trans. Dominican Nuns of Perpetual Rosary. Fatima, Portugal: Postulation Centre, 1976.

Kosicki, George W., C.S.B. *Born of Mary: Testimonies, Tensions, Teachings.* Stockbridge, Mass.: Marian Press, 1985.

Larkin, Francis, SS.CC. "Crawley-Boevey, Mateo". In *New Catholic Encyclopedia,* 4:16. New York: McGraw-Hill Book Co., 1967.

Laurenceau, J., O.P. "Aperçus sur l'histoire de la consécration à Marie". *Cahiers Marials,* no. 137 (1983): 66–84.

Laurentin, René. "Bulletin sur la Vierge Marie". *Revue des Sciences Philosophiques et Théologiques* 70 (1986): 101–50.

———, "Consecration and Entrustment: A Commitment to the Hearts of Jesus and Mary—Its Meaning for Our Personal Lives and the Life of Our People". Trans. Srs. Edita Telan, M.I.C., and Rachel de Mars, M.I.C. In *The Alliance of the Hearts of Jesus and Mary: The Inter-*

national Theological/Pastoral Conference, Manila, Philippines, 30 November–3 December 1987, Texts and Documents, 231–59. Manila: Bahay Maria, 1988.

———, *Essai sur le Développement d'une Idée Religieuse*. Vol. 1 of *Maria, Ecclesia, Sacerdotium*, 422–67. Paris: P. Lethielleux "Nouvelles Editions Latines," 1952.

———, "The Magisterium of the Church on the Alliance of the Hearts of Jesus and Mary". Trans. Srs. Edita Telan, M.I.C., and Rachel de Mars, M.I.C. In *The Alliance of the Hearts of Jesus and Mary: The International Theological/Pastoral Conference, Manila, Philippines, 30 November–3 December 1987, Texts and Documents*, 158–87. Manila: Bahay Maria, 1988.

———, *Queen of Heaven: A Short Treatise on Marian Theology*. Trans. Gordon Smith. Dublin: Clonmore & Reynolds; London: Burns Oates & Washbourne, 1956.

———, *The Question of Mary*. Trans. I. G. Pidoux. New York: Holt, Rinehart and Winston, 1965.

———, *Le voeu de Louis XIII: Passé ou avenir de la France 1638–1988*. Paris: O.E.I.L., 1988.

———, *A Year of Grace with Mary: Rediscovering Her Presence and Her Role in Our Consecration*. Trans. Msgr. Michael J. Wrenn. Dublin: Veritas, 1987.

Lebon, Henri, S.M. "Chaminade (Guillaume-Joseph)". In Marcel Viller, S.J., et al., *Dictionnaire de Spiritualité Ascétique et Mystique*, 2:454–59. Paris: Beauchesne et Ses Fils, 1953.

Lebrun, Charles, C.J.M. *Le Bienheureux Jean Eudes et le Culte Public du Cœur de Jésus*. 2nd ed. Paris: P. Lethielleux, 1918.

———, *The Spiritual Teaching of St. John Eudes*. Trans. Basil Whelan, O.S.B. London: Sands and Co., 1934.

Leeming, Bernard, S.J. "Consecration to the Sacred Heart". In *Pars Theologica*, 597–655. Vol. 1 of *Cor Jesu: Commentationes in Litteras Encyclicas Pii PP. XII "Haurietis Aquas"*, ed. Augustinus Bea, S.J., Hugo Rahner, S.J.,

Henri Rondet, S.J., and F. Schwendimann, S.J. Rome: Casa Editrice Herder, 1959.

Letourneur, Jean. "Dufriche-Desgenettes, Charles-Eléonor". In Marcel Viller, S.J., et al., *Dictionnaire de Spiritualité Ascétique et Mystique*, 3:1757–59. Paris: Beauchesne et Ses Fils, 1957.

Lewandowski, Bogumil. *Tutti consacrati alla Madonna.* Rome, 1988.

Little, Joyce A. "Redemptoris Mater: The Significance of Mary for Women". *Marian Studies* 39 (1988): 136–58.

Lohkamp, N. "Consecration, Personal". In *New Catholic Encyclopedia*, 4:209. New York: McGraw-Hill Book Co., 1967.

Lozano, Juan Maria, C.M.F. *Mystic and Man of Action: Saint Anthony Mary Claret.* Trans. Joseph Daries, C.M.F. Chicago: Claretian Publications, 1977.

Luis, Angel, C.SS.R. "La consagración a María en la vida y doctrina de Juan Pablo II". *Estudios Marianos* 51 (1986): 77–112.

MacDonald, Donald, S.M.M. "From the Slavery of Sin to the Total Consecration to Christ". *Queen of All Hearts* 40 (July–August 1989): 18–19.

Mai, Angelo Cardinal, ed. *Nova Patrum Bibliotheca.* Vol. 6 of *Pars Secunda.* Rome: Typis Sacri Consilii Propagando Christiano Nomini, 1853.

Manteau-Bonamy, H., O.P. *La Doctrine Mariale du Père Kolbe: plein feu sur l'Immaculée.* 2nd ed. Paris: Lethielleux, 1979.

———, *Immaculate Conception and the Holy Spirit: The Marian Teachings of Father Kolbe.* Trans. Br. Richard Arnandez, F.S.C. Kenosha, Wis.: Franciscan Marytown Press, 1977.

Marangos, J., S.J., "Le Culte Marial Populaire en Grèce". In *Maria: Études sur la Sainte Vierge*, ed. Hubert du Manoir, S.J., 4:810–11. Paris: Beauchesne et Ses Fils, 1956.

Marquis, Marie-Odile, and Jean-Hughes. *Spiritualità del Cuore di Cristo.* Trans. Sr. Clemente Moro. Milan: Editrice Ancora, 1986.

Marranzini, Alfredo, S.J. "L' 'Atto di Affidamento e Consacrazione' a Maria: Significato teologico". *Civilta Cattolica* 135:2 (1984): 12–29.

———, "Consacrazione a Maria in Prospettiva Teologico-Antropologica". *Madonna: Rivista di Cultura Mariana* 27 (August 1979): 51–76.

Martins, Antonio Maria, S.J., ed. and trans. *Memórias e Cartas de Irmã Lúcia.* Porto, Portugal: Simão Guimarães, Filhos, Lda., 1973.

Masson, Pierre-Reginald, O.P. " 'Ecce mater tua' (Jn 19, 25–27) selon l'interprétation des théologiens". In *De Beata Virgine Maria in Evangelio S. Ioannis et in Apocalypsi,* 201–23. Vol. 5 of *Maria in Sacra Scriptura: Acta Congressus Mariologici-Mariani in Republica Dominicana Anno 1965 Celebrati.* Rome: Pontificia Academia Mariana Internationalis, 1967.

Mathews, Stanley G., S.M., ed. *Queen of the Universe: An Anthology on the Assumption and Queenship of Mary.* Saint Meinrad, Ind.: Grail Publications, 1957.

McCarthy, Msgr. John F. "An Assessment of the Recent Extraordinary Synod". *The Wanderer,* 119, no. 11 (1986): 3.

McCurry, James, O.F.M. Conv. "Maximilian Kolbe and the Franciscan Marian Tradition". *The Cord* 33 (September 1983): 227–38.

McGratty, Arthur R., S.J. *The Sacred Heart Yesterday and Today.* New York: Benziger Brothers, 1951.

Meo, Salvatore, O.S.M. "La 'Mediazione materna' di Maria nell' Enciclica 'Redemptoris Mater' ". In *Redemptoris Mater: Contenuti e Prospettive Dottrinali e Pastorali,* 131–57. Rome: Pontificia Accademia Mariana Internazionale, 1988.

Mercado, Alphonsus, O.F.M. "De verbis Jesu ad Matrem et Discipulum (Io. 19, 26–27a) iuxta genus ioanneum. Adnotationes". In *De Beata Virgine Maria in Evangelio S. Ioannis et in Apocalypsi*, 123–37. Vol. 5 of *Maria in Sacra Scriptura: Acta Congressus Mariologici-Mariani in Republica Dominicana Anno 1965 Celebrati*. Rome: Pontificia Academia Mariana Internationalis, 1967.

Micewski, Andrzej. *Cardinal Wyszyński: A Biography*. Trans. William R. Brand and Katarzyna Mroczkowska-Brand. New York: Harcourt Brace Jovanovich, 1984.

Michaud, J. P., S.M.M. "Au service du Mystère de Dieu avec les Hommes". *Cahiers Marials*, no. 86 (1973): 15–22.

Mitchell, Valentine Albert, S.M. *The Mariology of Saint John Damascene*. Kirkwood, Mo.: Maryhurst Normal Press, 1930.

Molien, A. "Bérulle". In Marcel Viller, S.J., et al., *Dictionnaire de Spiritualité Ascétique et Mystique*, 1:1539–82. Paris: Beauchesne et Ses Fils, 1937.

Most, W. G. "Marian Consecration as Service: Historical, Theological and Spiritual Reflections". *Miles Immaculatae* 24 (1988): 441–63.

———, *Mary in Our Life: Our Lady in Doctrine and Devotion*. New York: P. J. Kenedy & Sons, 1955.

———, *Vatican II—Marian Council*. Athlone, Ireland: St. Paul Publications, 1972.

Murphy, John F. *Mary's Immaculate Heart: The Meaning of the Devotion to the Immaculate Heart of Mary*. Milwaukee: Bruce Publishing Company, 1951.

———, "Origin and Nature of Marian Cult". In *Mariology*, ed. Juniper B. Carol, O.F.M., 3:1–21. Milwaukee: Bruce Publishing Co., 1961.

Neubert, Emile, S.M. *Mary in Doctrine*. Milwaukee: Bruce Publishing Co., 1954.

Noye, Irenée, P.S.S. "O Jesus Living in Mary". Trans. Roger M. Charest, S.M.M. *Queen of All Hearts* 32, no. 5 (1982): 7–9, 36.

O'Carroll, Michael, C.S.Sp. "The Alliance of the Two Hearts". *Doctrine and Life* 38 (1988): 234–41.

———, *Mediatress of All Graces*. Westminster, Md.: Newman Press, 1958.

———, "Still Mediatress of All Graces?" *Miles Immaculatae* 24 (1988): 114–33.

———, *Theotokos: A Theological Encyclopedia of the Blessed Virgin Mary*. Wilmington, Del.: Michael Glazier; Dublin: Dominican Publications, 1982.

———, *Veni Creator Spiritus: A Theological Encyclopedia of the Holy Spirit*. Collegeville, Minn.: Liturgical Press, "A Michael Glazier Book", 1990.

O'Connor, Edward D., C.S.C. "Mary and the Holy Spirit". *Homiletic & Pastoral Review* 90, no. 8 (1990): 21–30.

———, *Pope Paul and the Spirit: Charisms and Church Renewal in the Teaching of Paul VI*. Notre Dame, Ind.: Ave Maria Press, 1978.

———, "The Roots of Pope John Paul II's Devotion to Mary". *Marian Studies* 39 (1988): 78–114.

O'Donnell, Timothy Terrance. *Heart of the Redeemer: An Apologia for the Contemporary and Perennial Value of the Devotion to the Sacred Heart of Jesus*. Manassas, Va.: Trinity Communications, 1989.

The Official Handbook of the Legion of Mary. Dublin: Concilium Legionis Mariae, 1961.

Ong, Walter J., S.J. *Fighting for Life*. Ithaca, N.Y./London: Cornell University Press, 1981.

Ordoñez Marquez, J. "La Cofradía de la Esclavitud en las Concepcionistas de Alcalá". *Estudios Marianos* 51 (1986): 231–48.

Pach, Jan, O.S.P.P.E. *Maria nell' Insegnamento del Cardinal Stefan Wyszyński*. Dissertationes ad Lauream in Pontificia Facultate Theologica "Marianum", no. 49. Rome, 1989.

Papàsogli, Benedetta. *Montfort: A Prophet for Our Times.* Trans. Ann Nielsen, D.W. Rome: Edizioni Monfortane, 1991.

Pelletier, Joseph A., A.A. *The Immaculate Heart of Mary.* Worcester, Mass.: Assumption Publication, 1976.

Peeters, Paul L. "*Dominum et Vivificantem*: The Conscience and the Heart". *Communio: International Catholic Review* 15 (1988): 148–55.

Philips, Gerard. "La Vierge au IIe Concile du Vatican et L'Avenir de la Mariologie". In *Maria: Études sur la Sainte Vierge*, ed. Hubert du Manoir, S.J., 8:42–88. Paris: Beauchesne et Ses Fils, 1971.

Poupon, M. T., O.P. *Le poème de la parfaite consécration à Marie.* Lyon: Librairie de Sacré-Cœur, 1947.

Pourrat, Pierre, P.S.S. "Abandon". In Marcel Viller, S.J., et al., *Dictionnaire de Spiritualité Ascétique et Mystique* 1:1–49. Paris: Beauchesne et Ses Fils, 1937.

———, *Christian Spirituality*, vol. 3. Trans. W. A. Mitchell. Westminister, Md.: Newman Press, 1953.

Prat, Ferdinand, S.J. *Jesus Christ: His Life, His Teaching, and His Work.* Vol. 2. Trans. John J. Heenan, S.J. Milwaukee: Bruce Publishing Co., 1950.

Pujana, Juan. "Simón de Rojas". In Marcel Viller, S.J., et al., *Dictionnaire de Spiritualité Ascétique et Mystique* 14:877–84. Paris: Beauchesne et Ses Fils, 1990.

Quéméneur, M., S.M.M. "Towards a History of Marian Consecration". Trans. William Fackovec, S.M. *Marian Library Studies* 122 (March 1966). Originally published as "La consécration de soi à la Vierge à travers l'histoire". *Cahiers Marials* no. 14 (1959): 119–28.

Resch, Peter A., S.M. "Filial Piety". In *Mariology*, ed. Juniper B. Carol, O.F.M., 3:162–67. Milwaukee: Bruce Publishing Co., 1961.

Ricciardi, Antonio, O.F.M. Conv. *St. Maximilian Kolbe: Apostle of Our Difficult Age.* Trans. Daughters of St. Paul. Boston: St. Paul Editions, 1982.

Robichaud, Armand J., S.M. "Mary, Dispensatrix of All Graces". In *Mariology*, ed. Juniper. B. Carol, O.F.M., 2:426–60. Milwaukee: Bruce Publishing Co., 1957.

Romb, Anselm, O.F.M. Conv., ed. *The Kolbe Reader.* Libertyville, Ill.: Franciscan Marytown Press, 1987.

Roschini, Gabriele M., O.S.M. "La Consacrazione del Mondo al Cuore Immacolato di Maria". In *Il Cuore Immacolato di Maria, Settimana di Studi Mariani*, 55–78. Rome: Edizioni Marianum, 1946.

———, *Dizionario di Mariologia.* Rome: Editrice Studium, 1961.

———, *Maria Santissima nella Storia della Salvezza.* 4 vols. Isola del Liri: Tipografia Editrice M. Pisani, 1969.

Salaville, S. A.A. "Marie dans la Liturgie Byzantine ou Gréco-Slave". In *Maria: Études sur la Sainte Vierge*, ed. Hubert du Manoir, S.J., 1:249–326. Paris: Beauchesne et Ses Fils, 1949.

Salgado, Jean-Marie, O.M.I. "Les appropriations trinitaires et la théologie mariale". *Marianum* 49 (1987): 377–448.

———, "Aux Origines de la Découverte des Richesses du Cœur Immaculé de Marie: du IIIè au XIIè Siècle". *Divinitas* 31 (1987): 186–232.

———, "La maternité spirituelle de la Sainte Vierge chez les Pères durant les quatre premiers siècles". *Divinitas* 30 (1986): 53–77.

———, *La Maternité Spirituelle de la Très Sainte Vierge Marie.* Vatican City: Libreria Editrice Vaticana, "Studi Tomistici", no. 36, 1990.

———, "La Maternité Spirituelle de la très Sainte Vierge Marie: Bilan Actuel". *Divinitas* 16 (1972): 17–102.

———, "Mise à Jour d'un Bilan: La Maternité Spirituelle de la Sainte Vierge Marie dans l'Écriture Sainte". *Divus Thomas (Piacenza)* 87 (1984): 289–323.

———, "La Visitation de la Sainte Vierge Marie: Exercice de sa Maternité Spirituelle". *Divinitas* 16 (1972): 445–52.

Schmidt, Firmin M., O.F.M. Cap. "Our Lady's Queenship in the Light of *Quas Primas*". *Marian Studies* 4 (1953): 118–33.

———, "The Universal Queenship of Mary". In *Mariology*, ed. Juniper B. Carol, O.F.M., 2:493–549. Milwaukee: Bruce Publishing Co., 1957.

Sebastian, Wenceslaus, O.F.M. "Mary's Spiritual Maternity". In *Mariology*, ed. Juniper B. Carol, O.F.M., 2:325–76. Milwaukee: Bruce Publishing Co., 1957.

Segalla, Giuseppe, Luigi Gambero, S.M., and Théodore Koehler, S.M. *Maria ai piedi della Croce*. Casale Monferrato: Edizioni Piemme, 1989.

Semmelroth, Otto, S.J. *Mary, Archetype of the Church*. Trans. Maria von Eroes and John Devlin. New York: Sheed and Ward, 1963.

Sennott, Thomas Mary. "Mary, Mediatrix of All Graces, Vatican II and Ecumenism". *Miles Immaculatae* 24 (1988): 151–67.

Sigrist, Paul. "Libermann (François-Marie-Paul)." In Marcel Viller, S.J., et al., *Dictionnaire de Spiritualité Ascétique et Mystique*, 9:764–80. Paris: Beauchesne et Ses Fils, 1976.

Sloyan, Gerard S. "Marian Prayers". In *Mariology*, ed. Juniper B. Carol, O.F.M., 3:64–68. Milwaukee: Bruce Publishing Co., 1961.

The Sorrowful and Immaculate Heart of Mary: Message of Berthe Petit, Franciscan Tertiary (1870–1943). Trans. Kylemore Abbey nun. Kenosha, Wis.: Franciscan Marytown Press, 1974.

Sparks, T. M., O.P. *Summarium de Cultu Cordis Immaculati Beatae Mariae Virginis*. Rome: Marietti, 1951.

Stasiewski, B. "Hlond, Augustyn". In *New Catholic Encyclopedia*, 7:41. New York: McGraw-Hill Book Co., 1967.

Stern, Karl. *The Flight from Woman*. New York: Farrar, Strauss and Giroux, 1965.

Tambasco, Anthony J. *What are they saying about Mary?* New York: Paulist Press, 1984.

Teologia e Pastorale della Consacrazione a Maria. Padua: Edizioni Messagero, 1969.

Thompson, William M., ed. *Bérulle and the French School: Selected Writings*. New York: Paulist Press, 1989.

Totus Tuus: attualità e significato della consacrazione a Maria. Rome: Santuario Madonna del Divino Amore, 1978.

The Treasury of the Sacred Heart. New York: D. & J. Sadlier & Co., 1879.

Triacca, Achille M. "*Sub tuum praesidium*: nella *lex orandi* un'anticipata presenza della *lex credendi*. La *teotocologia* precede la *mariologia*?" In *La mariologia nella catechesi dei Padri (età prenicena)*, ed. Sergio Felici, 183–205. Rome: Libreria Ateneo Salesiano, "Biblioteca di Scienza Religiosa" no. 88, 1989.

Trochu, Francis. *The Curé of Ars: St. Jean-Marie-Baptiste Vianney*. Trans. Dom Ernest Graf, O.S.B. Rockford, Ill.: Tan Books and Publishers, 1977.

Urquía Barroso, Juan Ramon, S.M. *The Theological Content of Consecration to Mary*. Trans. Robert Wood, S.M. Dayton, Oh.: Marianist Resources Commission, n.d.

Vagaggini, Cipriano, O.S.B. *Maria nelle Opere di Origene*. Rome: Pont. Institutum Orientalium Studiorum, "Orientalia Christiana Analecta", no. 31, 1962.

Valabek, Redemptus M., O.Carm. *Mary, Mother of Carmel: Our Lady and the Saints of Carmel*. Vol. 1. Rome: Institutum Carmelitanum, 1987.

Vallin, Pierre. "Ramière (Henri)". In Marcel Viller, S.J., et al., *Dictionnaire de Spiritualité Ascétique et Mystique*, 13:63–70. Paris: Beauchesne et Ses Fils, 1988.

Vandergheynst, Léon. *Le Pape et la Consécration du Monde à Marie*. Brussels: La Pensée Catholique; Paris: Office Général du Livre, 1968.

Vasey, Vincent R., S.M. "Mary in the Doctrine of Bérulle on the Mysteries of Christ". *Marian Studies* 36 (1985): 60–80.

Verheylezoon, Louis, S.J. *Devotion to the Sacred Heart: Object, Ends, Practice, Motives.* Westminster, Md.: Newman Press, 1955. Reprint. Rockford, Ill.: Tan Books and Publishers, 1978.

Villaret, E., S.J. "Marie et la Compagnie de Jésus". In *Maria: Études sur la Sainte Vierge*, ed. Hubert du Manoir, S.J., 2:936–73. Paris: Beauchesne et Ses Fils, 1952.

Vloberg, Maurice. "Le Voeu de Louis XIII". In *Maria: Études sur la Sainte Vierge*, ed. Hubert du Manoir, S.J., 5:519–33. Paris: Beauchesne et Ses Fils, 1958.

Walsh, Eugene A., S.S. *The Priesthood in the Writings of the French School: Bérulle, De Condren, Olier.* Washington, D.C.: Catholic University of America Press, 1949.

Ward, J. Neville. "Abandon". In *The Westminster Dictionary of Christian Spirituality*, ed. Gordon S. Wakefield, 1–2. Philadelphia: Westminster Press, 1983.

Wenger, A., A.A. "L'Intercession de Marie en Orient du VIe au Xe siècle". *Bulletin de la Société française d'Études Mariales* 23 (1966): 51–75.

Williams, George Huntston. *The Mind of John Paul II: Origins of His Thought and Action.* New York: Seabury Press, 1981.

Wiltgen, Ralph M., S.V.D. *The Rhine Flows into the Tiber: A History of Vatican II.* Rockford, Ill.: Tan Books and Publishers, 1985.

Winowska, Maria. "Le Culte Marial en Pologne". In *Maria: Études sur la Sainte Vierge*, ed. Hubert du Manoir, S.J., 4:684–709. Paris: Beauchesne et Ses Fils, 1956.

Wyszyński, Stefan Cardinal. "Oddanie Się Matce Boga Zywego". Trans. Seraphim Michalenko, M.I.C. Typescript from address at Warsaw Major Seminary Chapel on March 1, 1961.

Załęcki, Marian, O.S.P. *Theology of a Marian Shrine: Our Lady of Częstochowa.* Marian Library Studies, n.s., 8. Dayton, Oh.: University of Dayton, 1976.

INDEX OF BIBLICAL REFERENCES

Index of Persons

INDEX OF SUBJECTS